INTEGRATED MISSION-DIRECTED RESEARCH

EXPERIENCES FROM ENVIRONMENTAL AND NATURAL RESOURCE MANAGEMENT

WENDY PROCTOR

LORRAE VAN KERKHOFF

STEVE HATFIELD DODDS

CSIRO
PUBLISHING

National Library of Australia Cataloguing-in-Publication entry

Integrated mission-directed research: experiences from environmental and natural resource management/editors Wendy Proctor, Lorrae van Kerkhoff and Steve Hatfield Dodds.

9780643096943 (pbk.)

Includes bibliographical references and index.

Environmental management.
Interdisciplinary research.

Proctor, Wendy.
van Kerkhoff, Lorrae.
Hatfield Dodds, Steve.

333.7

Published by

CSIRO PUBLISHING
150 Oxford Street (PO Box 1139)
Collingwood VIC 3066
Australia

Telephone: +61 3 9662 7666
Local call: 1300 788 000 (Australia only)
Fax: +61 3 9662 7555
Email: publishing.sales@csiro.au
Web site: www.publish.csiro.au

Cover image by iStockphoto

Set in 10.5/13 Adobe Minion and Optima
Cover and text design by James Kelly
Typeset by Desktop Concepts Pty Ltd, Melbourne
Printed in Australia by Ligare

CSIRO PUBLISHING publishes and distributes scientific, technical and health science books, magazines and journals from Australia to a worldwide audience and conducts these activities autonomously from the research activities of the Commonwealth Scientific and Industrial Research Organisation (CSIRO).

The book has been printed on paper certified by the Programme for the Endorsement of Forest Chain of Custody (PEFC). PEFC is committed to sustainable forest management through third party forest certification of responsibly managed forests.

PEFC

PEFC/21-31-17

CONTENTS

LIST OF CONTRIBUTORS

Martin Bach
Institute of Landscape Ecology and Resources Management, University of Giessen, Heinrich-Buff-Ring 26–32, D-35392 Giessen, Germany

Gabriele Bammer
National Centre for Epidemiology and Population Health, ANU College of Medicine, Biology and Environment, Australian National University, Canberra, ACT, Australia; and Program in Criminal Justice Policy and Management, John F. Kennedy School of Government, Harvard University, Cambridge MA, USA.

Anthony Barr
CSIRO Land and Water, PO Wembley, WA 6913, Australia

Olga Barron
CSIRO Land and Water, PO Wembley, WA 6913, Australia

Lutz Breuer
Institute of Landscape Ecology and Resources Management, University of Giessen, Heinrich-Buff-Ring 26–32, D-35392 Giessen, Germany

Michael Burton
School of Agricultural and Resource Economics, University of Western Australia, Crawley WA 6009, Australia

Rajesh Daniel
Unit for Social and Environmental Research, Chiang Mai University, Thailand

Steve Hatfield Dodds
Australian Government Department of Climate Change (formerly CSIRO Sustainable Ecosystems), GPO Box 854, Canberra, ACT 2600, Australia

Hans-Georg Frede
Institute of Landscape Ecology and Resources Management, University of Giessen, Heinrich-Buff-Ring 26–32, D-35392 Giessen, Germany

Stefan Gäth
Institute of Landscape Ecology and Resources Management, University of Giessen, Heinrich-Buff-Ring 26–32, D-35392 Giessen, Germany

Russell Gorddard
CSIRO Sustainable Ecosystems, GPO Box 284, Canberra ACT 2601, Australia

Emma Jakku
CSIRO Sustainable Ecosystems, Queensland Bioscience Precinct, St Lucia, Qld 4067, Australia

Gail Kelly
Inland Revenue Department, Hamilton, 3240, New Zealand

Elizabeth Kington
CSIRO Land and Water, Wembley, WA 6913, Australia

Friedrich Kuhlmann
Institute for Agricultural and Food Economics, University of Giessen, Giessen, Senckenbergstr. 3, D-35390 Giessen, Germany

Louis Lebel
Unit for Social and Environmental Research, Chiang Mai University, Thailand

Jaroslav Mysiak
Fondazione Eni Enrico Mattei, Venice, Italy

Richard B. Norgaard
Energy and Resources Group, University of California, Berkeley CA, USA

Jo Pluske
School of Agricultural and Resource Economics, University of Western Australia, Crawley, WA 6009, Australia

Thorsten Pohlert
Institute of Landscape Ecology and Resources Management, University of Giessen, Heinrich-Buff-Ring 26–32, D-35392 Giessen, Germany

Mark Pridham
Department of Food and Agriculture Western Australia, South Perth, WA 6151, Australia

Wendy Proctor
CSIRO Sustainable Ecosystems, GPO Box 284, Canberra ACT 2601, Australia

Wolfgang Reiher
Institute of Landscape Ecology and Resources Management, University of Giessen, Germany; now at DR. KNOELL CONSULT GmbH, Marie-Curie-Str. 8, D-51377 Leverkusen, Germany

Patrick Sheridan
Institute for Agricultural and Food Economics, University of Giessen, Germany; now at Agro Risk Euro Scan GmbH, Wilhelmstr. 25, D-35392 Giessen, Germany

Alexander Smajgl
CSIRO Sustainable Ecosystems, Townsville, Qld 4810, Australia

Trevor Smales
CSIRO Land and Water, PO Wembley, WA 6913, Australia

Peter Thorburn
CSIRO Sustainable Ecosystems, Queensland Bioscience Precinct, St Lucia, Qld 4067, Australia

Prasnee Tipraqsa
Hohenheim University, Stuttgart, Germany

Jeffrey Turner
CSIRO Land and Water, PO Wembley, WA 6913, Australia

Lorrae van Kerkhoff
Fenner School of Environment and Society, ANU College of Medicine, Biology and Environment, The Australian National University, Canberra ACT, Australia

Chapter 1

Introduction

Wendy Proctor, Lorrae van Kerkhoff and
Steve Hatfield Dodds

The idea of sustainability has posed new challenges for all sectors of society – government, community, industry and business – and also for science. New forms of science are emerging that attempt to retain and capitalise on the established analytical strengths of traditional science, but also address the concerns and values inherent in efforts to move towards sustainability. These concerns and values are wide ranging, but include social justice, intergenerational equity and a more balanced approach to understanding the consequences of human action, which includes ecological, economic and social dimensions.

The consequences for research are extensive, and have been discussed at length over the past two decades. In this book, we characterise two major dimensions of these consequences – that research has become more *integrated* – in counteraction to traditional scientific approaches that favour fragmentation – and that it has become more *mission-directed*, or targeted towards achieving innovative solutions to complex problems. This book documents and reflects on these two dimensions of science in the context of sustainability. We describe the challenges, the lessons and, in some cases, the rewards of taking an integrated mission-directed approach to research. By documenting these efforts, we hope to contribute to a larger 'mission' of learning that focuses not on questions of *what* research contributes to sustainability, but *how* – and how we can collectively make that contribution more effective, more innovative and better attuned to the demands of sustainability.

In this chapter, we will outline the broad context for integrated mission-directed research and list some key themes and questions identified by the authors as challenges we confront in this territory. These themes and questions form the basis for the following chapters, which we summarise in an overview at the end of this chapter.

THE NATURE OF INTEGRATED MISSION-DIRECTED RESEARCH

The idea of integrated mission-directed research arises from discussion of the nature of science and the design of appropriate policies that generate tangible outcomes and support innovation. This literature reveals that attitudes towards research and research funding have shifted, from primarily valuing academic outputs, such as peer-reviewed papers, to the assessing and valuing of research outputs and the economic, social and environmental benefits (which are fundamental to reaching 'sustainable' outcomes) achieved through research investments.

Gibbons, Nowotny and colleagues argue that this social context requires a rethinking of past presumptions about science governance and the drivers of innovation (Gibbons *et al.* 1994; Nowotny *et al.* 2001). Old-fashioned science thinking, they argue, emphasised the distinction between pure and applied science, and presumed that science breakthroughs are generally achieved through deep specialisation and research guided by self-generated disciplinary research agendas. Taking this view, innovation is thus directly correlated with withdrawal into highly compartmentalised specialist science communities. These authors contrast the curiosity driven research paradigm (termed 'Mode 1' science) with 'Mode 2' mission-directed research, which is characterised by transdisciplinary integration, strong stakeholder engagement in framing research goals and the use of heterogeneous research teams that marshal and integrate the methods required to address externally defined goals.

The important message for the traditional science community from these influential authors is that mission-directed research, not traditional curiosity driven research, will be the source of the outstanding science breakthroughs in the next century. Engagement with the difficult and complex problems of others is presented as the crucible of innovation. New insights and innovation are driven by deep engagement with stakeholders, respect for their views and insights, and commitment to addressing their issues and problems. Accountability to others – at least if done well – has the potential to drive better science outcomes, rather than being a distraction from the core business of science, or a necessary evil to be endured.

In practice, many of the outstanding innovations of the past were the result of mission-directed research – such as the development of antibiotics, new food solutions and improved transport technologies. Others were curiosity driven. Some were a fortuitous blend of both. It seems likely that curiosity driven and mission-directed research will both continue to be important sources of innovation, and that both will continue to contribute to improvements in our quality of life and sustainability.

THE SCIENCE–SOCIETY–POLICY INTERFACE: THE NEED FOR INTEGRATION AND STAKEHOLDER ENGAGEMENT

Attention to the instrumental value of research outputs (rather than a presumption that research is intrinsically valuable) raises wider questions about the role of knowledge in shaping human action. It is clear that 'mental models' have a significant role in shaping human action, including through perceptions of cause and effect relationships, and the ways in which people learn over time (see Gintis 2000, 2003). The adaptive governance literature identifies a number of general conditions that facilitate the development of rules and management practices that meet the evolving needs and desires of a specific community (see Dietz *et al.* 2003, Arrow *et al.* 1995). In the context of managing common environmental resources, such as a fishery or urban air quality, this literature suggests that collective action is most likely to be effective when:

(1) the major determinants of resource condition and resilience are well known, including key cause and effect relationships; and
(2) the condition of the asset or resource is subject to human influence, including the fact that any damage inflicted is not irreversible; and
(3) formal or informal arrangements can be crafted that are supported and valued by (or result in net benefits to) key constituencies.

Science and scientists have important roles in relation to each of these conditions, and thus have key roles in underpinning effective collective action and promoting sustainable development.

Much sustainability-oriented mission-directed research is focused on public good outcomes: raising issues around science and public policy engagement. Gibson (2003) provides a useful review of different perspectives on the research-policy nexus, critiquing the widespread 'two communities' view that emphasises the different roles, focus, values, cultures and operating environment of scientists and policy makers. Most of the insights from this review relate more generally to the relationships between science and key stakeholder communities, including business.

In very general terms, one of the key contributions of research to our wider society is its ability to provide new insights and better understanding, particularly through linking cause and effects, providing early warning of impacts and consequences, and exploring wider system interactions. These insights enable the identification or development of new technologies, management strategies and collective policy approaches. Paul Oquist (1978) provides a more formal typology of research modes:

- **Descriptive research**, which describes phenomena within typologies of facts and events *(positive)*, and describes or advocates attitudes or evaluative systems *(normative)*.
- **Prediction and assessment** (termed nomothethic research), which explains or predicts the consequences of specific events in terms of key variables and assesses or evaluates impacts against nominated criteria.
- **Policy research**, which involves the production of knowledge that guides policy practice, achieving impact through communication of research outputs.
- **Action research**, involving the production of knowledge that guides practice, where change occurs as part of the research process through engagement of stakeholders.

The contribution of scientists is somewhat broader than the contribution of science, and includes providing specialist expertise and advice (drawing on the stock of knowledge), undertaking new research (expanding or deepening the stock of knowledge), acting as an honest broker and helping to build capacity (both involving aspects of assisting access to knowledge). Scientists also potentially connect to goals of social justice, by identifying and making visible those communities who are not well represented in existing governance or decision-making structures.

Insights from this literature include that knowledge is crucial to effective decision making and action, and is influential in public debate. Expert knowledge is used selectively by competing interests, however, and communicating science findings and participating in public debate requires specific skills. More generally, researchers have strengths and weaknesses in contributing to policy, and constructive impact depends on clarity, relevance (of both form and content), rigour and perceived integrity.

OVERVIEW

The chapters in this book are divided into three main parts to reflect their different orientations. Part 1 deals with 'Theoretical perspectives' and contains four chapters describing case studies from Australia and the world. In Chapter 2, lessons from the Millennium Ecosystem Assessment provide the historical context of currently held beliefs about environmental systems and management and how dominant beliefs are intertwined with our environmental problems so that we can move beyond them to new institutional solutions. Chapter 3 provides a detailed explanation of what integrated research means and how it is done. Chapter 4 then provides some theoretical perspectives as well as challenges and success factors in undertaking integrated research in a 6-month review of this research within the Commonwealth Scientific and Industrial Research Organisation (CSIRO). Chapter 5 provides a different perspective on integrated research in the context of environmental conflicts arising from the re-introduction of large carnivores in European landscapes.

The second part of the book covers 'Engaging individuals and communities' and comprises three chapters that give an international perspective of various methods incorporating participatory techniques to enhance integrative research and outcomes. Chapter 6 reviews a case study involving communities from Thailand and incorporates issues concerning ethical considerations in such research. Chapter 7 provides an overview of the role of technologies to enhance interactions between scientists and communities in integrated research using agricultural decision-support systems. Chapter 8 discusses two projects that used a regional development framework based on systems thinking in two Australian coastal regions (Augusta-Margaret River Shire in Western Australia, and the Central Coast in NSW) facing intense development pressures.

Part 3 is based on the theme of 'Supporting policy development and decision making', with Chapter 9 providing a systems approach to integrated research in a policy context by reviewing a program aimed at designing a Water Management Plan that will be used by decision makers within a town to improve the water supply. Chapter 10 details the Integrated Tool for Economic and Ecological Modeling (ITE^{2}M): a network of several models addressing agro-economy, agricultural policy and environmental services with respect to soil, water, floral and faunal biodiversity. This model is used in Europe to assess different agricultural land use scenarios. Chapter 11 – the last chapter in Part 3 – covers multiple governance scales in integrated modelling and decision support, and argues that scales of decision making are a 'meta-level' for integration.

The book ends with Chapter 12: a set of conclusions that reflect on integrated mission-directed research and draw out important lessons from the theory and practice presented here.

REFERENCES

Arrow K, Bolin B, Costanza R, Dasgupta P, Folke C, Holling CS, Jansson B-O, Levin S, Mäler K-G, Perrings C and Pimental D (1995) Economic growth, carrying capacity, and the environment. *Science* **268**, 520–521.

Dietz T, Ostrom E and Stern PC (2003) The struggle to govern the commons. *Science* **302**, 1907–1912.

Gibbons M, Limoges C, Nowotny H, Schwartzman S, Cott P and Trow M (1994) *The New Production of Knowledge. The Dynamics of Science and Research in Contemporary Societies.* Sage, Thousand Oaks, California.

Gibson B (2003) Beyond 'two communities'. In: *Evidence-based Health Policy. Problems and Possibilities.* (Eds V Lin and B Gibson) pp. 18–30. Oxford University Press, Oxford.

Gintis H (2000) *Game Theory Evolving: A Problem Centred Introduction to Strategic Interaction.* Princeton University Press, New Jersey.

Gintis H (2003) 'Towards a unity of behavioural sciences'. Santa Fe Institute Working Paper #03-02-015, March 2003.

Nowotny H, Scott P and Gibbons M (2001) *Rethinking Science. Knowledge and the Public in an Age of Uncertainty.* Polity Press in association with Blackwell Publishers, Cambridge, UK.

Oquist P (1978) The epistemology of action research. *Acta Sociologica* **21**(2), 143–163.

Rittel HJ and Webber MM (1984) Planning problems are wicked problems. In: *Developments in Design Methodology.* (Ed. N Cross) pp. 135–144. John Wiley & Sons, Chichester, UK.

Part 1

Theoretical perspectives

Chapter 2

Understanding and managing complex systems: historical perspectives and lessons from the Millennium Ecosystem Assessment

Richard B. Norgaard

ABSTRACT

Throughout human history, people have shared experiences and knowledge. However, since the rise of both economic specialisation through markets and scientific specialisation a century and a half ago, people no longer share as many experiences or as much knowledge. Environmental management requires shared understanding across stakeholders and with the public at large. Although most scientists and the public believe that science will someday lead to some sort of universal understanding available to all, in fact no such unified, accessible understanding exists. The Millennium Ecosystem Assessment organised more than a thousand scientists from multiple disciplines to work together to collectively understand environmental complexities and suggest management options.

INTRODUCTION

Integrated mission-directed research (IMDR) both draws on and contributes to how we – applied researchers, scholars, environmental managers and policy makers – think about how we relate to environmental systems. This is an ongoing, iterative process. How we think we relate to environmental systems is framed by modern beliefs that were established during the past few centuries. These beliefs frame not only how we understand these systems but also how environmental science, policy and management have been structured in institutions. In this sense, the nature of our historic beliefs helps to explain why some environmental management has been successful as well as why other environmental problems remain unsolved. These are the problems IMDR is still working on. Taking an historical perspective helps us see how dominant beliefs are intertwined with our environmental problems so that we can move beyond them to new institutional solutions.

The Millennium Ecosystem Assessment (MA) exposed the nature of modern beliefs and there consequences very clearly. The MA was a review extending over 5 years by some 1400 scientists from around the world of what is known about how people transform ecosystems, how ecosystem services promote human well-being, and what are the prospects for human well-being in the future. The MA entailed a participatory, deliberative process that provides an example of why the dominant historical beliefs about the nature of reality, science and management are incomplete. It also provides some interesting lessons on how the dominant framework might be dramatically expanded.

This chapter provides historical context for this critically important expansion in how we do science and management, describes the MA as an example of this expansion and draws lessons from the MA to facilitate a better understanding of the nature of the expansion.

HISTORICAL CONTEXT

For the vast majority of human history, people lived as hunter-gatherers in small groups of 50 to 200. Each person did similar things: there was relatively little specialisation in tasks. People shared the same myths passed down from their ancestors. With very little hierarchy or differentiation, it was relatively easy to act together because they saw the same things together and interpreted their meaning together. People were hunter-gatherers for 99.5% of human history, until the rise of agriculture began some 15 000 years ago.

Agriculture brought a surplus of production that facilitated investments in physical structures and the rise of social hierarchy and diversification. Thus, along with irrigation projects, defensive walls, temples and castles, we begin to see the rise of full-time leaders and their differentiation into rulers, priests and philosophers. Specialisation in craftsmanship and the arts also arose, as well as full-time warriors. Nevertheless, the vast majority of people worked the land and, through this shared experience, they retained a common understanding of the natural world.

The transition to agriculture facilitated a tremendous increase in human population, from some 5 million people worldwide 15 000 years ago to 1200 million people around 1850. Thus, before the implementation of modern science in agriculture, the human population increased by a factor of 240. We slowly occupied different niches around the globe, using novel approaches to agriculture. Well-being and longevity increased as well. People did this through experiments and mistakes, observing outcomes and adjusting how they interacted with nature. We now denigrate this as *trial and error*, yet *learning-by-doing* still plays an extremely important role in the age of modern science and technology. Indeed, with respect to the indirect consequences of technology – the social and environmental consequences – this is especially true. The surplus from traditional agriculture supported early explorations and conquests across Asia, the European voyages of discovery, the development of imperialism through colonisation and the beginnings of Western science.

Five critical and complementary transitions took place during the middle of the 19th century, merely 150 years or so ago. These important transitions occurred 99.995% of the way through human history.

First, the idea of material progress went from being a possible scenario explored by a few utopians to becoming both a widely accepted aspect of modern life and a dominant expectation for the future. It also became common wisdom that material abundance would reduce the wants that drive theft and the conflicts that drive war. In this way, the idea of material progress complemented long-standing, religious hopes for moral progress. Yet material progress also soon became an end in itself, swamping the moral ever since.

Second, the industrial revolution got fully underway as we switched from using renewable energy – animal, biomass, water and wind power – to non-renewable fossil hydrocarbons. The increases in population and well-being ever since have arisen largely through technologies that deplete coal, petroleum and natural gas: the fossil stocks of solar energy captured over millennia by life itself. Historically, life processes took carbon dioxide from the atmosphere; environmental processes sequestered it as fossil hydrocarbons, changed atmospheric gas composition and created the environment we know today. By using fossil fuels, we have literally been reversing the historical processes that made the environmental conditions in which today's life forms and ecological systems evolved.

Third, the role of markets in people's lives became increasingly important: the economic philosophy of markets arose, and markets became more systematically institutionalised. The rise of markets, combined with fossil-fuel-driven industrialisation, facilitated the rise of specialisation in the economic lives of more and more people.

Fourth, natural philosophy divided into the separate, specialised sciences of physics, chemistry, geology and other disciplines we know today. Moral philosophy split into the social sciences. And it became standard practice for individual scholars to learn more and more about less and less. No mechanisms were established to bring the splintering sciences into a coherent whole.

And fifth, progressive governance was invented. In the second half of the 19th century, western societies brought scientists and engineers into the process of governance as agents of progress. We created agricultural schools, departments of agriculture and agricultural extension services, and during the 20th century these were replicated around much of the globe.

It is important to acknowledge two beliefs about progressive governance that are widely known but rarely properly addressed. First, western societies typically believed that agencies could be separately established along professional and disciplinary lines with agricultural scientists, water engineers, and fisheries experts, for example, housed in different agencies, and yet still work systematically together. This belief was rooted in the idea that the sciences would naturally fit together into a unified whole. In fact, historic problems that fit the foci of the original agencies are handled reasonably well. Problems that fall between their mandates, as well as some of the consequences of their projects that were outside their purview, become known as 'environmental' problems. In fact, however, environmental problems are not a separate and distinct type of problem. Rather, they are the problems that remain insufficiently addressed because of the divisions created by the gains of specialisation both in science (i.e. the disciplines) and in social institutions (i.e. the organisational advantages of charging particular branches of government with solving particular types of problems).

The second belief is that the agencies provide expert advice to the policy process and implement public projects in a manner that is value free. The values and will of the people are supposed to be exercised democratically through the selection of policies and projects, not through the progressive agencies and their scientists. Both the divided structure of science and progressive governance and the presumption of the objectivity of science and progressive governance have proven highly problematic, yet they remain dominant modern beliefs that affect how we think about science and environmental governance.

The key point here is that modern beliefs about nature and science were only institutionalised in the structure of science, our social organisation, and the relations between them a mere century and a half ago: a mere wink of time in any serious gaze at human history. Of course, during this 'mere wink', material well-being advanced tremendously, but so did serious environmental problems. Many now see environmental problems foreclosing options for material well-being for future generations – one of the conclusions of the MA – so a little deeper analysis of our beliefs about nature, science and environmental management is in order.

EMBRACING UNIVERSAL PRINCIPLES OR THE COMPLEXITY OF EVOLVED SYSTEMS

Early Greek and Roman philosophers argued that everything was composed of a few basic components such as earth, water, air and fire. Some argued that the complexities of the universe reduced to geometric golden means. The idea that everything can be explained in terms of underlying basic parts and a fairly simple rule book for their assembly and operation is a part of Western tradition.

Having spent a fair amount of time among physicists, I am accustomed to the phrase 'you can deduce that from first principles.' Some things can be deduced from the laws of thermodynamics, the properties of materials and a few empirical constants. A little over a century ago, Svante Arrhenius determined from first principles and a few parameters how the doubling of carbon dioxide in the atmosphere would affect the temperature of the Earth. With far more sophisticated global circulation models, also running on a few first principles, we have added a few important details to his initial estimates, but they are still just additional details. However, now that climate science is beginning to incorporate the dynamics of ocean currents and the interactions of diverse terrestrial ecosystems over time, our understanding of climate change is becoming immensely more complicated and not reducible to first principles at all.

Underlying the claim that one can deduce the complex nature of reality from 'first principles' hides the belief that all science builds up from a relatively few basic principles. Once we know these, everything will fall into place. So far, however, this has not been the case. Physics explains some things about chemical phenomena, but one cannot derive the periodic table from physics. And how different types of atoms combine into different types of molecules is the very essence of chemistry. Similarly, organismal biologists are constantly complaining that ecology neither builds on principles of organismal biology nor incorporates its substantive knowledge. So, the idea that underlying principles explain complexity at higher levels simply has not born out. Some argue that at new levels, new basic principles must be introduced. But the nature of science thus far suggests otherwise. At higher levels of organisation, multiple new theories emerge that only explain different parts of the greater complexity. Thus, ecology has many frameworks of analysis: population biology, food webs, energetics, biogeochemical cycles, hierarchy analysis, ecosystem ecology, evolutionary ecology, behavioural ecology and landscape ecology, and so on. Similarly, diverse ways of thinking about people and social systems can also be found in the social sciences. Although the first principles of physics and chemistry hold at higher levels of complexity, new first principles have not emerged to explain these higher levels.

When we speak of biological diversity, we quickly point out that biodiversity can only be understood as genetic diversity, organismal diversity and ecosystem diversity working together. This is because the way we understand genetic biodiversity is not nested in organismal and ecosystem diversity. Rather, our understandings of the three levels of biodiversity are interactive. Some scientists who acknowledge that biological systems are tightly interlinked with social systems also argue that biological diversity can only be understood as interactive with social diversity. This means that if all of our social and economic systems operate on the same beliefs and rules, social diversity will be reduced, the range of human pressure on biological diversity is narrowed and the possibilities for biological diversity are greatly reduced.

We need to embrace diversity and complexity at each of these levels, including diversity and complexity in human systems, and see them as interrelated. While this is increasingly understood, we also live in an age of rising fundamentalism: in a search for first principles, whether from science or religion. While we need to accept that some things can be explained by universal underlying principles, we need to realise that underlying principles do not explain everything. Yet arguments from first principles carry strong appeal. The case for globalisation is argued from underlying economic principles of exchange alone, universally applied. Why have we so strongly embraced the principle of exchange and proceeded to transform our economic organisation in spite of everything else we know from the social sciences and practical understanding? Why do we build organisations that end up pushing particular underlying principles rather than organisations that embrace the diversity of our world and of how we understand it? How can we organise ourselves so that we can use the multiple frameworks and information from the multiple disciplines and combine this with experiential knowledge?

FINDING HOPE IN A RENEWAL OF SHARED LEARNING AND COLLECTIVE UNDERSTANDING

During the 1980s, we collectively began to realise the nature of our environmental problems and how we have perpetuated them through narrow thinking and action. The philosophy of sustainable development arose, arguing how we needed to go about development in a more holistic way. We realised that we could not move forward without resolving material differences between rich and poor. Resolving complex problems requires us to work across the specialised knowledge of different people. Sustainable development is about coming to a shared understanding between rich and poor, urban and rural, and scientific and traditional people.

The parable of the three blind men touching different parts of an elephant teaches young people that we see different things from different positions. This is important, but not sufficient. The message of the parable for adults is surely that we need even more hands on the elephant, that we had better talk together and feel some more to move beyond the differences in what we are feeling and determine that we have an elephant on our hands. The philosophy of sustainable development encourages pragmatic reaching across different communities of scientists, practitioners and interest groups to come to such a shared understanding.

For a few years, the philosophy of sustainable development and the importance of bringing different peoples into a collective understanding of development emerged and dominated our thinking. Then the continued rise of free market fundamentalism – a phenomenon that had begun only somewhat before the emergence of concern with sustainability – grew sufficiently strong to out-compete the more holistic philosophy. Sustainable development has not been forgotten, but free market fundamentalism reigns, bolstering the ideas that markets can solve everything, that individual choice is almost always better than collective choice, and that the burden of proof for exercising collective responsibility lies on those who are concerned about the direction we are headed.

Yet, even as free market fundamentalism gained strength, another phenomenon also emerged. Scientists began deliberately working together in a new way to understand the climate system on which we all depend. Atmospheric physicists thinking in milliseconds and microns, evolutionary ecologists thinking in continental scales and millennia, and economists thinking in dollars and discount rates began to talk together. These ways of thinking do not naturally fit together. Large computer models help these scientists think through the systemic complexities, while smaller models help them see the whole system. Much of the shared understanding of the scientists actually comes through talking together, then doing their individual research around new assumptions and learning how to interpret their results in the context of what those in other disciplines know. Furthermore, the process of understanding climate science has not simply been one of bringing together the separate disciplines but also of connecting scientists from around the globe who can interpret the significance of climate science in their own environmental and social contexts. In this collective and interactive process, a large group of scientists has come to a shared understanding of climate change. Thus climate science spans the disciplines because there are scientists who are willing to spend the time with, and to learn from, each other. In this way, they are building a collective understanding of the whole system and what are thought to be its most important feedbacks.

The MA is even more phenomenal in that it tackled the interactive complexities from all of the multiple drivers of ecosystem change, not simply those primarily driving climate change. The MA scientists developed a systemic framework (Figure 2.1), assessed the scientific literature and synthesised a four-volume report on the conditions and trends of ecosystems, social systems and the interactions between them and what these mean for human well-being over the next half century.

The general framework for the analysis was one of the most important accomplishments of the MA. It systemically illustrates the key issues while at the same time it highlights the difficulties of understanding ecosystem change in more than a qualitative way. Ecosystem change occurs through a great number of mechanisms. Few of the individual processes can be represented in a mathematical model: none with parameters that hold from one locale to the next, let alone around the globe. Ecologists have nothing comparable to the relationship between the stock of carbon dioxide in the atmosphere and equilibrium global temperatures. Without a central relationship to build on as in the IPCC assessments, computer models played a much smaller role in the MA. Although climate scientists probably overemphasise the importance of formal models to their basic understanding of climate change, the role of formal models in the MA was so limited that no use could be made of them at all.

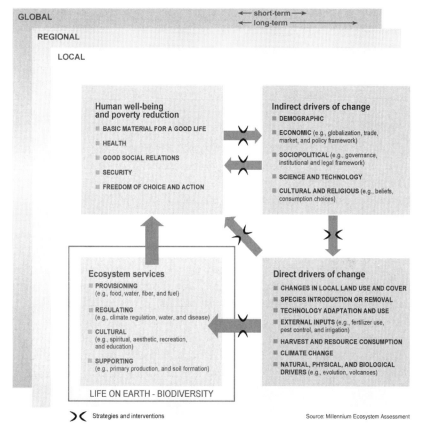

Figure 2.1. A framework for understanding ecosystem services and ecosystem change.

There is another important difference between the IPCC assessments and the MA. Economic organisation and incentives are at the centre of the complementary unfolding disasters of both climate change and ecosystem change, yet the MA veered significantly from the approach taken in the IPCC. Economic growth models using gross domestic product (GDP) as a core metric are central to the IPCC scenarios. Human well-being, technological responses and levels of damage are all tied to GDP growth. While the nature and tightness of the tie of these variables to GDP are discussed in the IPCC assessments, the economic models themselves remain at the core of the analysis, on a par with the physical science models that relate the accumulation of greenhouse gases to climate change. Indeed, the whole approach of scenarios with quantitative projections of GDP evokes 'predictable precision' that climate science cannot deliver. The MA took a decidedly different approach by decoupling human well-being, as well as technological change and other phenomena, from GDP. With human well-being uncoupled from GDP in the MA, economic reasoning with its formal models did not dominate the discussion of well-being. Indeed, other social scientists probably had a comparative advantage at 'looking around' the economy and thinking directly about ecosystem services and human well-being.

The MA picked up where the IPCC had reached after a decade and started with scientists from the developed and the developing countries participating almost equally. This exposed tensions over equity and Western visions of the future right from the beginning. Interpretive social scientists were never able to append themselves to the core climate models and hence worked apart from the IPCC process, whereas interpretive social scientists were welcomed from the beginning into the MA. Thus feedbacks from 'softer' analyses of social change were treated with as much respect as the analyses economists had quantified for the IPCC. Although climate scientists are now becoming serious about the complexities of feedback from diverse terrestrial ecosystems and are incorporating the dynamics of ocean currents, the MA started with such complexity and more. In short, climate assessment reflects the initial framing and order in which additional frames of analysis were added, while the MA reflects what happens when complexity and the need for multiple frames are acknowledged from the start.

For solid scientific reasons, the MA had to be methodologically pluralistic. Ecologists have multiple ways of framing relations and dynamics between species. The multiple ways economists understand economic systems were brought into the MA from the beginning. The MA – once it had been accepted that all frames of analysis come to the table on an equal footing – had to be a deliberative process of learning together. Let me highlight the reasons why deliberation was a necessity.

First, the literature that was assessed reflects the fragmented, disciplinary nature of science. Environmental scientists rarely make the linkages identified in the MA general framework to the social system, while social scientists rarely make adequate linkages in their analyses to the environmental system. Thus, natural scientists and social scientists had to interpret each other's literatures together, clarify the linkages from what they each knew through experiential knowledge, and come to a common understanding of the significance of the literature to the more systemic questions being addressed by the MA.

Second, ecology consists of formal frameworks such as food web models, more-interpretive frameworks, such as landscape ecology, and metaphors such as 'environmental engineer'. The different ecological ways of thinking do not fit together within an overarching meta-model of an ecosystem. Which framing seemed most powerful was case specific and, in many cases, several framings were important. Similarly, the literature on the relations between the environment and human well-being are framed by neoclassical, as well as Marxist, political economists, anthropologists from cultural ecology and ethnobiology, geographers from different schools of thought, and political ecologists whose original training could have been in anthropology, geography, political science or sociology.

Third, neither social systems nor ecosystems have 'inherent' scales for analysis. Although many social models are applicable at any scale, the situation in ecology is much messier. Researchers select the spatial and temporal extent and the grain of an analysis depending on the problem focus, the chosen ecological or other framework, and the constraints of obtaining appropriate data. The differing spatial and temporal extents and grains of analysis of the cases assessed made it very difficult to summarise the literature as a whole and interpret its general applicability globally, including to situations yet to be analysed.

Fourth, MA participants became increasingly aware of the historical contingencies and local contextualities of the dynamics between social and ecological systems. Everything had multiple causes and multiple effects, although particular analyses typically emphasised but one or two. The variety of factors and their interrelations across spatial and temporal scales that could have contributed to a crash of a population or shift in the structure and processes of an ecosystem could not be documented. There were parallel difficulties for explaining changes in social systems.

Fifth, and closely related to the fourth, we know very little about ecosystem thresholds owing to the complex nature of ecosystems and their dynamics. Identifying thresholds – a concept critical to both popular notions and formal stock-flow models of sustainability – was not possible because no ecosystem and the ways it is embedded in larger systems has been so completely modelled and empirically calibrated that the distinction between sustainable flows and degradation can be made. Thus, neither the MA conceptual framework nor the empirical literature reviewed distinguished between ecological services generated by sustainable ecosystem flows and those that were generated through degrading ecosystem properties that would result in reduced future flows. Although participants were well aware that populations crash and ecosystems go through transitions that are difficult, if not impossible, to reverse, the shared concern that future generations would have fewer ecosystem services – a concern that seemed to have increased for most participants through the MA – could not be deduced scientifically.

Sixth, although concern was shared, values, especially those rooted in economics, were actively disputed. Although the relative impacts of different greenhouse gases can be compared and aggregated reasonably well with respect to their impact on warming, it was impossible to compare or aggregate drivers of ecosystem change. Some biologists were intrigued by the possibilities of devising relative weights for ecosystem services through economic valuation, and some economists were prepared to use valuations in the literature. Participants from developing countries, however, argued that economic valuation methods weight the dollars the rich spend on eco-tourism the same as the dollar-equivalents the poor spend on food and bus fares. The MA addresses future generations out of a concern that the current socioeconomic system does not weight them adequately. Thus, it would be illogical to use current preferences, behaviour or replacement costs from a system that is on the wrong course to weight and aggregate details to inform new policies to protect the future. Others pointed out that for there to be any rationality to relying on stated preferences or human behaviour, one would have to assume that lay people were sufficiently informed of the very complexities the MA scientists were struggling to understand. This assumption contradicted the objective of the MA to provide much needed knowledge to decision makers. In short, the problems of using monetary values to weight phenomena are tightly embedded in the very socioeconomic system driving the problems of ecosystem degradation the MA sought to understand in order to design new policies

Thus, for clear scientific reasons, to the extent that the MA brought scientists' fragmented knowledge together into a coherent whole, it was through collaborative learning and collective judgment. This is a new way of doing 'big science.' The three blind men are not simply announcing their separate findings about the elephant but many scientists are feeling, talking to each other, thinking together, going back to feel again, and expanding the number of people participating in the process.

EXPANDING OUR NOTION OF SCIENCE

Reductionist science assumes that scientists can address smaller and smaller questions without losing time linking what they are learning to the other sub-fields of their disciplines, let alone other disciplines. The vast majority of scientists still believe the parts will all come together 'naturally' and, if not, it will be some one else's responsibility to bring them together. Of course, we now know that this is not true. The MA provides documentation as to why this is not true and what can be done to overcome it. Yet our universities and research institutions continue to be structured as if the separate sciences will somehow merge into a coherent whole, long after empirical evidence has documented otherwise and new approaches have emerged for which scientists could be better prepared.

Similarly, our environmental management institutions are largely structured around historic notions of how science works. The expanded way that science is working to understand complex environmental problems raises serious questions with respect to bureaucratic accountability. Environmental agencies derive authority from science, are held accountable for basing their decisions on the best science, and have found themselves in a power vacuum when the science is not clear. And our standards of clear science are historic; that is, coherent combinations of established laws or unchallenged theories backed by empirical documentation. Judgment is regarded with suspicion. As scientists become more deliberate in how they collectively understand complex systems, and public consciousness of this new way of doing big science increases, environmental policy and management agencies will probably be able to adapt to it. But a systematic effort needs to be made.

On the positive side, these relatively recent developments in science complement experiments initiated somewhat earlier to bring user groups and traditional people with experiential knowledge into a participatory role with science. Action research, participatory research, rapid rural appraisal, citizen science and related efforts entail experiential knowledge, deliberation and judgment comparable to that used by scientists in the IPCC assessment and MA process. Scientists certainly have an edge in interpreting the scientific literature, but local people have an edge when it comes to local conditions.

We think of ourselves as the smartest and most social of all species. I do not know whether either of these qualities is more characteristic of people than porpoises or whales. Perhaps the key distinction is that people also have opposable thumbs because many other species, from ants to wolves, are social. But, I am certain that our smartness and sociality need to work more effectively together. Our ability to communicate and organise ourselves in disparate tasks as social beings, and our ability to understand as smart beings, are inseparable. They cannot be described, measured, analysed or evaluated separately. Our smartness only works through the ways we communicate, organise and build knowledge together. The approach we began to take around 150 years ago to being smart and social is not working; we need to change the institutional structures and understandings of science that guide our smartness and sociality, but we should not give up being smart and social.

Yet, unfortunately, the lure of answers rooted in first principles remains strong. We have scientific fundamentalists who interpret reality through the lenses of particular parts of science. We have free market fundamentalists who see everything in economic terms. Others rely on religious fundamentalism and faith-based knowledge. Yet surely each of these, and any combination of fundamentalist approaches, will hasten the collapse of the very multi-levelled diversity on which we depend.

FURTHER READING

Note: This chapter summarises the key points from a lecture by the author at the CSIRO-SEI Integration Showcase on 27–28 June 2006 and a 'Master Class' presented on June 29, Canberra, Australia. The author is in the process of augmenting and linking the following articles for a book. Further reading and references can be found in the articles listed below.

Lélé S and Norgaard RB (2005) Practicing interdisciplinarity. *BioScience* **55**(11), 967–975.

Norgaard RB (2004) Learning and knowing collectively. *Ecological Economics* **49**(2), 231–241.

Norgaard RB and Baer P (2005) Collectively seeing complex systems: the nature of the problem. *BioScience* **55**(11), 953–960.

Norgaard RB and Baer P (2005) Collectively seeing climate change: the limits of formal models. *BioScience* **55**(11), 961–966.

Chapter 3

Improving integrated research: tools for analysis and learning

Lorrae van Kerkhoff and Gabriele Bammer

ABSTRACT

Analysis of the integration approaches taken by two Australian Cooperative Research Centres – the CRC for Greenhouse Accounting and the CRC for Coastal Zone, Estuary and Waterway Management – is used to reflect on (a) six heuristics for understanding integration and (b) a framework of six questions for describing integration. The heuristics are connecting across research silos, a jigsaw, purchaser–provider relationships, extension work, value adding across multiple scales and 'locked door' serendipity. The questions examine what the integration is aiming to achieve, what is being integrated, who is doing the integration and how, and investigating the context for the integration and success measures. Both the heuristics and the questions have broader applications. We also examine what integration in research is, along with contexts in which integration occurs, by examining projects, programs and organisations. We conclude by examining institutional aspects of integration, especially governance, funding and accountability, and incentives.

INTRODUCTION

Integrated research is commonly seen as a pathway to achieving different, more practical outcomes from research than is the case in typical academic research, or even applied research, and has become a popular catch phrase in natural resource management (NRM). But what does integrated research really mean? How is it done? And how can learning from emerging activities and practices embodying an integrative approach be promoted? These questions lie at the heart of the challenges facing integration researchers who are striving to craft a coherent research tradition, often in isolation and without a common ground for sharing experiences and ideas (Bammer 2005). In this chapter we present some of our ideas and experiences to help shape that common ground. We are interested in fostering mutual learning to enhance the quality of integrated research and in enthusing researchers to engage in, and improve, methodologies.

We present some of the diverse ways in which research can be integrated, and discuss some of the innovations and experiments that people have undertaken to implement the idea of integration in practice. We then draw on a case study of two Australian Cooperative Research Centres (van Kerkhoff 2008) as organisations that embody many of these different aspects of research integration. We use this as a basis for demonstrating the value of taking a structured approach to learning about integration, by asking and answering six targeted questions (Bammer and LWA Integration Symposium Participants 2005). We argue that reflecting on integrated research practice is an essential component of learning to get better at it, and that structured approaches offer more systematic and comparable lessons. Although these questions are primarily directed at the 'unit of integration' – in other words, the project or program of research – there are also additional issues that affect our understandings of, and capacity to do, integrated research. We conclude by proposing a complementary set of questions that start to unpack the institutional and organisational dimensions of integration.

WHAT IS INTEGRATION?

This question has many different answers. At the most general level, of course, it implies bringing disparate things into something more whole. However in a research context, those 'things' can be many and varied, including:

- **Multiple disciplines:** multi-, inter- and transdisciplinary research approaches all seek to integrate (to varying degrees) across the conceptual boundaries posed by disciplines; e.g. ecological economics explores the overlaps and spaces between ecology and economics.
- **Problem-solution framing:** narrow problem framings can lead to narrow solutions, so integration can be concerned with building broader, more systemic understandings of problems and their pos-

sible solutions. For example, shifting thinking from 'the problem' of localised food shortages to thinking about the dynamics of food production and distribution opens up a wider set of possible solutions for hunger and famine, such as market reform or changes to property rights.

- **Organisational units:** building connections across organisations, or across units within one organisation, is also a setting for integration. Within universities, these units may sometimes map onto disciplines but can also include more applied multi-disciplinary schools or centres. Attempting to construct a course in environmental health, for example, may require efforts to integrate across an Environment Department and a School of Public Health. Successfully teaching such a course requires not only integration of knowledge, but also integration of administrative structures to allow remuneration, for example, to be shared across different academic units.

- **Multiple sectors:** this includes integration between science and policy, or between science and community or other stakeholders, often with the intention that such integration will result in research that is more useable and useful in application. Involving farmers in the development of a computer-based decision-support system for their production practices, for example, helps to ensure that the final product will be relevant to other farmers, and presented in an understandable and useful format.

- **Resources**: this involves collaborative research that brings together a range of resources (funds, time, infrastructure and knowledge) to do research that is not possible with each group operating independently. This need not involve a specific organisational structure, and can range from relatively informal arrangements, such as involving local stakeholders to gain access to their specific historical knowledge, through to large-scale, formal research agreements to share high-cost equipment, such as those found in nuclear physics.

Thus, integration encompasses both integration *within* the research sphere, as well as integration *beyond* the research sphere; it also encompasses the *activities* of doing research, as well as the organisational and institutional *structures* that surround them (van Kerkhoff 2005a). Any given project may include one or more of these types of integration. The choices that are made regarding which of these dimensions of integration are most critical – and most problematic – are often also not well articulated, but assumed under a broad banner of integration. In the worst case scenario they are not well thought through, leading to effort and resources being directed to integration that may not actually be confronting the main integration challenges at all. This lack of articulation also means that key aspects of integration remain hidden, hindering evaluation and learning.

The diverse ways in which a research project, program or organisation (recognising that some of the above dimensions of integration, including organisational integration and problem-solution framing integration need not be based on a specific project) can be integrative also highlights the need for learning from experience, because questions of how to decide which tools are most appropriate for these different contexts for integration are currently few and far between. Fortunately, there are many experiments in integration taking place across diverse settings that can form a rich basis for this learning.

CONTEXTS FOR INTEGRATION

Reflecting the observation that there are many 'things' that can be usefully integrated in a research context, there are likewise many different forms of experimentation – in crossing disciplines, in linking organisational forms, in fostering cross-sectoral relationships, and so forth. These present many different opportunities to learn from integration in practice. These experiments usually occur within the following contexts:

- **Integrated projects**: these are projects that seek to bring together a range of collaborators, such as researchers from different disciplines or research paradigms (empirical researchers and modellers, for example); or seek to bring stakeholders into the project as co-researchers or advisors. Individually, most projects represent relatively small investments in integration, and can often be flexible in their approach.
- **Integrated programs**: these are groups of projects that may take conventional research approaches individually, but together form a strongly interconnected suite of work and/or perform an integrative function, such as informing identified policy needs. An example is a suite of projects designed to feed results into a single model. These are less flexible than individual projects, because changes to any component of the program may affect the overall goal.
- **Integrated organisations**: structures to connect organisations (beyond those implied by more transient cross-organisational projects or programs) or to create new, integrated organisations are also important. These may include new organisational forms, such as the Santa Fe Institute (www.santafe.edu), where economists work

alongside physicists, ecologists, and so on, each sharing an interest in complexity. Although they may not be working together on a specific project, the 'discipline-less' organisation is structured so that thinking and ideas from one field can connect with the others. The Australian Cooperative Research Centres (https://www.crc.gov.au/Information/default.aspx), discussed in more detail below, also represent a 'quasi-virtual' new organisational form that brings together disparate groups.

These three contexts can be regarded as complementary, but not necessarily as hierarchical or nested. It is entirely possible – indeed, perhaps far more common – to do integrated research at the project level without being part of an integrated program. Likewise, having an integrated organisation at the formal level does not automatically translate into integrated projects or programs; these can be facilitated by organisational structures, but integration at the program and project scales needs additional effort and planning.

This is not a complete list of all integrated research contexts, but it does highlight that integration can take place at different scales and in different practical settings. The ways in which people who participate in these settings understand what integration is, and how to achieve it, offer useful lessons for those trying to improve integrated research practice. But how can we structure this learning so that the lessons drawn are comparable, allowing us to start to build a comprehensive set of understandings about integrated research?

EXAMPLE: COOPERATIVE RESEARCH CENTRES

In this section we draw on a case study of two Australian Cooperative Research Centres (CRCs) to illustrate what insights we might gain from taking a more structured approach to learning about integration. The analysis we present is based on our previous work in identifying how participants in integrated research understood their practices, from their own perspectives. We then compare this practice-based understanding with the insights that emerge by taking a more theoretically oriented approach using a framework based on the systematic analysis of six questions. Although both of these are presented quite briefly here for the purpose of illustration, they can be followed up in more extensive detail elsewhere (van Kerkhoff 2008; Bammer 2006a; Bammer 2006b; Bammer 2008).

The two centres were the CRC for Greenhouse Accounting and the CRC for Coastal Zone, Estuary and Waterway Management (the Coastal CRC), which were in operation from 1999 to 2006. CRCs are research partnerships formed between universities, government research agencies and stakeholder partners. They are partially funded by the Australian Commonwealth Government and co-funded by the partners. They are generally structured into a small number of research themes or programs, with several projects in each. Most importantly, however, they have a formal mandate to do integrated research and to be integrated research organisations, supported by formal contracts and overarching governance arrangements (van Kerkhoff 2005b). Consequently, they embody the multiple contexts for integration we described in the previous section: projects, programs and organisations.

This study was concerned with how people understood the concept of integration, and how they applied it from the perspective of their own role in the CRC (van Kerkhoff 2008). It was based on interviews with a diverse range of partners and participants in the CRCs, including researchers, program managers, chief executive officers, students and a range of stakeholders. The ideas they offered reflected a number of heuristics; that is, the concepts people use to understand and guide their actions in relation to achieving integration. These heuristics formed six main groups.

1. Connecting across research silos

In this heuristic, research is primarily conducted in self-referential silos, and the role of integration is to draw connections between them. For example, both CRCs had computer-based modelling projects that were seeking to bring together the research conducted in various other sections of the CRC.

2. Jigsaws

Many researchers used the metaphor of a jigsaw puzzle to describe integration: bringing all the fragmented pieces of the puzzle together to provide a complete picture. This was viewed by many as desirable, as well as desired by practitioners such as policy makers. It implies that such a complete picture is possible, and was the concept underlying much of the modelling effort.

3. Purchaser–provider relationships

CRCs were expected to operate at least in part as research service-providers, so the purchaser–provider heuristic also formed a way of thinking about integration. Contracted research is regarded as effectively integrating across the research-policy (or other implementation) divide, because the purchasers decided what research products they required. The purchasers also have a vested interest in implementing the results.

4. Extension work

'Getting results out there' through effective extension was also seen as a form of integration, where researchers worked with specialist communicators or extension agents to shape relevant messages. This was regarded as integrative, in the sense that research was being put together with practice, and there were opportunities for users to provide feedback to the researchers.

5. Value adding across multiple scales

This was a more complex model of integration, where research-based knowledge could be progressively integrated as there was movement 'up' scales, from empirical knowledge of, say, specific species up to an ecosystem scale, then to an ecosystem-management scale, then to an ecosystem-society scale and finally to a fully integrated understanding. At each scale, the new level of research 'adds value' to the previous one, and there may be application in practice at all scales. This was an innovative model, which was unique to one of the CRCs.

6. 'Locked door' serendipity

The final model was the most simple: namely that integration occurs by placing people in the same space and letting them sort out how they can best work together. It allows for serendipity and encourages 'organic' projects to emerge. The CRCs as a whole reflected this model in many respects, with emphasis on gaining formal commitments that the partners will work together – 'locking' the relationship – but then providing substantial flexibility regarding how they achieve that.

These six heuristics illustrate the diverse ways in which people understood what integration is in the context of these two CRCs. These are significant in the context of learning, because what people learn from their experiences depends strongly on their existing understanding of what they are trying to do, and how they are trying to do it. Consequently, these models also illustrate the problems that may emerge when such diverse understandings are at play – different lessons and largely incompatible conclusions.

A STANDARD WAY TO DESCRIBE INTEGRATION

Bammer and LWA Integration Symposium participants (2005) have proposed a set of six questions that offer a structured approach to describing integration. They make key aspects of integration that are often not described explicit, and thereby create a more comparable environment for learning. These questions are:

- What is the integration aiming to achieve and who is intended to benefit?
- What are the elements being integrated?
- Who is doing the integration?
- How is the integration being undertaken?
- What is the context for the integration?
- How is success measured?

We apply these to the CRC cases.

What is the integration aiming to achieve and who is intended to benefit?

This helps us think about the aims of the integration, rather than the aims of the research project or program.

In the CRC for Greenhouse Accounting, although the main aim of the research was to build a better understanding of carbon in the environment, the main aim of the integration was to contribute to the development of policy tools by their major stakeholder, the Australian Greenhouse Office (an agency of the federal government). In contrast, the Coastal CRC's research had far broader aims of improving coastal management across varying geographic scales. The integration therefore aimed to build effective relationships with community groups: local, state, federal governments and their agencies; and large industry. In both cases, the stakeholders were seen as the major beneficiaries, and the integration was a way of increasing the accessibility and relevance of the research to those stakeholders.

What are the elements being integrated?

This helps us think about the boundaries inherent in our problem definition and what is being included, excluded and marginalised. Is the boundary defensible?

In the Greenhouse Accounting CRC, the primary elements being integrated were fragmented areas of scientific research – by bringing together knowledge on carbon in soils (below-ground parts of plants) and carbon above ground (in above-ground parts of plants). This was an important component of understanding that also underpinned the application they were concerned with, in creating national carbon accounts. The Coastal CRC emphasised the boundaries between science and policy, adopting an explicit mandate of 'bridging the gaps' between these two domains. In the process of meeting this mandate, they also worked across disciplines; for example, by building conceptual models of estuarine systems that incorporated marine biology, microbiology, chemistry and geomorphology.

Who is doing the integration?

This need not be collaborative – integration can be done by an individual, or by the whole group, or sub-group.

In the Greenhouse Accounting CRC, the integration was largely the responsibility of the modelling group in a specific program, where all the other research (such as those projects measuring carbon in trees and carbon in soils) was intended to feed into a final, whole-of-system model. In the Coastal CRC, all project leaders were held to be responsible for integration, designing research that involved relevant stakeholders in appropriate ways.

How is the integration being undertaken?

We propose that there are five primary classes of integration methods: dialogue-based, model-based, vision-based, product-based and common-metric-based (Bammer *et al.* 2007).

In the Greenhouse Accounting CRC, integration was largely model-based. Model-based integration relies on using a mathematical or conceptual model as the focus for bringing knowledge together. The Australian Greenhouse Office then incorporated the CRC's mathematical models into their own work on measuring carbon. The CRC also provided other specific outputs to their major stakeholder, where key reports required the researchers to develop a strong understanding of their stakeholder's needs. Integration in the Coastal CRC was predominantly vision- and dialogue-based. The Centre's vision of bridging the gaps between science and policy drove the impetus for integration. Dialogue and participation were the preferred methods for integrating, with even the computer models being devised to facilitate dialogue with and among stakeholders rather than to provide absolute answers.

What is the context for the integration?

This especially includes political, historical and organisational context; indeed anything that might affect the aims, methods or success of the integration.

The Greenhouse Accounting CRC was working on a politically controversial issue, in a contested national and international context – neither the Australian government nor the international community were settled in their ideas regarding the control of greenhouse gas emissions, and there were strong vested interests and scientifically sophisticated stakeholders who wanted to see particular forms of greenhouse accounting. This context was also characterised by rapid change and unexpected delays in decision making, as when Kyoto Protocol negotiations were suspended in 2001. In contrast, coastal management in Australia did not have the administrative equivalent of a single, overarching federal agency. There were many jurisdictions responsible for different drivers of coastal degradation. This created the context where the Coastal CRC needed to engage across these diverse stakeholder groups if they were to achieve their goal of improving coastal management.

How is success measured?

Measures of success should include both outcomes and processes.

In the timeframe of the study, which focused on the earlier years of the CRCs, there were few measures in place to try to identify the success or otherwise of integration. In a general sense, the Greenhouse Accounting CRC's success was measured largely by outcomes including clearly identified advances in sequestration modelling and a satisfied major stakeholder. The process by which this was achieved was largely by direct negotiation with that stakeholder. In the Coastal CRC, the outcomes sought were improved coastal policy and/or management, and the process to achieve that was the active involvement of stakeholders throughout the research. More specifically, they also conducted a benchmarking study on project leaders' attitudes and actions towards stakeholder participation in research projects. A follow-up study at the end of the CRC's life found an increase in the proportion of projects that actively involved stakeholders. This measured process, but did not offer any conclusions regarding either the researchers' or the stakeholders' satisfaction with these processes.

WHAT DID WE LEARN (THAT HEURISTICS DIDN'T TELL US)?

Thinking about integrated research in this more structured way offers different insights from those afforded by the heuristic models used by the interviewees in the study.

First, it illustrates the fundamental importance of the stakeholder landscape. The presence of a single, powerful stakeholder versus a large number of small stakeholders generated a very different set of challenges and appropriate actions for each of the CRCs. The more conventional research model adopted by the CRC for Greenhouse Accounting suited an environment where they were working with a scientifically sophisticated stakeholder organisation, whereas the highly engaged model suited the Coastal CRCs mandate to 'bridge the gaps' with stakeholders who had highly variable scientific capability. Similarly, the controversial policy environment faced by the CRC for Greenhouse Accounting also shaped their emphasis on modelling and other similar scientific products as their main integrative activity. In a controversial environment, it can be risky to work too closely with any single stakeholder, because it may reduce the credibility of the science to others, so opting for a more distanced relationship based on providing products was a better strategy than actively involving the stakeholder in their research. This indicates that understanding stakeholders is vital: a message that was far less clear in the intuitive models of integrated research.

Second, there are few indicators of success or failure. It is difficult to measure performance if goals are too broad or too narrow, and therefore difficult to judge the appropriate allocation of resources. The Coastal CRC's broad goal of 'bridging the gaps' was aspirational, but provided little tangible guidance for project leaders. The CRC for Greenhouse Accounting's narrow goal of developing tools for national greenhouse policy was more mundane, and was felt by some to be restrictive because it implied that successes outside that narrow mandate did not 'count'. Indicators for success or failure, whether broad or detailed, can play a strong role in shaping the ways integrated research is approached and understood.

Third, this approach starts to focus attention on the importance of the specifics of a particular problem and the context in which it has arisen – people work out who to integrate with, and how, in the context of seeking a solution to a particular problem or striving to attain a specific goal. As a result, much integrated research activity is context specific, where both understandings of the past (how did we get into this situation?) and visions for the future (what do we want to achieve?) come into play (see also van Kerkhoff 2008). This means that learning from experience is fraught with difficulty, as when researchers imagine that the interests held by a group of stakeholders in one project will be similar to the interests held by stakeholders in a different project.

Fourth, historical heuristics (those concepts that people are familiar with) can be misleading. Heuristics tend to be based on concepts people are familiar with, which may not be adequate to the task of describing integration fully. For example, the concept of extension or outreach, which many researchers invoked to describe integration, characterised stakeholders as passive recipients of research-based knowledge. Yet the stakeholders themselves were often far more actively engaged in the research than an extension model implies. As a result, the ideas surrounding integration may be end up being confusing and contradictory, rather than helping us to understand and learn effectively from experience.

CONCLUSIONS

In this chapter we have argued that we can benefit from being more systematic about our approaches to understanding, describing and doing integrated research. The case study of the two CRCs illustrates the practical application of taking a systematic approach, in terms of minimising inefficiencies. Being clear about the goals of the integration, and articulating them in relation to the context and particular problem-solution setting, is a fundamental step in refining the practice of integrated research. If we are going to continue to build on our practice-based experiences in integrated research – and through that maximise our potential to learn from those experiences – structured reflection that draws on, and informs, emerging theories of integration is important.

To date these structured, theoretically oriented approaches to integration have tended to focus inward toward the project or program, rather than outward to better understand integrated research in its organisational or institutional contexts. We propose that the next step in building robust reflection to improve the practice of integrated research is to look beyond the project towards the institutional structures and arrangements that foster (or inhibit) integration. In this context "[i]nstitutions are systems of rules, decision-making procedures, and programs that give rise to social practices, assign roles to participants in these practices, and guide interactions among the occupants of the relevant roles. Unlike organisations, which are material entities that typically figure as actors in social practices, institutions may be thought of as the rules of the game that determine the character of these practices" (Institutional Dimensions of Global Environmental Change 2005). As a preliminary set of institutional considerations, we propose close examination of governance, funding and accountability, and incentives:

Governance arrangements for integrated research, both formal and informal:

- Who makes which decisions?
- How is power shared or concentrated?
- Are these structures appropriate for integration?
- How are they shaped by organisational history and context?

The governance of integrated research processes and decision-making includes the formal rules and processes that support or hinder integrated research. University norms that tend to promote discipline-based research (and researchers) over research and researchers who span disciplines do not favour integration; whereas formal policies that seek to break down traditional discipline-based structures within the university may help it to flourish.

Funding and accountability:

- Who is funding the integrated research?
- Who are participants primarily accountable to?
- Do participants have multiple accountabilities?
- What are they accountable for?

If integrated research is funded primarily by industry or government departments seeking solutions for immediate problems, integrated researchers may not have the resources to develop new methodologies or frameworks for tackling longer-term challenges or refining processes and practices over time. Yet, where they are funded solely by academic research councils, researchers may be discouraged from actively engaging in activities concerned with application. Some analysts have suggested that research projects that are formally accountable to both stakeholders and research institutions are more likely to effectively connect research and action (Guston 2001).

Incentives for people to participate in integrated research:

- Why do people want to participate in integrated research?
- Are there conflicting incentives in relation to a particular project?
- Can these be resolved? How?

Although this may be changing, formal academic reward systems typically encourage narrow, disciplinary research rather than complex, integrated research. Rewards for publication in peer-reviewed journals are rarely matched by equivalent rewards for stakeholder reports or news media coverage. As a result, researchers can be deterred from taking on or participating in integrated research projects, even if interdisciplinary, problem-oriented research is encouraged in institutional rhetoric.

Understanding these dimensions of integrated research is also critical to understanding why it is challenging, and what we may learn from working in integrated projects, programs or organisations. These questions offer a different perspective on integration that seeks to identify its place within wider academic or other social structures, and ultimately to offer ideas on how those wider structures may need to adjust to better accommodate integrated research.

We have presented in this chapter some conceptual tools that may help integrated research practitioners take a more structured and analytical approach to reflecting and learning from what we do. Sharing these lessons is critical to avoid reinventing the wheel and replicating errors, but also for building a more nuanced understanding of what integrated, mission-directed research entails and how to navigate these complex waters. Through the combined processes of looking inward to the unit of integration, and outward to the institutional and organisational settings within which that integration is taking place, we may collectively start to build substantial improvements in integrated research and, ultimately, in improved natural resource management.

REFERENCES

Bammer G (2005) Integration and implementation sciences: building a new specialization. *Ecology and Society* **10**(2), 6 [online] <http://www.ecologyandsociety.org/vol10/iss2/art6/>.

Bammer G (2006a) A systematic approach to integration in research. Integration Insights #1, September. Available at <http://i2s.anu.edu.au>.

Bammer G (2006b) Illustrating a systematic approach to explain integration in research – the case of the World Commission on Dams. Integration Insights #2, October. Available at <http://i2s.anu.edu.au>.

Bammer G (2008) Enhancing research collaboration: three key management challenges. *Research Policy* **37**(5), 875–887.

Bammer G and LWA Integration Symposium Participants (2005) Guiding principles for integration in natural resource management (NRM) as a contribution to sustainability. In: Australian case studies of integration in natural resource management (NRM). (Eds G Bammer, A Curtis, C Mobbs, R Lane and S Dovers). *Australasian Journal of Environmental Management* **12** (Supplement), 5–7.

Bammer G, MacDonald D and Deane P (2007) Dialogue methods for research integration. Integration Insights #4, May. Available at <http://i2s.anu.edu.au>.

Guston DH (2001) Boundary organizations in environmental policy and science: an introduction. *Science, Technology and Human Values* **26**(4), 399–408.

Institutional Dimensions of Global Environmental Change (2005) 'Science plan'. IHDP Report Series. Human Dimensions of Global Environmental Change, Bonn, Germany.

van Kerkhoff L (2005a) Integrated research: concepts of connection in environmental science and policy. *Environmental Science and Policy* **8**, 452–463.

van Kerkhoff L (2005b) Strategic integration: the practical politics of integrated research in context. *Journal of Research Practice* **1**(2), Article M5.

van Kerkhoff L (2008) *'Making a Difference': Science, Action, and Integrated Environmental Research*. Sense Publishers, Rotterdam, The Netherlands.

Chapter 4

Challenges and success factors in undertaking integrated research

Elizabeth Kington

ABSTRACT

A 6-month review of current research within the Commonwealth Scientific and Industrial Research Organisation (CSIRO), which sought to explore the interface between science and societal change, has revealed many practical challenges for researchers, the research process and the institutional environments in which this research is managed and funded. Semi-structured interviews were used to elicit, from the experiences of individuals involved in six case study projects, the success factors, challenges and lessons to be learnt by CSIRO within an area of emerging science. The study showed that project teams were engaging and interacting with challenging community, government policy and industrial institutional settings. The process of engaging with people, their experiences and needs confronted traditional 'top-down' scientific research dissemination and the way researchers needed to think about tackling research problems.

These projects have shown CSIRO researchers how to stretch themselves across disciplinary boundaries, work cooperatively and to interact with socially complex environments and people. This has encouraged new forms of learning, brought systems understanding to research domains and, through building community consensus and participation processes, has influenced 'real world' issues.

Accommodation of this research within the many CSIRO Divisions' cultural environments brings into focus the transition needed to better accommodate the pursuit of knowledge that is often considered to be less scientifically rigorous, more intellectually challenging and too interpretive in the light of past CSIRO practice. High levels of time, effort and funding are required, and sufficient lead time is needed to plan and organise the research process. The study participants suggested that the existing academic reward system was inadequate and an impediment to the pursuit of integrative research by CSIRO scientists.

INTRODUCTION

Social and economic integration, as it is referred to by the CSIRO's 'emerging sciences' documentation, has been described as contributing to a new 'paradigm shift' in the way CSIRO conducts its research. The CSIRO Social and Economic Integration Emerging Science Area Business Plan (2002–2006) recognises *'science organisations face 'drivers' at the business operations level and in the actual science they perform.'* It suggests social and economic integration is fundamental to all research, as *'pursuing science without reference to its social and economic context is like choosing to be deaf or blind'.*

This emerging science is concerned with increasing research relevance in human affairs, developing marketable knowledge and social learning. It necessarily embraces systems analysis, action learning and decision-support modelling, as well as the more straightforward disciplinary collaborations. This transition is not easy to achieve and involves 'doing things differently' as well as 'thinking differently' about research.

THE REVIEW

In June 2002, a short-term contract was awarded to conduct a review of social and economic integrated (SEI) best-practice research in the CSIRO. The objective of the study was to ensure future investment in integrated science was underpinned by a rigorous understanding of internal and external best practice, and to assist in the development of 'flagship' projects, through which large CSIRO investment was to be made. The contract was overseen by the four-member SEI Forum Steering Committee and the final report was presented to the SEI Board in March 2003.

The material for this chapter is based on the findings of this review, which can be found in a report titled 'The review of contemporary SEI best practice in CSIRO: SEI stories – reflections and lessons from a selection of SEI science in CSIRO' (Kington 2003).

BACKGROUND – INTEGRATED RESEARCH IN THE CSIRO

The CSIRO is Australia's national science agency and one of the largest and most diverse research agencies in the world. CSIRO operations span seven sectors: Agribusiness, Energy and Transport, Health, Information Communication and Services, Manufacturing, Mineral Resources and Environment and Natural Resources, with more than 6500 people conducting and assisting with scientific research. Within the CSIRO, approximately 70 projects were identified to have integrated social and economic research.

The Division of Sustainable Ecosystems (CSE) was distinct from other CSIRO Divisions in having the greatest number of integrated research projects and many CSE researchers and teams who were familiar with engaging with social and economic practitioners. Projects were predominantly 'driven' by sustainable resource use and land-use planning. Some involved group learning processes, usually with resource users, while others had chosen adaptive research techniques to learn and evolve research through its implementation. Multi-disciplinary team approaches, decision-support frameworks, stakeholder participation, geographical information system modelling and social surveying were commonly employed methodologies.

The Division of Land and Water (CLW) had the second greatest number of integrated research projects, although the manner in which projects were undertaken was distinctly different. Within this Division, social and economic research was being predominantly undertaken by two principal research groups: The Policy and Economic Research Unit and The Australian Research Centre for Water in Society. These groups had specialised in the economic and social-psychological aspects of land and water management research, respectively. These groups also contained the majority of economic and social researchers, who worked collectively as part of multi-disciplinary teams, as well as separately – for example, to develop social and economic decision tools for policy.

Within other divisions, such as the Division of Mathematics and Information Systems (CMIS) and Health Science and Nutrition (HSN), multi-disciplinary teams that provide whole-of-system/cycle perspectives had been principally used in integrated research and, within the Division of Minerals and Energy (CME) community consultation processes had been employed to complement industrial decision making. Many other projects embraced collaborative processes and partnerships with stakeholders to develop 'best-practice' processes. Others employed tools such as decision-support modelling software.

Overall, it was proposed that these integrated research projects resulted in increased research relevance, closer interaction with stakeholders and enhanced the value of research outcomes. Analysis of the social and economic environments and adaptive research approaches provided greater insights about 'whole' systems and more control of the research process.

Integrated research projects were perceived as being particularly useful for natural resource decision-making issues, where multiple stakeholders, environmental objectives and economic development needs required planning consensus. An integrative approach to understanding these issues collectively, and as part of a collaborative process, ensured greater success in achieving desired outcomes.

A key challenge was in projects with policy implications. It was believed that outcomes from these projects could be confronting to existing organisational structures, but it was noted that progress was being made towards achieving them.

The success of the projects reported here was mixed, but many of the novel, and often innovative, research processes being used were described as improving the researchers understanding of 'real' systems and providing inspiration for ongoing research work. From the limited details obtained from researchers, it was possible to observe new forms of satisfaction, as well as some frustration and disappointment regarding the time required to conduct this research and the ability to produce appropriate (and acceptable) outcomes.

Some research areas identified settings where integrated research might play an important role, including telecommunications, IT, agriculture, natural resource management, policy, sustainability, complex systems, market institutions and governance, water reclamation and life-cycle analysis.

THE CSIRO CASE STUDIES

Out of the 70 identified projects, six were chosen as case studies by the SEI Forum. The purpose was to evaluate these projects as examples of SEI research 'best practice' and for important practical experience to be shared.

Semi-structured interviews were used to examine aspects of the research processes being employed by these selected projects and draw out some of the key lessons. Findings from the personal experiences of the people involved highlighted the strengths of each project structure and some of the frustrations and challenges being faced.

These experiences were compiled into a narrative of the research process for each project, highlighting issues encountered, together with background information of the research objectives and project history. Each story revealed differences in how research problems were constructed, how research was organised and managed, and how the research connected with 'real' people, systems and markets.

The six projects were chosen broadly from seven CSIRO research divisions and were methodologically different. Whole-of-system analyses and sustainability were important 'drivers'. Out of the six projects, four embraced computer modelling technology to examine decision-making processes and encourage organisational change. Four of the projects used multi-disciplinary teams, and one used collaborating research teams from three quite different CSIRO Divisions. Despite their differences, common themes and issues emerged.

Projects were participatory, engaging with relevant communities and organisations, with one of these employing an action research process and three applying social surveying techniques. Two projects were funded in partnership with industry and one in partnership with a state government. All six projects interfaced with practitioners and stakeholders to improve decision making.

CHRRUPP

The Central Highland Regional Resource Use Planning Program (CHRRUPP) was a 'real' resource-use planning exercise. CSIRO scientists facilitated the development of a process that would be a collaborative partnership of sector interest and community groups, which aimed to last beyond the life of the research-funded project. Building sector capacity was a key aspect of this process that ensured participants came to the planning process with a clear idea of all the issues at a regional scale. Critical, too, to its success was identification and nurturing of local champions and to set the project up from its inception on the ground. A 1-year scoping exercise ensured that the project management team could develop a successful planning process. The researchers recognised that 'change occurs by working through people, building capacity and working on the social dimensions, rather than simply developing more scientific knowledge'. The strength of CHRRUPP was that it developed 'tools' that would support the process, rather than presenting pre-conceived solutions. It sought to undertake planning in an integrated and participatory way, engaging all sectors in all aspects of the planning process, while paying attention to their social and economic issues.

NWShelf JEMS

The North West Shelf Joint Environmental Management Strategy (NWShelf JEMS) arose out of concerns that the basis for management decisions for a major coastal environment were being made without access to all the necessary information. Originally, a scientifically based environmental management project to develop a multiple-use planning framework for sustainable management of the North West Shelf resources was proposed. After scoping this idea, it evolved into a more integrated and coordinated management framework, which would also engage the views of the local communities affected by future resource management decisions and the economies they depended upon. Multiple sector interests were engaged through a steering committee that guided the research work, and the Government of Western Australia was engaged to facilitate a coordinated management strategy at the end of the project. Throughout their work, scientists communicated to others their progress and justified why they were doing each piece of research. A leading scientist suggested '... *This continually exposed scientists to "real" issues and ensured the research work remained relevant and focused*. It was explained '... *Engagement of sector interests took time and initially ...there was a tendency for them to sit back and be critical*'. Further, '*It took years to explain the Management Strategy Evaluation model to all the people involved, and because it is was based on a Decision Support Software model, there was a risk that it would be seen as too new and complicated for real joint management decisions and scenario exploration*'. To overcome this, the project intended to introduce an additional step that would allow the model to be more user-specific and operational.

FARMSCAPE

The Farmers Advisors and Researchers Monitoring Simulation Communication And Performance Evaluation (FARMSCAPE) program essentially grew out of an investigation into why there was such a low adoption among the farming community of decision-support software technology. Over the 10 years since it began, the program has incorporated about 20 different funded projects. The researchers had worked in a participatory way with farmers and farming systems to understand and lower the barriers to farmers' adoption of a decision-support tool. A principal scientist suggested '... *During this time the team has undergone a transformation in their awareness of the social dimensions of farming, a product of holistic thinking, which has been more important to the success of the team's practice than staffing with specialists from social science disciplines'.* The team has evolved to become operationally leaderless: leadership being distributed among team members depending on activity. Time was spent understanding the emergent approach, learning about agricultural scientists and instigating a 'cultural' shift in the way research was being done.

FIA

The Food Into Asia Aleurone (FIA) project developed out of the discovery of a safe way to extract the aleurone layer from wheat bran, and the chance discovery that this aleurone contained folate. The CSIRO Division of Heath Science and Nutrition, in partnership with the food industry, established an integrated research program to determine the efficacy and marketing potential of this product within Asia. A high-profile management team coordinated and set directions for the research, which was overseen by a steering committee. Analytical and clinical trials were followed by consumer analysis and community acceptance of the product to determine the best way it could be used. The final marketing was left up to the industry partners. With all the necessary research skills held 'in-house', coordination of divisional teams and communication was maximised, with all research achieving objectives and deadlines.

JUNIPER

'Juniper', a decision-support computer software tool, grew out of mining industry research, where major decision making by industry was often premised on reliability factors, not experimentation. Important social and economic factors were not always being considered in these decisions. The software tool was developed as a way of enhancing decision making in the context of incomplete information. A CSIRO researcher suggested '... *This process promised to "take the blinkers off" technicians and scientists with respect to their engagement with social and economic practitioners and real world decisions by allowing all players to examine decision-pathways and the assumptions upon which decisions were being made'.* An experienced facilitator, conversant with industry needs, and comfortable with 'fuzzy' math-logic, grounded-theory and de-briefing techniques, was necessary to run industry personnel through the Juniper process. Recruitment of the right researchers for this work was therefore crucial, as was the right way to commercialise this software package. A challenging institutional environment had affected the implementation of Juniper, despite its non-threatening way of exploring decisions, and senior level champion support had been an invaluable driver for this research.

UWSP

The Urban Water System Program (UWSP) was built upon the lessons of its predecessor, and benefited operationally from being more independent and flexible in its industry-partnered research into alternative sustainable urban water design. As well as obtaining a greater input from industry, a lot of effort was put into the research proposals – from a broad spectrum of people and disciplines. Ambitious research objectives were set for a major multi-divisional project: engaging the water consumers and industry developers. Researchers from three divisions, representing a broad spectrum of disciplines, collaborated equally and were negotiated through a management committee with industry partners. The research developed and tested inter-divisional relationships and broadened researchers understanding of the complexity of resource management issues.

All six case studies were considered to be 'ahead of their time' and this was perceived to be consistent with the research role of the CSIRO. Evaluation of the different types of integrated research was measured by its ability to influence individuals, communities, business and industry, and governments in order to effect 'change' in the way they made decisions. Evaluation was perceived to be an important research component to build into research projects to measure this impact.

PRACTICAL CHALLENGES

Creating meaningful change within different social environments

Creating research processes that encourage change takes time and commitment. Research projects require leverage within social environments and a number of strategies were employed within the case study projects to bring greater relevance to research outcomes.

Policy environments where researchers had developed state-level decision tools for planning future resource management and alternative policy choice benefited, it seems, from 'champions' and leadership conversant with both technical language and the political environment. Even then, there was no guarantee within the political environment that even well-researched alternatives would be endorsed.

Resource management research and planning within state government and regional environments was shown to require processes that engaged the relevant sector interests in an equal capacity, and in an ongoing way, so that it facilitated learning and shared understanding.

Industry research partners and environments were shown to require service efficiency and clear rules set on intellectual property ownership, and adequate industry input and control of research objectives and direction. Timely reporting and goal-driven efficiency was shown to be compelling attributes of a research team when meeting these industry needs.

Creating meaningful change within the individual farm business environment was shown to require one-on-one engagement in order to understand how these individuals operated, as well as improving how well they understood emerging research and technology.

What consideration should be given to the needs of social and economic practitioners within projects?

Building working relationships with communities, industry and sector interests that serve the needs of these partners within research, while remaining 'ahead of the game', is a vital research contribution for society and requires the careful balancing of multiple research goals. Research must necessarily remain innovative, problem-oriented and serve the public good, while also bringing value to these partners and inevitably to their economic interests. The distinction between service science and the pursuit of science for the public good warranted some clarity within integrated research when there was close interaction with 'real' social issues, people and partners.

Engaging the social and economic practitioners within these research project environments required an understanding of how they operated in order to develop appropriate ways to interact with them. This often required the development of new research skills for the individual researcher and different research methodologies, including the confidence to orientate research practice to give this new interface value within the research process. An example of this within multi-disciplinary research is the requirement for social research outcomes to better inform the research objectives of the technical research. When this didn't occur, strategic social research planning and integration was compromised.

What are researchers confronting?

In attempting to forge these new relationships, many researchers are confronted personally with a new challenge. They are not only responsible for innovation and depth in the understanding they bring to new fields, but also the strength of the relationship they build with the relevant social environment, where what they have to offer must be perceived as useful, marketable and promoting change. The various research processes studied in this review approached this challenge in different ways.

Smaller research teams perceived themselves as providing this interface, and with this often came the need to cross disciplinary boundaries to better understand how people made decisions and develop methodologies that embrace this. Individuals were required to have social skills and the ability to converse with client groups, which is not something all scientists possess, or want to learn.

Larger research teams developed these relationships often through bringing in relevant social disciplines to conduct social surveying and market research, in order to orientate research goals appropriately. Communication among research groups and with relevant social environments was highlighted as pivotal to each project's success, and emphasis was placed on continuing research where this communication had worked well. Pioneering change through the strength of effective research leadership was also emphasised, as was the necessity to maintain a research role where 'change' was seen to be occurring. The limitation of research project funding 'cycles' to maintain support for capacity building processes was a source of frustration and loss.

Provision by the research organisational environment to accommodate the emerging science needs, as experienced by researchers interviewed within this review, was considered to be critical to its future success. Methodologies employed by them to engage with social and economic practitioners have been noted by other scientists as lacking scientific rigour. The cultural resistance experienced within some divisions, particularly to the 'softer' research approach, was apparent.

For the researchers involved in these projects, often as part of large team environments, the issue of receiving appropriate and equivalent academic reward compared with the hypotheses-oriented science was also noted. Being part of successful team environments was attributed to factors such as equity – in all being part of designing research goals, communication among the team, and efficiency in the transfer of information – as well as personal achievement.

Pursuing integrated research has required scientists to engage with issues rather than act purely as a specialist. Interviewees suggested that a limited number of publications was one of the costs of doing this. Involvement in large multi-disciplinary groups and multi-divisional projects took time and effort and was not always matched in terms of personal publications or time post-project to capitalise on the new skills, knowledge and experience. Flexible promotion systems, which rewarded people for doing well in what was in the organisations interests, and some accommodation for rewarding systems thinking within the reward structure, was considered necessary.

Creating research environments that nurture integrated science

The transaction costs in undertaking integrated and 'interfacing' research projects were high. Long planning phases, where no research outcomes were evident, were necessary in order to scope the 'right' research question, thus ensuring research relevance. A lot of time and resources were required to establish engagement processes, and to administer and manage large research teams. Research team reliance on a supportive environment within the many CSIRO Divisions and support from senior management was recognised as an important factor in achieving successful outcomes. Cultural acceptance of these new scientific pursuits appeared to play an important role, as well as the ability to defend 'process' as opposed to simply outcomes-based research results with senior managers.

CONCLUSION

Despite the growing need to understand and solve complex societal problems scientifically, break new ground in terms of the relationship between science and societal change, and examine whole-of-system processes, it has been revealed that this comes at a cost to the research environment and challenges the traditional research culture. This cost is also borne by the individual researchers, whose career pathways can become less rewarding. These costs must be offset by the benefits of research outcomes, in terms of its relevance and significance, as well as accommodated by the research organisational structure, in terms of them providing a cultural environment for this research to flourish.

REFERENCES

Kington EA (2003) 'Social and economic integration. A review of contemporary SEI best practice in CSIRO and SEI stories – reflections and lessons from a selection of SEI science in CSIRO'. CSIRO Land and Water, Perth.

Chapter 5

If there is a bear: conservation in the midst of conflicts

Jaroslav Mysiak

ABSTRACT

Nature conservation is an area with a high propensity for the collision of values, interests, norms and beliefs. The return of large, charismatic but potentially dangerous predators to their former habitats epitomises many of the conflicts that emerge around environmental issues: scientific uncertainty, conflicting values, divergent interests, and high-profile, often emotive community action: both in favour and against. Yet these conflicts can also present opportunities for engagement and change. This chapter briefly examines theories about environmental conflicts, and draws on the reintroduction of bear species as an example of approaches to conflict resolution. It summarises main challenges faced by researchers attempting to broker good outcomes for both bears and the communities the bears need to live with.

INTRODUCTION

Environmental management and nature conservation are areas with a high propensity for the collision of values, interests, norms and beliefs. The list of conflict-prone issues is long; prominent examples include genetically modified organisms, species and ecosystem conservation, environment-related diseases, hazardous waste, and pollution and health risks. Primary sources of tension and conflict are the environmental changes such as global warming, the increasing human population and per capita consumption, and the resulting demand on scarce natural resources.

Initiatives to return large predators to areas from which they were driven out create a demand for habitat, which frequently results in severe conflicts. One of the most charismatic species among these predators, the bear, has been making headlines around the world, albeit for different reasons. In France, the attempts to repopulate the Central Pyrenees with the brown bear (*Ursus arctos*) from Slovenia were met with violent protests from thousands of shepherds and other anti-bear activists who fear that the bears would attack sheep flocks and humans. In Germany, the shooting of 'Bruno', a descendent of the bears reintroduced into the Italian Alps, raised a sharp controversy and seriously damaged the credibility of community pledges to support the return of the large carnivores. In other countries with abundant bear populations, such as Romania, people's fears are warranted and, although the attacks on human are rare, they are sufficient to heat up the conflict. The bear population in Romania is kept down intentionally, according to some, in an effort to limit the threats posed to humans and livestock, while others suspect that economic interests are at play. In the US, conflict was sparked over the Yellowstone distinct population segment of grizzly bears (*Ursus arctos horribilis*) losing their status of 'threatened' under the US Endangered Species Act (ESA). The intention to do the opposite –that is, to attribute the polar bear (*Ursus maritimus*) with 'threatened' status under the ESA – evolved into an argument between climate change sceptics and the advocates of action on climate change.

These and other conflicts prompted by conservation policies have similar patterns, although in apparently analogous situations examples of both cooperation and conflict can be found (Sidaway 2005). Conflicts are perpetuated by divergent perceptions of the threats and damages, and the legitimacy and urgency of policy responses. Scientific knowledge can, in some cases, alleviate the conflict by dispelling doubts and concerns. For example, some species came off the ESA species list because new, more precise data suggested their listing was not compulsory. More often than not however, scientific knowledge is a part of the problem. Similar to the science of climate change, conservation science is afflicted by uncertainties that are difficult to reduce, at least in the short term. There is a lack of knowledge about, for example, how ecological processes influence population survival, and the field is rife with value judgments. All these things make it difficult to determine exactly where science ends and policy advocacy starts.

For many, conflicts are tied to negative associations such as verbal or physical violence, troubled relationships, frustration, the violation of rights and rules, and delays in policy implementation. Yet conflicts also play a positive role through the release of hostilities, the establishment of social groups and by helping to facilitate the adjustment of social norms and power relations (Coser 1956; Simmel 1964). As result of a number of hard and persistent conflicts, conservation policies have shifted to voluntary programs for species protection and cooperative, community-based approaches. How successful are these policies in terms of conflict resolution and bringing about agreement and consensus? What is the prospect of disputes turning into intractable conflicts and persistent frustration and under what conditions does conflict become a disorder and a permanent disturbance to sustainable development? And, most importantly, what is the role of scientists in conflict resolution when the pursuit of objective knowledge must be reconciled with emotional disputes in which opposing parties hold seemingly irreconcilable views on the matter of conflict? This chapter briefly examines theories about environmental conflicts, gives an overview of the approaches to conflict resolution and summarises main challenges faced.

In the 1984 US election campaign, one of Ronald Reagan's television ads showed a bear – an allusion to the USSR – roaming in a forest. An ominous male voice accompanied the clip, suggesting that it was smart to be strong as a bear because nobody knows for sure whether the bear – if there was a bear – was tame or vicious. This chapter highlights how many conflicts about the management of bear populations are fuelled by fears about the unknown levels of threat to both humans and bears. The re-settlement projects in the French Pyrenees and the Central Alps (Italy and Austria) and the management practices in bear-rich countries such as Slovakia, Slovenia and Romania provide practical cases that illustrate the challenges to conflict resolution.

CONFLICTS AND CHALLENGES OF THEIR RESOLUTION

Conflicts attract the attention of scholars from different disciplines who are interested in how attitudes and positions tied to ethnicity, religion, politics, personality, gender and values play a role in the evolution of disputes. Given the range of various manifestations of conflict, it is not surprising that there are different interpretations of what constitutes a conflict. A divergence of values, needs, interests, opinions and goals is not sufficient to explain why conflicts come up in some situations and not in others. According to Barki and Hartwick (2004), a conflict requires disagreement, antagonistic behaviour (e.g. competition, hostility or debate) and negative emotions (e.g. anxiety, jealousy, frustration, fear or anger) at the same time. Others believe that any or a particular combination of disagreement, hostility and negative emotions lead to conflict (Jehn 1994; Amason 1996; Hellström 2001). This conceptualisation of conflict is not consistent with the term 'human wildlife conflict' (HWC) in which the needs or behaviour of wildlife is seen alongside human goals or interests (Madden 2004). In this chapter, the focus is on social conflicts exacerbated by people's perceptions of wildlife and its value, and the damage and threats posed to humans.

With respect to causes of conflicts and their settlement, many people distinguish between values and interests (Amy 1987). The former are deeply held beliefs that are not negotiable. The most inviolable among them – the sacred values – incorporate moral beliefs that are beyond any individual or material pay-off (Altran *et al.* 2007). The Black Hills, for example, are believed to be a sacred place for the Lakota tribe who persistently refuse the compensation money for dispossession, which now amounts to three-quarters of a billion dollars. Interests encompass material or non-material benefits with variable relative priorities (Acland 1995). The value-driven differences can be suppressed in a bid for consensus (Sidaway 2005), allowing interest groups to reach settlement. Nevertheless, in practice, interests and values may not be easily separable and the typologies of conflicts that are based on such a separation may have a weak empirical standing (Sidaway 2005). Gray (2003) suggests other, more practical, categories along which to describe conflict. These include categories (or frames) referring to how disputants characterise themselves (identity frames), how they describe other parties' interests and motivations (characterisation frames) and what they suggest to do about the conflict (conflict-management frames). In addition, she proposes a set of auxiliary frames such as social control, risks, whole story, power and loss versus gains.

Equally important is to understand how conflict evolves. Conflicts are dynamic, path-dependent constructs in which 'future developments are influenced, enabled and constrained, by structures which have grown out of specific historical developments' (Voss and Kemp 2006, pp. 13–14). Some people distinguish between *disputes* as temporal peaks or escalations of animosity, and more complex *conflicts* persisting over a longer time horizon and describing a broader context in which the disputes rise (Mbonile 2005). Some conflicts are never settled completely and rise up all over again. Even a successful settlement does not prevent a series of subsequent disputes - with peaks of lower intensity (Honeyman 2001).

Just as for conflict definition, there are various accounts of what it means to resolve a conflict. For example, in Boulding (1962) conflicts are resolved by reconciliation, compromise or award. Reconciliation presumes the opposing parties will come to shared preferences and values. Compromise, on the other hand, means that the achieved outcomes are less than ideal for all. Finally, award refers to a situation when parties accept the verdict of an external person or agency. Burton (1990), on the other hand, equates resolution with a change in relationship, which is attained by solving the causes of conflictual behaviour. Barton's definition differs from that of Boulding in various aspects: it is narrow, it excludes compromise and adjudication, and explicitly addresses the causes of conflict (Schoeny and Warfield 2000).

Resolution or settlement in the broadest sense can be achieved by different means. In Rijsberman (1999), these are aligned in a spectrum ranging from voluntary, consensus-building techniques to strategies in which the opposing parties entrust the formal control over the case to an external authority. In-between are approaches that involve the assistance of a third party, which, however, does not take control over the negotiation. In Meyer and Konisky (2005), the collaborative institutions are distinguished by their degree of governmental participation. One end of the spectrum is characterised by settlement efforts that go beyond the mandate of a regulatory framework or governmental agency. At the opposite end, an agency devolves the authority for policy implementation to local participants.

Conflict resolution can be achieved by different means. Alternative discourse resolution ADR (Harashina 1995; Rose and Suffling 2001; Sidaway 2005) includes techniques used as an alternative to litigation. Among them, arbitration describes settlement in which the choice of a solution is delegated to a third, impartial party. In mediated agreements, the third party facilitates the process but the solution needs to be agreed upon by the parties in conflict. In negotiation, the parties bargain without being assisted by a third party. Besides ADR, a number of other approaches devised for environmental planning and policy making fall within the scope of conflict resolution. Social learning (Maurel *et al.* 2007), for example, fosters mutual appreciation of conflicting parties' views and perspectives, and this is expected to favour compromise-building and constructive attitudes to conflict reconciliation. In Elliot *et al.* (2003), attention is paid to reframing as a technique to change understandings and interpretations of the issue in conflict. The extent to which the conflict can be reframed depends on the ability of the people to inquire into the intentions and meanings of the other parties involved in the conflict (Schoen and Rein

1994; Elliot *et al.* 2003). Deliberative policy making (Chess *et al.* 1998) is based on the mutual exchange of arguments and a process of seeking balance between conflicting arguments and claims (Renn 2006). An active involvement of all policy actors is expected to increase acceptance of the chosen policies and pave the way for policy implementation. Community-based environmental protection (CBEP) (Meyer and Konisky 2005) encompasses a variety of activities that have the empowerment of local communities to design and implement environmental protection policies in common. Through this empowerment, CBEP creates opportunities for policies to be sensitive to local concerns and preferences. The contributions of each of the above techniques to conflict resolution may not be the same, but they overlap and to large extent coincide with the general principles distinguishing successful negotiations (Lewicki *et al.* 1999): they reduce tension and manage the de-escalation of hostility; they enhance communication and improve each party's understanding of the other's perspectives; they control the number and size of issues; they establish a common ground as a basis for agreement; and they enhance the desirability of the options and alternatives.

The need to address both the process of settlement and the outcomes achieved makes the assessment of resolution processes a difficult task. Such an assessment has to consider different features such as fairness (e.g. legitimacy and inclusion), efficiency (compared with litigation for example) and changes in relationships (e.g. trust developing among the adversaries) (Susskind and Cruikshank 1987; Moore 1996; Todd 2001; Todd 2002). Characteristics of the settlement process that are criteria for success include, among others, an improved understanding of the issues and generated cooperative behaviour. The outcomes, on the other hand, can be evaluated on the basis of whether or not the parties reached an agreement, the quality and stability of the consensus, and the environmental effects of the agreement.

A few studies have compared and assessed collaborative management processes and conflict resolution across different case studies. Although the benefits of ADR and collaborative institutions were substantiated, some have cautioned against overconfidence and expectations that cannot be met. Instead of creating opportunities to resolve conflicts, the CBEP can exacerbate conflict, increase the state's control over contested resources and marginalise local communities (Castro and Nielsen 2001). Lubell (2004) observes that the collaborative institutions may increase the level of consensus and produce favourable changes in attitudes and social relations, but these, however, do not necessarily translate into a higher level of cooperation among the parties. In fact, they can create 'perceptions of progress in the absence of any real change, thereby reducing the expressed political demand for policy change without addressing the environmental and social conditions that generated that demand' (p. 550). Meyer and Konisky (2005) suggest that community-enforced environmental protection may not perform as well as state regulations and may put a disproportionate burden on poor communities. Finally, the success of collaborative institutions is believed to depend on local circumstances (Leach and Pelkey 2001) and this approach provides limited opportunities to reach actors who are not already involved in local policy making (Abel and Stephan 2000).

Conservation programs draw legitimacy from science. But science that strives to be an objective and disinterested (i.e. value free) source of knowledge cannot determine all choices conservation policies have to make. It can back these choices, for example, by providing plausible assessments of species' vulnerability to habitat alteration or management changes. These assessments are as reliable as the data and knowledge on which they rely, but even the most reliable assessments are conditioned by the best knowledge available. Moreover, the decision to put a species into protection, or deciding upon where and how these species can or should be protected, involves a host of value judgments, in addition to scientific knowledge. The variety of indicators describing the ecological significance, such as endemism, taxonomic uniqueness, usual phenomena, global rarity or vulnerability, requires additional choices to be made. What's more, the subjectivity of choices and the extent to which opinions and judgments substitute missing data and gaps in knowledge are not transparent to non-scientists. In this respect, the authority drawn from science – one that does not account sufficiently for the uncertainty and value judgments pervading conservation efforts – may create tensions and exacerbate conflicts. As observed by (Johnston and Soulsby 2006), the local or contextual knowledge is often used as a form of resistance, promoting a different account of what constitutes good management against the scientific knowledge that underpins the conservation programs.

MAKING CONSERVATION EFFORTS BEARABLE

If bears symbolise the harmony between nature and mankind in ancient cultures (Kellert *et al.* 1996), this is hardly the case nowadays. Few species have incited such fierce conflicts as various species of bear have over recent years. The aim here is not to investigate each specific case in full detail, but to reveal similarities in the patterns of argumentation in the different contexts.

The scientific knowledge of bear ecology and biology is not reported here: it is handled in full detail (Breitenmoser 1998; Graham *et al.* 2005).

In France, the bear reinforcement program was first completed in 1996–1997. Three bears were released in the Central Pyrenees to stop the local population from dwindling away. The program met staunch resistance and only the Constitutional Council prevented an amendment to hunting laws that would have given local authorities the power to demand the removal of the introduced specimens. Further releases were decided after the last native female bear was shot dead and the West Pyrenees population was left with only males. Five bears were set free in 2006, upon approval from France's highest administrative court. The release of the first of them, Palouma, was protected by around 150 police officers. Still, the protestors managed to block the first attempted release and Palouma was not released until the next day elsewhere in the region. A few months later when Palouma died falling from a cliff, many suspected foul play. The discovery of old bullet wounds in the body of another bear that died in a car accident fuelled suspicion.

Programs similar to the one in France were carried out in Austria (1989–1992) and Italy (1999–2002). In Austria, three bears were re-settled to the Ötscher region in Lower Austria. A sharp increase in damage to property and livestock changed the initially positive public attitude and prevented further releases. In Italy, 10 bears were released in the Adamello Brenta national park in Trentino. The successful translocations opened doors to a natural immigration to the neighbourhood regions in Germany and Switzerland. However, in May 2006, when a young male bear, baptised Bruno by the media, crossed the boundary to Germany, the initial enthusiasm of the environmental authorities faded with the first damage. When even a special Finish bear team failed to capture him alive, the initially suspended hunting permit was reopened and Bruno was shot soon afterwards. In Italy, Bruno's death was considered as a backlash against conservation policy.

In Romania there are several thousand bears. The city of Brasov is known for the bears that raid foothill suburbs in an effort to find food. The situation escalated when, in October 2004, a rabid bear killed two men and injured six others in the forested area on the edge of the city (BBC 2004). Although bear attacks have been rare in recent times, between 1987 and 1992 more than 20 people were killed and many more injured. Since then, bear numbers have significantly decreased, partly as a result of regressive policy. According to some environmental associations, the drop in numbers was much higher than reported by the government. The dispute is indicative of conflicts in other bear-rich countries. In Slovenia, the culling controversy broke out over the government plans to increase the hunting quota to over one hundred. Major national and foreign wildlife conservation groups objected to the proposal, questioning the scientific justification. In Slovakia, the hunting quotas are lower but hard to meet, as the hunters complain, due to the restriction on bear-hunting methods. A high officer of the state environmental agency caused additional uproar by suggesting there was not enough space for the current number of bears and recommended halving their population.

The episodes of conflict escalation have a similar pattern of emotionally coloured outbreaks of animosity and confrontation, accompanied by verbal and physical abuse. Infuriated Pyrenees farmers and anti-bear activists besieged local institutions, destroyed equipment, exhibited carcasses of sheep killed by a bear, smashed bottles of sheep blood against the facade of the town hall and scattered honey jars containing bits of broken glass in the forest. Thousands took part in the protest demonstrations. Bruno's death prompted similar reactions from bear supporters. Death threats were made against the hunter whose identity was not disclosed, against the public officers who issued the hunting permit and against the staff of the university department where the carcass was deposited and examined. Hunting facilities were damaged in distant places in the country because hunters were held collectively responsible. Vacationers cancelled their advanced bookings in the area where Bruno was shot to death.

In the aftermath of these episodes, legal complaints were filed and appeals were made for the demise of high-level political representatives who were held directly or indirectly responsible. The weekly journal *Die Zeit* portrayed Bruno as a symbol of the 'double moral of preserve and punish': the desire for unspoiled nature along with the fear of incursion from what is strange and non-conformist (Diez 2006). Others depicted Bruno as a victim of the globalised world, and the Italian newspaper *Repubblica* saw in Bruno's case yet another strain on the turbulent relationship between Italians and Germans. The resistance of the Pyrenees farmers was brought into connection with 'guerre des demoiselles': an uprising of Ariège's peasants in the 19th century against the king's control of forest resources.

In some ways these cases could not be more different. In the French case, the environmental authority campaigned for the conservation program, which was opposed by local population. In the German case, the authorities are caught in a dilemma over whether to tolerate damage and risk human accidents, or to preclude bears, and risk compromising their own mandate and credibility. In the Romanian and other cases, the authorities' policy of population management is criticised from both within and outside the country as lacking a sound scientific basis. Despite these differences, the cases have much in common. They all consist of a web of arguments that tap into identity of place, culture, the species' ecological value and the threat/damage inflicted by the bears. One moves between these arguments, intentionally or not, while seeking to advance one's own position.

A prominent element in these conflicts is the contrast of values, lifestyles, preferences and norms in rural and urban societies. The former are directly exposed to the risk and have to cope with the bulk of the damage, and are thus inclined to more critical and negative attitudes towards large predators (Breitenmoser 1998). Most fierce opponents of the conservation programs are, not surprisingly, among shepherds, honeybee farmers and members of the local mountain communities, because they see their rights violated and their habitual way of life threatened. Urban dwellers' image of bears as 'lovable, funny and good natured' (Ecco 1994) is put down to a result of wrong worldviews. The investigations into the people's perceptions of large predators display a more complex picture, with a range of factors such as age, sex, level of knowledge and perceived fear as predictors of attitudes, although their importance varies between specific contexts. For the bear supporters, all the hue and cry uses bears as a scapegoat for the economic recession of pasture farming. Paradoxically, the bear symbolises both the identity of the Pyrenees Mountains and the complex of problems the Pyrenees farmers experience.

The resentment of mountain communities is fuelled by perceptions of being excluded from decision making about their own environment and life. Governments are believed to be more responsive to strong lobby groups and not very concerned with the living conditions in the rural world. Bears are returning into a changed setting: the herding practices have changed along with people's conceptions of predators. What's more, the gaps in administrative and legislative frameworks make it difficult to assign liability for damage.

There are a few who challenge the merits of conservation in general. Still, excessive attention to a single species is seen by some as detriment to preservation of an entire ecosystem. The bear is seen as a typical, flagship or umbrella species, which accentuates its conservation value. More intense disputes arise over the question of where bears should be allowed to establish a population that is viable, socially acceptable and ecologically sustainable. The question of 'where' is not only connected to the opposition to having large predators in the 'backyard'. Brown bears are not endangered globally and, although they are strictly protected in Europe, there are countries with abundant populations. So, many people ask why it is necessary to protect, re-stock or introduce bears in areas where they cause much greater troubles. Those inclined towards conservation consider it a moral duty to protect the species or to help it to establish in suitable areas. The international obligations to protect the species are seen by some as reducing the flexibility to deal with local concerns and oppose any initiative that goes beyond basic compliance.

The concerns associated with the population size include reproduction and mortality rates, composition according to age and sex, and vulnerability to poaching, diseases or habitat alteration. The population size is rarely known precisely, and data is criticised as being wrong, methodologically flawed, politically biased, selective in avoiding contrary evidence or not reliable for other reasons. The conclusions are not deemed warranted, or the data is equally consistent with different interpretations.

Damages to sheep, cattle and beehives are unavoidable but, for the supporters of the conservation policies, they are an acceptable price to pay. They suspect that farmers exaggerate actual damage and attribute to bears losses that are due to other reasons including inappropriate livestock husbandry, diseases and storms. In their view, damage can be prevented or kept at low levels by the use of special herding dogs, electric fences and by attending the herds with professional shepherds. Alpine pasture farming is facing an economic recession and for many the predators and threats they epitomise are the last straw. In the eyes of many shepherds and farmers the damages are large and unacceptable. The financial compensations and incentives to prevent damages do not account for secondary costs and damages such as livestock injuries, costs for sheep guardian dogs, and the additional work that is difficult to quantify (Kaczensky *et al.* 2004).

The management/reduction of bear populations is believed to be premature because the population is not (yet) stable, the goal of protection has not been attained or there are additional factors threatening the viability of the population or negatively affecting the bears' habitats or food sources. For some, killing bears is not morally or ethically justifiable at all; others are just opposed to commercial and trophy hunting. The reasons for management are seen as wrong or lacking scientific basis. Management is opposed also because it is perceived as ineffective in reducing damage and attacks on humans, which are not due the population density but to inappropriate pasturing practices or careless behaviour of people. Supporters of bear conservation believe that regulation can further exacerbate the conflicts because it interferes with the social organisation of the population.

The criteria for changing the protection status (either to attribute a population with threatened or endangered status or to remove such status) are not agreed upon, just like the criteria by which nuisance behaviour is defined and permits are issued to deal with nuisance specimens. The reason for disagreement provides many concerns regarding the population size, dynamics and ecology or assessment of risk posed by the specimens in question. Attitudes towards killing are conditioned by the success or failure of non-lethal approaches such as translocation, aversive conditioning and detailed monitoring. Yet, the period when hunting permits are issued may cause discontent because it puts female bears with cubs at risk, and hunting methods (e.g. hunting with bait) may be questioned.

Are there any closer connections among the arguments in the different cases? Are they just instances of a cycle of conflict evolution? The specific situations can at least give hints about the challenges one may expect to come further down the track. The natural immigration of predators can attract broad public consent initially. The legal or illegal killing of such specimens – especially when they leave behind orphaned cubs – upsets many people, creating an atmosphere from which the reintroduction or reinforcement projects may benefit. As the damage increases – and here it is often the orphaned cubs which, in order to survive, often develop food-conditioned behaviour – the acceptance dwindles. Staunch opposition from those who are negatively affected – who are small in number but strongly determined – can disintegrate political commitment or provide opportunities for political exploitation. Negative media coverage accelerates the process. At the later stage as the population spreads out, and management becomes indispensable, those who initially supported the conservation unconditionally, oppose the management.

BEARING UP UNDER CONFLICTS

Any change is likely to adversely affect some people more than others. Conservation efforts thus provide many opportunities for conflicts and contrasting accounts about what is at stake. Because the conflicts draw upon the beliefs, perceptions, values and interests of many – creating a 'maze' that is difficult to disentangle – defining or categorising the conflict unambiguously and identifying solutions that satisfy everybody is not straightforward.

Bear populations are managed according to plans whose development is assisted by conservation and planning guidance (Servheen *et al.* 1998; Swenson *et al.* 2000). These can, if implemented sensitively, help to prevent or alleviate conflicts. It is recommended, for example, that population areas be divided into zones with detailed management prescriptions for each of them. The management strategy should be supervised by a steering panel: assembling competent authorities, experts and representatives of communities (e.g. hunters, land owners and environmental NGOs) affected by the policy. Local opposition is seen as a major threat to population survival; hence public participation is encouraged to bolster the acceptance of predators and to make management plans responsive to local needs and concerns. Recommendations are given about how to prevent or reduce damage and what should be taken into account when designing compensation systems. Active information policies and education programs are necessary, in any case, to balance the news coverage of negative, emotionally charged incidents. Further research and monitoring are necessary in support of all above recommendations.

The implementation of these recommendations is not straightforward, so successful conflict resolution requires the combination of analytical skills, intuition and social competence. Consequently, resolution in some cases does not guarantee the same success in others. Nevertheless, a pioneering approach to public relations has been set up in Austria in form of *bear advocates* (BAs). These are 'independent mediators between humans and bears' (Länderübergreifende Koordinierungstelle für Bärenfragen 2005): experts knowledgeable in bear biology and ecology who listen to, appreciate and advise people who come to harm or suffer from property or livestock damage. Yet designing compensation systems able to increase acceptance of predators is not easy. More often than not, the schemes are deemed inflexible and tedious. A more flexible approach is based on negotiated agreements mediated by state authorities who, in case the parties are not able to find agreement, determine the extent of compensation at their own discretion. The parties can still decline the arbitral judgment and file a lawsuit.

An investigation into public attitude disclosed more support for the bear reinforcement program in the Pyrenees than in Trentino, where, however, no such animosity was experienced afterwards. More than a thousand people took part in the public hearing in the Pyrenees and many others submitted comments online and 70 institutions were consulted individually. The comments included a broad range of concerns and constructive suggestions for program implementation. However, the consultation was focused on the modality of population reinforcement, and the decision about whether or not to continue the program was not put up for discussion. Hence, public hearings were boycotted by some farmers and shepherds associations.

Bruno's roaming in Austria and Germany was closely watched by experts and bear advocates. During the 2 months he killed 32 sheep, some chickens and damaged 9 beehives. This is not much compared with damage attributed to some specimens in France or Italy. His behaviour was classified in 24 cases ordinary, in 22 cases suspicious and in 8 dangerous (Austrian Bear Emergency Team 2006). The decision to shoot Bruno may have protected the conservation efforts in neighbourhood countries from a wave of animosity should Bruno have gone on to cause a serious accident. However, the decision left little policy leeway for another bear with an even higher propensity to livestock predation and posing a higher risk to humans.

With the aim of coordinating bear management and the handling of nuisance bears across Alpine counties, a policy workshop was initiated. It involved experts and decision makers from different administrations. The workshop sought to inform policy making. It seems, however, that the initiative fell short of bringing together policy makers and experts to discuss the management issues and the forum fell back on separated science/policy factions (Molinari and Breitenmoser 2007). The decisions about how many bears should be admitted in the Alps, the range of viable and sustainable populations, and where bears should be allowed to settle are political choices. Preferably, these decisions should be made at national level (Swenson et al. 2000), taking local needs and concerns into account. An agreement coming out of such a policy process would most probably settle on much less than the 700–1100 specimens estimated by WWF (2007) as the carrying capacity of the East Alpine region.

The cases described here and elsewhere show that provision of better data/knowledge cannot settle the conflicts or compel policy closure, except in the simplest cases. For some, the solution is to shift scientific practices to socially distributed, application-oriented and trans-disciplinary approaches (Gibbons 1999; Jasanoff 2003). These practices build upon a scientist's accountability and awareness of the social implications of research. Under this perspective, the full objectivity of scientific pursuit is not attainable and needs to be substituted by 'a dialogic process, an intense (and perhaps endless) "conversation" between research actors and research subject …' (Nowotny et al. 2003, p.187). Others, somewhat more pragmatically, see the role of science as explicitly addressing what policy options are consistent with scientific knowledge (contrary to being policy neutral) (Pielke 2002). Political stalemate can be overcome only in politics, 'engaging in process of persuasion, reframing, disaggregation and devolution, to locate areas of value consensus, overlapping interests or low stake options … that enable actions in the absence of a comprehensive political solution or scientific understanding' (Sarewitz 2004, p.400). Both these standpoints have some common ground in recognising the failure of the end-of-pipe-line model of science–policy interface (get the data right first, then act), although they differ in the role attributed to scientists in policy making.

REFERENCES

Abel TD and Stephan M (2000) The limits of civic environmentalism. *American Behavioral Scientist* **44**(4), 614–628.

Acland AF (1995) *Resolving Disputes without Going to Court: A Consumer Guide to Alternative Dispute Resolution.* Century Business Books, London.

Altran S, Axelrod R and Davis R (2007) Sacred barriers to conflict resolution. *Science* **317**(5841), 1039–1040.

Amason AC (1996) Distinguishing the effects of functional and dysfunctional conflict on strategic decision making: resolving a paradox for top management teams. *Academy of Management Journal* **39**, 123–148.

Amy D (1987) *The Politics of Environmental Mediation.* Columbia University Press, New York.

Austrian Bear Emergency Team (2006) *JJ1 "Bruno" in Austria and Germany 2006 – Protocol and Risk Assessment.* Austrian Bear Emergency Team, Vienna, Austria.

Barki H and Hartwick J (2004) Conceptualising the construct of interpersonal conflict. *International Journal of Conflict Management* **15**(3), 216–244.

BBC (British Broadcasting Association) (2004) *Romanian Killer Bear had Rabies.* BBC, London. <http://news.bbc.co.uk/2/hi/europe/3756078. stm>.

Boulding KE (1962) *Conflict and Defenses. A General Theory.* Harper & Row, New York.

Breitenmoser U (1998) Large predators in the Alps: the fall and rise of man's competitors. *Biological Conservation* **83**(3), 279–289.

Burton J (1990) *Conflict: Resolution and Prevention.* St Martin's Press, New York.

Castro AP and Nielsen E (2001) Indigenous people and co-management: implications for conflict management. *Environmental Science & Policy* **4**(4–5), 229–239.

Chess C, Dietz T and Shannon M (1998) Who should deliberate when? *Human Ecology Review* **5**(1), 45–48.

Coser LA (1956) *The Functions of Social Conflict.* The Free Press, New York.

Ecco U (1994) *Il secondo diario minimo*. Bompiani, Milan.

Elliot M, Gray B and Lewicki RJ (2003) Lessons learned about the framing and reframing of intractable environmental conflicts. In: *Environmental Conflicts: Concept and Cases*. (Eds RJ Lewicki, B Gray and M Elliot) pp. 409–436. Island Press, Washington DC.

Gibbons M (1999) Science's new social contract with society. *Nature* **402**(6761), C81–4.

Graham K, Beckerman AP and Thirgood S (2005) Human-predator-prey conflicts: ecological correlates, prey losses and patterns of management. *Biological Conservation* **122**(2), 159–171.

Gray B (2003) Framing of environmental disputes. In: *Environmental Conflicts: Concept and Cases*. (Eds RJ Lewicki, B Gray and M Elliot) pp. 11–34. Island Press, Washington DC.

Harashina S (1995) Environmental dispute resolution process and information exchange. *Environmental Impact Assessment Review* **15**(1), 69.

Hellström E (2001) *Conflict Cultures – Qualitative Comparative Analysis of Environmental Conflicts in Forestry*. Silva Fennica, Monographs 2. The Finnish Society of Forest Science, The Finnish Forest Research Institute, Vantaa, Finland.

Honeyman C (2001) The wrong mental image of settlement. *Negotiation Journal* **17**(1), 25–32.

Jasanoff S (2003) Technologies of humility: citizen participation in governing science. *Minerva* **41**(3), 223–244.

Jehn KA (1994) Enhancing effectiveness: an investigation of advantages and disadvantages of value-based intragroup conflict. *International Journal of Conflict Management* **5**, 223–238.

Johnston E and Soulsby C (2006) The role of science in environmental policy: an examination of the local context. *Land Use Policy* **23**(2), 161–169.

Kaczensky P, Blazic M and Gossow H (2004) Public attitudes towards brown bears (*Ursus arctos*) in Slovenia. *Biological Conservation* **118**, 661–674.

Kellert SR, Black M, Rush CR and Bath AJ (1996) Human culture and large carnivore conservation in North America. *Conservation Biology* **10**, 977–990.

Länderübergreifende Koordinierungstelle für Bärenfragen (2005) Managementplan Bär Österreich- überarbeitete Version 2005. WWF Österreich, Vienna.

Leach WD and Pelkey NW (2001) Making watershed partnerships work: a review of the empirical literature. *Journal of Water Resources Planning and Management* **127**(6), 378–385.

Lewicki RJ, Saunders D and Minton J (1999) *Negotiation*. McGraw-Hill Higher Education, Burr-Ridge, Illinois.

Lubell M (2004) Collaborative environmental institutions: all talk and no action? *Journal of Policy Analysis and Management* **23**(3), 549–573.

Madden F (2004) Creating coexistence between humans and wildlife: global perspectives on local efforts to address human–wildlife conflict. *Human Dimensions of Wildlife* **9**, 247–257.

Maurel P, Craps M, Cernesson F, Raymond R, Valkering P and Ferrand N (2007) Concepts and methods for analysing the role of information and communication tools (IC-tools) in social learning processes for River Basin Management. *Environmental Modelling & Software* **22**(5), 630.

Mbonile MJ (2005) Migration and intensification of water conflicts in the Pangani Basin, Tanzania. *Habitat International* **29**(1), 41.

Meyer SM and Konisky DM (2005) 'Community-based environmental protection: a status report and some new evidence'. Paper presented at the annual meeting of The Midwest Political Science Association, Palmer House Hilton, Chicago, Illinois. <http://www.allacademic.com//meta/p_mla_apa_research_citation/0/8/6/3/4/pages86342/p86342-1.php>.

Molinari P and Breitenmoser U (2007) *Brown Bear in the Alps: 3rd International Workshop. Proceedings.* National Office of Forests, Nature and Land Management, Triesenberg, Lichtenstein. <http://www.lcie.org/Docs/Regions/Alps/BrownBearAlps_Proceedings.pdf>.

Moore SA (1996) Defining 'successful' environmental dispute resolution: case studies from public land planning in the United States and Australia. *Environmental Impact Assessment Review* **16**(3), 151.

Nowotny H, Scott P and Gibbons M (2003) Introduction: 'Mode 2' revisited: the new production of knowledge. *Minerva* **41**(3), 179.

Pielke RA (2002) Science policy: policy, politics and perspective. *Nature* **416**(6879), 367.

Renn O (2006) Participatory processes for designing environmental policies. *Land Use Policy* **23**(1), 34–43.

Rijsberman F (1999) 'Conflict management and consensus building for integrated coastal management in Latin America and the Caribbean'. Inter-American Development Bank, <http://www.iadb.org/sds/publication/publication_1532_e.htm>.

Rose M and Suffling R (2001) Alternative dispute resolution and the protection of natural areas in Ontario, Canada. *Landscape and Urban Planning* **56**(1–2), 1.

Sarewitz D (2004) How science makes environmental controversies worse. *Environmental Science & Policy* **7**(5), 385–403.

Schoen D and Rein M (1994) *Frame Reflection: Toward the Resolution of Intractable Policy Controversies.* Basic Books, New York.

Schoeny M and Warfield W (2000) Reconnecting system maintenance with social justice: a critical role for conflict resolution. *Negotiation Journal* **16**(3), 253–268.

Servheen C, Herrero S and Peyton B (1998) 'Bear. Status survey and conservation action plan'. IUCN The World Conservation Union, Gland, Switzerland.

Sidaway R (2005) Resolving environmental disputes: from conflict to consensus. Earthscan, London.

Simmel G (1964) *Conflict and the Web of Group Affiliations.* Free Press, New York.

Susskind L and Cruikshank J (1987) *Breaking the Impasse.* Basic Books, New York.

Swenson JE, Gerstl N, Dahle B and Zedrosser A (2000) *Action Plan for the Conservation of the Brown Bear (Ursus arctos) in Europe.* Council of Europe Publishing, Strasbourg, France.

Todd S (2001) Measuring the effectiveness of environmental dispute settlement efforts. *Environmental Impact Assessment Review* **21**, 97–110.

Todd S (2002) Building consensus on divisive issues: a case study of the Yukon wolf management team. *Environmental Impact Assessment Review* **22**(6), 655.

Voss J-P and Kemp R (2006) Sustainability and reflexive governance: introduction. In: *Reflexive Governance for Sustainable Development* (Eds J-P Voss, D Bauknecht and R Kemp). Edward Elgar Publishing Limited, Cheltenham.

UK WWF (2007) *Status und Zukunft des Braunbären in Europa und den Alpen.* Vienna, Austria. <http://www.wwf.at/de/view/files/download/forceDownload/?tool=12&feld=download&sprach_connect=214>.

Part 2

Engaging individuals and communities

Chapter 6

Identification, engagement and influence: research for development and the environment in the uplands of northern Thailand

Louis Lebel, Rajesh Daniel and Prasnee Tipraqsa

ABSTRACT

The conventional approach to mission-directed research assumes that once the problem is framed correctly by development experts, science can get on with its work in exploring solutions that eventually will be forthcoming. This model has serious limitations both for describing how the world actually works and for what might be desirable. In this chapter, we explored three longer term projects conducted in the uplands of northern Thailand that attempted to bring research-based knowledge to bear on problems of development and the environment. From these analyses, we infer a different model: one in which issues of problem definition, scientific discovery and development policy re-making are tangled, at different times informing, challenging and by-passing each other. Further reflection leads us to three broader conclusions: (1) identification of problems is a critical ongoing negotiation in which it pays to be understandable to as wide a range of stakeholders as possible; (2) the effectiveness of engagement by researchers with narrowly defined stakeholder groups or a wider public in their dealings with public policy issues is contingent on the sensibility they bring with them; (3) mission-directed research, because it can be very influential, carries with it ethical responsibilities that may not apply so strongly or frequently as in other kinds of research.

INTRODUCTION

Mission-directed research aims to solve a specific problem or deliver a particular outcome. Adoption or uptake of research is managed 'aggressively' because success is judged by results. It is common to contrast mission-directed with investigator- or curiosity-driven research. Increasingly, in the field of development and the environment, it is being claimed that a greater emphasis on mission-directed research is needed, because it will pay off – both in practical outcomes and in more fundamental advances in knowledge.

The conventional, technocratic, approach to mission-directed research adopts a pipeline perspective on science-to-policy or knowledge-to-practice exchanges (van Kerkhoff and Lebel 2006). It assumes that once the problem is framed correctly by development experts, science can get on with its work in exploring solutions that eventually will be forthcoming. Integration is the catchword (van Kerkhoff 2005) for getting technologically driven solutions accepted socially and for research where different disciplines work in the same place.

But there are several limitations to this model, both for describing how the world actually works and for what might be desirable. First, development experts are often wrong or may only view a problem from the particular angle of the organisations they serve rather than from those who will have to live with the 'development solutions'. Second, scientists are often interested, even passionate about, connections or ideas that are only obliquely relevant to the immediate problems at hand, and so are forever redirecting their real work in other directions. Third, the targets and other stakeholders are not passive recipients of plans, proposals and advice, but strategically engage with development experts and the knowledge-producing communities to forward their interests insofar as they are able. Fourth, technologies and management innovations are transformed when they are embedded in new social systems and, in turn, may effect those social institutions. Fifth, mission discourses of projects may be there to gain access to government officials, donors and places, whereas mission practices may be something altogether different; for example, driven by concerns for social justice.

The result is a series of interactions around 'mission-directed' that can be far from straightforward. Rather, the issues of problem definition, scientific discovery and policy development can be extremely complex and challenging and may sometimes by-pass each other. Integration is inconsistent: in-depth when convenient and circumscribed otherwise. Social context and power relations are altered by interventions and technologies. The missions initially used to promote investments or particular policies eventually becomes less and less like targets and more and more like processes of negotiation – a way of doing business and of getting things done.

That is one of the main conclusions we draw from our exploration of three longer-term projects conducted in the uplands of northern Thailand that attempted with varying degrees of sophistication and specificity to bring research-based knowledge to bear on problems of development and the environment. The three projects considered in detail were the Thai-German Highland Development Programme (Box 6.1), set of collaborations coordinated by the World Agroforestry Centre (Box 6.2) and collaborations under the Uplands Program of Hohenheim University (Box 6.3) in northern Thailand.

The peoples and landscapes of the uplands in northern Thailand have been the subjects of environmental and social development discourses and the targets of policies for several decades. From the 1960s, the focus on reducing opium cultivation, countering support for communism and national security in the Cold War dominated the state's agenda (Renard 2001). Then came another modern push to develop 'primitive people' and 'agriculture' and integrate those who spoke different languages, worshipped in different ways and wore different clothes into a nationalist culture of Thai-ness that the lowlands were creating (Winichakul 1994; McCaskill and Kampe 1997). Throughout, Christian missionaries had seen the opportunities to add to their subjects. After conversion came conservation movements with nowhere left to put their parks except on the tops of mountains where these different people were living. Nature conservationists decried all kinds of swidden farming and forest use as deforestation and forest degradation, paving the way for the state to step right back in to protect watersheds, biodiversity, and so on (Laungaramsri 2002a). But they didn't have it all their own way either. Concerned individuals and groups fought to strengthen rights to use and access land and water for agriculture and forests in the uplands for various products that they provide for daily life (Laungaramsri 2002b; Sato 2003). They argued for a community forestry law and the rights of people to participate directly in land-use planning or the management of water resources (Hirsch 1997; Missingham 2003;

Walker 2003). Through several decades of discrimination, conflict and debate, science was deployed when it was convenient to justify actions, buttress arguments and dismiss alternatives (Forsyth 1998, 2003). At other times it was just ignored.

The rest of the chapter is organised around three threads, which lead us to our conclusion. The first is the notion that identification of problems is a critical ongoing negotiation in which it pays to be understandable to as wide a range of stakeholder as possible. The second is that the effectiveness of engagement by researchers with narrowly defined stakeholder groups or a wider public in their dealings with public policy issues is contingent on the sensibility they bring with them. The third is that mission-directed research, because it can be very influential, carries with it ethical responsibilities that may not apply so strongly or frequently as in other kinds of research.

IDENTIFICATION AND UNDERSTANDING

The way problems for research and development are first identified and framed may have long-term implications. Huge inequalities in the capacity to exploit natural resources, and brute force to control the movements of people, has meant that the voices of people living in the uplands has rarely been heard against the din made by experts in development bureaucracies. The questions asked during development research on farming systems and forest management were determined by political considerations, such as control of timber and land (Vandergeest and Peluso 1995), as much as concerns with ecosystem services, biodiversity or livelihoods (Lebel *et al.* 2004). The Thai state, by treating conservation of upland forests as a national security mission and drawing on international environmental discourses, could guide domestic research programs and outside agency assistance to serve its own strategic policy interests.

Most groups engaged in research for development strive to make what they do understandable to others in particular ways. Research programs are circumscribed to be read and satisfy international donors, agencies that control access to people, land and budgets, and, more rarely, the target or affected communities. Legibility matters because without it commitment and support for the mission is hard to achieve. To achieve legibility, many actors resort knowingly to simplifications about cause and effect and bury real complexity inside sweet mission statements and technical integration. Defining development problems as needing integration to solve them can put them out of reach of the communities to be developed and into the domain of experts or it can be an argument for greater engagement with people in specific places.

Shaping contexts

Missions are shaped by the wider social and political context in which they emerge. Thailand was considered to be a major illicit opium drug produc-ing country in the Golden Triangle. The Thai–German Highland Develop-ment Programme (TG-HDP) emerged from the efforts by the Thai government, beginning in the 1960s, to stop the cultivation of opium poppy (Renard 2001), counter sympathy for communist movements, and deal with other rural development challenges in the uplands of northern Thailand (Box 6.1). In 1969, King Bhumibol Adulyadej initiated the Royal Project using development projects for the integration of ethnic minorities into the mainstream of the Thai state. These projects got additional sup-port from the Thai government and donor agencies (Tapp 1986).

Over 12 major internationally donor-assisted projects followed during the 1980s, which included the TG-HDP whose mission idea was initiated at the Third Thai–German Government Conference on Financial and Tech-nical Cooperation held in Bangkok from 30 April to 4 May 1979. At the conference, the German delegation wanted to make technical cooperation funds available for a highland development project, with the emphasis on crop replacement and community development (Dirksen 2002). In this chapter, we emphasise the work of the TG-HDP on natural resources man-agement and its linkages with pursuit of other objectives.

Advocacy–science balance

The international program ICRAF (now relabelled as The World Agrofor-estry Centre) had been concerned more about advocacy than science, especially in terms of agroforestry that was focused largely on alley-crop-ping that itself had some mechanistic weaknesses. So, when Pedro Sanchez became director general of ICRAF, and ICRAF joined CGIAR in 1991, his mandate was to bring more science into ICRAF. The global 'alternative to slash and burn' (ASB) programme was based on the slash-and-burn farm-ing practices in Latin America and Africa. In these locations, it really was slash and burn – the land was cleared and burnt for conversion to agricul-ture. Then CGIAR opened the South-East Asia office in 1992–93 and ASB SE Asia was started with ICRAF (Box 6.2). The term ASB suited the mind-set of central governments in South-East Asia who tended to view upland especially ethnic community populations and their farming practices

BOX 6.1. THAI–GERMAN HIGHLAND DEVELOPMENT PROGRAMME

Players

The Thai–German Highland Development Programme (TG-HDP) was a regional rural development project jointly executed by the Thai Office of the Narcotics Control Board (ONCB) and the Deutsche Gesellschaft fuer Technische Zusammenarbeit (GTZ) of Germany (Prasong Jantakad and Carson 1998). The TG-HDP began in 1981 and ended in September 1998 (Dirksen 2002).

Key agencies include the United Nations Fund for Drug Abuse Control (UNFDAC), the United Nations Development Programme (UNDP), the United States Department of Agriculture (USDA) and, later, the World Bank, USAID and other bi-laterals such as the Australian and Danish governments.

Objectives

The overall goal of the project was 'the quality of life of the highland population is improved, the drug abuse problems are reduced and the ecological balance is maintained better' (Prasong Jantakad and Carson 1998; Dirksen 2002).

Activities

The TG-HDP operated in three project sites in Chiang Rai and Mae Hong Son provinces of northern Thailand. (TG-HDP 1991). The TG-HDP began its work in the first project area of Tambon Wawi, Chiang Rai province in 1982. Work began in the second area of Nam Lan, Mae Hong Son province in 1984, and in the third area of Huai Poo Ling, Mae Hong Son province in 1990 (Dirksen 2002).

The TG-HDP implementation (especially in the final phases) focused on four main issues:

(1) community-based land-use planning and local watershed management
(2) community-based drug abuse control
(3) rural financial management
(4) off-farm income generation.

Germany invested 20 million euros – matched by the Thai government – in the Programme (Dirksen 2002, p. 334).

Outcomes

According to Dirksen, the TG-HDP was instrumental in introducing:

• community-based and integrated social development program activities including gender issues and drug abuse prevention
• a savings and credit scheme

- community-based land-use planning and local watershed management measures, as well as sustainable farming and social forestry
- highland handbooks, media and training curricula
- systematic and integrated planning methods and procedures (Dirksen 2002, p. 341).

with suspicion. However, the region's farming practices were not the slash and burn as in Latin America, but comprised diverse types of rotational shifting cultivation (Clark and Tomich 2007). This deviation from the state mindset about slash and burn proved a challenge early on, which the ICRAF Thailand office not only adeptly took on but eventually resulted in making it the defining statement of its Thailand agroforestry research.

At first, attracting the attention of the higher levels of the Royal Forest Department (RFD) was difficult for ICRAF. Finally, after a workshop in 1989, Plodprasop Suraswadi, who later became the RFD Director-General, became interested and involved. Another challenge was to fit the research programme in Thailand into the ASB, to be consistent with donor requirements. The RFD was interested in improving land-use management in mountainous areas because these were the prime locations for both forestry and agriculture.

In the 1980s, the concept of agroforestry in Thailand and South-East Asia was thought of as alley-cropping.[1] Researchers at ICRAF turned out to be the leading wave of *landscape agroforesters* – that is '*to understand agroforestry, we have to understand the landscape: the agriculture, the forests, how they interact, and how they are managed*'. They were trying to get people to think outside the box in terms of what agroforestry was, and how to do it.

The Chiang Mai office started work in Mae Chaem District with a preliminary scope: what are the major kinds of agro-ecosystems involved? They ended up selecting some areas and doing some studies that would represent the range of variations in Mae Chaem (Box 6.2); for instance, looking at the different fallow areas of the forests and the different stages that they become fallow.

Scientific foundations

Much like ICRAF in the Mae Chaem Watershed, the need for better supporting science and scientific capacity was the cornerstone of the Hohenheim Uplands Program. To start their new Uplands Program in South-East Asia, most of the Hohenhiem scientists involved in the program in West Africa agreed to adopt a more farmer-oriented approach (Box 6.3). The

BOX 6.2. THE INTERNATIONAL CENTRE FOR RESEARCH IN
AGROFORESTRY (ICRAF) IN NORTHERN THAILAND

Players

The International Centre for Research in Agroforestry, ICRAF, is an autono-
mous, non-profit organisation established in 1977. ICRAF is a member of the
Consultative Group on International Agricultural Research (CGIAR). It is governed by an international board of trustees and funded from voluntary contributions from a host of bilateral, multilateral and private donors. ICRAF carries
out research in six ecoregions – in collaboration with National Agricultural
Research Systems (NARS) – one of which is in South-East Asia.

Objectives

ICRAF's goal is to help to alleviate tropical deforestation, land depletion and
rural poverty through the development and promotion of improved agroforestry systems. ICRAF initiated a regional research programme in South-East
Asia in 1992. The objective is to implement ICRAF's mission in the unique agr-
oecological and institutional circumstances of the nations of South-East Asia.
With its regional headquarters in Bogor, Indonesia, ICRAF's South-East Asian
Regional Research Programme is developing alternatives to unsustainable slash-
and-burn agriculture and ways to rehabilitate degrading uplands. It engages in
this mission with many partner institutions, including government research centres in forestry and agriculture, universities and non-governmental institutions.
The target ecosystems are: forest margins or zones of current forest conversion
– here we focus on 'comp agroforests' as a sustainable land use; imperata grass-
lands, where small-scale agroforestry methods contribute to reclamation of currently underutilised land; and hill slopes, where natural vegetative strips and
other contour hedgerow practices provide a foundation for agroforestry to sus-
tain farming on sloping land (ICRAF 2007).

Activities

In northern Thailand, ICRAF started in Mae Chaem district in Chiang Mai province developing partnerships with other field-based organisations that had
experience in the field but were weak in technical areas. CARE International
was already doing work in Mae Chaem (MC) and also ran the (Royal-supported)
Suan Paa Sirikit Project for uplands development.

Outcomes

The Thailand project implemented the agroforestry project with a unique 'landscape' context: taking the larger landscape ecosystem, but with site locations

and using methods for estimating plant biodiversity, carbon stocks, methane emissions, and so on. It built a detailed digital evaluation model, digitised from 1:50 000 scale map overlays and aerial photos from 1954. ICRAF Thailand also decided to put aside existing land-use categories in order to have more open-ended categories so that people could add to them and that the project's samples reflected these different land-use systems.

The mapping of the local systems became hugely popular and the project ended up mapping 1400 sq km of MC – almost 40% of the subdistrict. Everybody who saw the maps wanted them. The maps had local names and they showed intention: not just 'forest cover', but 'this is our conservation zone, this is our forest fallow zone, and so on'. Their local land-use system has evolved through use of our mapping systems (*David Thomas, pers. comm.*).

target groups of the program are small resource holders living in the upland areas. The rationale and assumptions, much like the TG-HDP, was that uplands were fragile ecosystems and that the consequence of unsustainable resource use in the uplands was affecting lowland people.

The preparatory phase started in 1997 as interdisciplinary study projects. Teams of Thai, Vietnamese and German masters students were supervised by senior team leaders. They conducted intensive field studies for 3 months, combining both collective inquiries and individual fieldwork. Students were trained intensively in participatory research methods. The results of integrated study projects were fed back to farmers immediately after the completion of field study and finalised the report (Neef and Heidhues 2005).

Priorities for research, as identified by the farmers and stakeholders, were then used to define the research concepts. In the next step, the interests and priorities that had been identified by the farmers in the uplands, stakeholders and scientists were then considered. This was because scientists have different disciplinary backgrounds. During this period, several meetings were held with national representatives of different research intuitions and international experts from various development projects, including researchers from ICRAF (Box 6.2) and the TG-HDP (Box 6.1).

The final objectives of the program were developed after more than 3 years of preparation (Box 6.3). The final version of the research proposal was then a compromise between the disciplines of the participating scientists', farmers' and other stakeholders' priorities, and other factors, such as the political situation in these countries (Neef and Heidhues 2005).

BOX 6.3. THE HOHENHEIM UPLANDS PROGRAM

Players

The collaborative research program 'Sustainable Land Use and Rural Development in Mountainous Regions of South-east Asia' is also known as 'The Uplands Program' or HUP. The program was initiated by the University of Hohenheim (Stuttgart, Germany) in July 2000 in cooperation with four Thai universities – Chiang Mai University, Kasetsart University, Mae Jo University and Silpakorn University – and four Vietnamese universities – Hanoi Agricultural University, Thai Nguyen University of Agriculture and Forestry, Vietnam Agricultural Science Institute and the National Institute of Animal Husbandry (Uplands Program 2006).

Objectives

Primary and long-term objectives of the Uplands Program are the creation of a scientific basis for:

(1) Developing and testing sustainable land use, production and processing systems in ecological sensitive and economically disadvantaged mountainous regions of South-East Asia.

(2) Identifying innovative methods and approaches for research of ecological systems and their dynamic with special consideration of complex interactions between ecological heterogeneity, ethnic diversity and institutional frameworks.

(3) Developing concepts for rural institutions and policies addressing rural poverty and food insecurity in mountainous regions, and to improve the resilience of rural households in dynamic economic environments of South-East Asia (Uplands Program 2006).

Activities

The Uplands Program is a large interdisciplinary research program that combines various sub-projects from 12 disciplines ranging from soil, plant and animal sciences to economics and sociology (subprojects). In the first phase, the program combined 13 sub-projects of which six did research in Thailand, three in Vietnam and four in both countries. In the second phase, the program combined 18 sub-projects of which eight conducted research in Thailand, five in Vietnam and five in both countries (Uplands Program 2006).

The maximum duration of the program is 12 years. The program started its first phase from 1 July 2000 and ended on 30 June 2003. The second phase was from 1 July 2003 and ended on 30 June 2006. The program's third phase started from 1 July 2006 and ended on 30 June 2009. After each phase, the program is evaluated by DFG and the proposal for the next phase is submitted (Uplands Program 2006).

The program is funded by the Deutsche Forschungsgemeinschaft (German Research Foundation or DFG) and co-funded by the National Research Council of Thailand (NRCT) and the Ministry of Science and Technology (MOST), Vietnam. The budget in Thailand was about two million Euros for each phase (Neef A 2007, *pers comm.*). Support was provided from NRCT (co-funding), which was important to involve Thai researchers.

Outcomes

From the first and second phases, the program produced different outputs: workshops, seminars and conferences; and its materials, newsletters, journal articles, working papers, five bachelor theses (in Thailand), 43 master theses (in Thailand) and 29 PhD theses (in Thailand).

In phase I and II, the program was clearly successful at generating knowledge, understanding of the complexity of upland agriculture, institutions and natural resource management practices. The less successful part was that the knowledge could not directly solve most of the problems.

The project is nearing the end of the second of three planned phases. The difference in objectives between the two phases was that in the first phase the program tried to develop new methods to understand complexity, analysed the status quo, worked at the plot and farm-household level, whereas in the second phase, the program tried to develop technical options, models and scale up from plots to the community and landscape unit level (Uplands Program 2006; Neef A 2007, *pers. comm.*).

Evolving missions

Multiple agendas, contested views and underlying complexity transform missions in the real world.

The TG-HDP also reframed and elaborated its mission as the project matured. According to Hagen Dirksen, the former Senior Advisor to the TG-HDP – after a first bilateral arrangement between Thailand and Germany was concluded in 1981 – between the initial planning and the start of the TG-HDP, '*understanding of the highland situation in northern Thailand had become more profound. It was realized that the problem of narcotics could not be solved in isolation. Opium production is closely connected with the entire livelihood of the highland population; poverty, health, nutrition and education are issues of prime concern*' (Dirksen 2002, p. 333).

It was also understood that other issues were connected to upland development such as agricultural development and environmental issues in the highlands – forest destruction, soil erosion and sedimentation. Moreover, issues of citizenship and land use permits for the hilltribe population have always been important factors. Given these overarching issues, *'to deal with these concerns effectively, an integrated multi-sectoral rural development program approach was required'* (Dirksen 2002, p. 333).

Over the 17 years, the key development concepts and approaches of the TG-HDP were modified, reflecting both changes in conditions in the highland areas as well as understanding of them and broader paradigms of development intervention (Prasong Jantakad and Carson 1998). Initially a top-down crop-extension and crop-replacement approach introduced coffee and red kidney beans and their farming techniques. By 1990, the same extension approach introduced farmers to 'integration of perennials', where coffee and fruit trees were grown. But by 1990, there was some recognition that this 'did not address farmers' problems', so 'participatory extension' with farmers training farmers was also introduced, involving paddy rice farming, livestock raising and small-scale irrigation. This soon evolved into Community Based Land Use Planning and Local Watershed Management (CLM) where farmers did topographic model building and participatory mapping as tools for land-use planning, and village meetings were held on land-use plan and land management (Prasong Jantakad and Carson 1998, p. 11).

'TG-HDP was never designed as a fixed 'project'. Rather it was conceived as a flexible programme able to respond to changing requirements and reinforce existing institutions' (TG-HDP 1991).

Identification of the problems and objectives of research, both initially and later, if programs are allowed to evolve through crisis–evaluation–reformulation cycles, is a key step in mission-directed integrated research. Many researchers find it pays to be understandable to as many of the important stakeholders they must engage with as possible. Integration provides one method for assessment and understanding; negotiation provides another, emphasising the contingent character of research–development relationships. Despite various degrees of 'participation' involved in planning (such as land-use) or knowledge building (as in mapping exercises), in none of the three programs we studied were the subjects and targets of research and development prominent in *defining* the missions, although each program would claim they had the 'people's' interests at heart or in mind.

Table 6.1.   Engagement profiles of the three upland research and development programs.

Indicators of engagement styles	TG-HDP	ICRAF	HUP
Dominant research – policy logic	Use research for implementation and policy support	Research for negotiation and alternative policy	Research for understanding and informing policy
Key knowledge instruments	Expert-official inputs, reviews	Community consultation, mapping	Experiments, surveys, training students
Key engagement or boundary objects	Coordination plans and evaluation reports	Mapping exercises, maps and assessment or technical reports	Research papers
Venues	State-centred: government agencies	Mixed: community, government and scientific	Science-centred: scientific conferences

ENGAGEMENT AND SENSIBILITY

Engaging government agencies, other research groups, affected stakeholders or the broader public requires different skills, is done with different purposes and can achieve different outcomes (Table 6.1). The three programs vary somewhat on where they positioned themselves on the research–development applications spectrum with the TG-HDP having the strongest links to implementation and the HUP the least. The knowledge base varied. HUP had the most conventional academic scientific program. The TG-HDP relied most heavily on expertise within the Thai bureaucracy and development agencies.

The three programs also illustrate how engagement of different sorts makes use of different tools. The ICRAF project was the most innovative in terms of using mapping and maps as boundary objects, while the two other programs focused on conventional planning and reporting. The primary arenas where research ideas were formulated and findings exchanged also varied across programs (Table 6.1).

Integration as coordination

Despite an initial objective for a broad and holistic rural development approach, the TG-HDP was primarily concerned with integration as an administrative or coordination challenge. The project's working assumption was the need for integration of highland areas in northern Thailand into the administration system of the Thai government. Thus, the project planned and implemented its work with the national, provincial and lower-level government agencies that were mandated for specific tasks in the highlands. For example, the Department of Public Welfare (DPW) of the Ministry of Labor and Social Welfare, the Department of Agriculture (DOA), agencies under the Ministry of Interior (MOI), Ministry of Agriculture and Cooperatives (MOAC), Ministry of Public Health (MOPH), Ministry of Education (MOE) and later, the Ministry of Commerce (MOC), set up offices and assigned staff in highland areas.

In the early period, there was little coordination and teamwork among the various agencies. Things improved after a Management Unit (MU) was established in Chiang Mai (Dirksen 2002, p. 336). The medium term and yearly planning exercises they conducted with participating agencies led to better integration of plans and program activities at the provincial, district and village levels.

The project's close coordination with the Bureau of Budget ensured that the Thai government funded more than 80% of the program costs in Wawi and Nam Lang subdistricts. An assessment carried out between 1983 and 1994 in Nam Lang showed that the number of roads and tracks increased, piped water and electricity was introduced to the area, and state services in administration, agriculture, health, education and community development expanded rapidly, *'with the presence of government officials rising six-fold'* (Dirksen 2002, p. 341). The TG-HDP *'acted as the catalyst for institutional development'* (Dirksen 2002, p. 335). Thus, the TG-HDP research base comprised both information from the government agencies that it worked with at the central and local level as well information from its efforts at participatory land-use mapping with village communities through its 'Land Use Planning Teams'.

Engaging maps

In contrast, for ICRAF, engagement was necessarily with a broader mix of researchers and participants, with liaison with government agencies remaining very important. ICRAF used maps and landscape notions widely to engage with different groups of stakeholders.

ICRAF had people based in Mae Chaem as well as in Chiang Mai. They hired some local ethnic people. One Karen man who worked as a member of the initial teams was especially valuable to the program because he was highly respected for his local knowledge and advice and travelled widely in the region. ICRAF also teamed up with local development groups: NGOs, such as CARE, and a Royal Project – the Suan Paa Sirikit Reforestation Project – that helped in facilitating local introductions.

Similarly, an important feature of the TG-HDP approach was to employ villagers in Contact Teams to assist the MU in raising awareness, building confidence, identifying priorities and problem solving in the villages. Later on, the MU also set up a Women Action Team and two agricultural coordinators in the project areas to strengthen the integration of rural women into the overall development process (Dirksen 2002, p. 337).

ICRAF started with the challenge of making Geographic Information Systems useful to people at the local level, adopting a participatory land-use mapping approach like Sam Mun. However, what they found was that people in Mae Chaem were '*far more aware of all this, and they had already done it. They just hadn't put it on maps. So what we needed to do was not to facilitate the planning process, we needed to be able to try to put their information into a form and domain where it could be used as a basis for negotiation.*' The task was to try and raise the level of discussion by making effective use of technology and information that comes from this.

The need to better understand spatial variation and distribution of land uses and vegetation cover in Mae Chaem became obvious early, so the ICRAF group did more mapping and remote sensing that aided the initial exploratory work, from thinking about categories of land use through to the dynamics of change and its impacts on people and on the environment.

For a map to provide boundaries in negotiations over land-use in watershed management, it needs to be accurate enough, to include classes of land use that are understandable to the different parties and to cover a large enough area (Saipothong and Thomas 2007). Many village-level mapping exercises are too small in extent for use in watershed management, although they may be appropriate for other land management activities (Saipothong *et al.* 2005). Map boundaries and classes made without participation of local people may not be understood properly because they do not capture actual patterns and use of management, such as 'community' forests (Saipothong and Thomas 2007). Capturing the subsequent information about land use and land cover maps in digital form using GIS techniques then allows flexible presentation and a higher, more standardised, quality output for negotiating with government and outside agencies and for further analysis (Saipothong *et al.* 2005).

TG-HDP also had a history of exploring community-based planning, but this was often in a much more top-down style. In its highland development activities, the project used participatory approaches called '*Community Based Land Use Planning and Local Watershed Management or CLM*' (Anonymous 1998). This was done both to protect forests while also supporting hilltribes in the transition towards permanent agriculture and residence. The participatory process included classification and mapping of natural resources at village level and was initiated in Mae Hong Son province. The aim of the classification and mapping was to improve sustainability in the use of land, water and forests, enable rehabilitation of watershed catchment areas and allow intensified agricultural production on suitable land.

Three-dimensional topographic models on a scale of 1:5000 were used to demarcate village areas, including outer user boundaries for village registration, permanent cultivation areas, community forest areas to be used and conservation/watershed forest areas for environmental protection. As planning approaches became more concerted, it was possible to experiment with new technologies (Puginier 1999). But doubts remain as to what extent the CLM approach was genuinely participatory or whether it was '*a modification of extension efforts to replace shifting cultivation with permanent farming and to increase reforestation areas*' (Puginier 2002). The TG-HDP thereby had the role of a mediator between hilltribes and government agencies (Puginier 2002).

HUP placed a greater emphasis on understanding than on directly influencing farming practices. This affected how it approached engagement with subjects and agencies. In some research projects, we were told, scientific instruments needed to be installed in the fields of the farmers. The participating farmers sometimes interrupted measurements, despite having been given instructions by scientists not to do so. Further explanations allowed measurements to continue. But a few projects in the HUP program had more in-depth engagement with farmers. One project, for example, used the multi-agent systems to simulate the situation of water scarcity for local stakeholders in upper and lower reaches of a sub-catchment in the Mae Sa watershed. This exercise stimulated dialogue among stakeholders and demonstrated that researchers could help a group to think through scenarios to improve resource allocation and water conservation (Neef *et al*. 2006), in part, because the scientists were seen as neutral (according to the scientists involved).

Constructive engagement

Given that the northern Thai uplands region is a highly charged political arena where different actors, discourses and perspectives intersect and collide, research or development efforts can face a range of local reactions from resigned tolerance to vocal opposition. Building and gaining the trust of local communities can be crucial. Not surprisingly, our review of the three case studies and other related programs in the uplands shows that, although hard to measure, the sensibility of researchers towards others mattered a lot. Respect and tolerance for the beliefs, practices and values of others is an important starting point to a deeper understanding of the environmental management options and local development aspirations and opportunities. Indicators include: efforts to engage local stakeholders in their own language; starting from a working assumption that people in a place probably know useful things about it that outsiders do not; openness to possibility that aspirations, needs of a 'group' or 'class' of people are not homogeneous; recognition that a history of discrimination and continuing structural barriers to self-representation and determination must be at least acknowledged, if not addressed. In policy terms, this meant addressing – when talking about farming practices or the environment – issues of citizenship, education, health service access, community forest, land title and local government representation. None of these indicators do away with the need for quality research, based on evidence and sound reasoning, but they do underline the difference in outlook that comes from empathy with the subjects. Researchers who adopt a constructive approach to engagement that is sensitive to needs and aspirations of others can co-produce knowledge that is relevant and valued.

INFLUENCE AND RESPONSIBILITY

Integrated mission-directed research about, and for, the development of the uplands frequently raises ethical and power issues. Two modes of research and development cycles can be distinguished and observed (Figure 6.1). The first studiously avoids these issues and the second constructively engages them. In our view, researchers in development have an ethical responsibility and moral obligation to consider not only the uncertainties, limitations and biases in their own work and interpretations but also how their scientific findings might be used by others. Researchers involved in each of the three programs we studied were pushing for something like mode 2 cycles even when the wider context of the work had many competing programs with mode 1 practices. Mode 2 research cycles should be fairer.

Real needs and aspirations

The TG-HDP encountered two issues important for the upland ethnic communities involved in the project: citizenship cards and land rights. After the project, the majority of villagers in the TG-HDP areas have

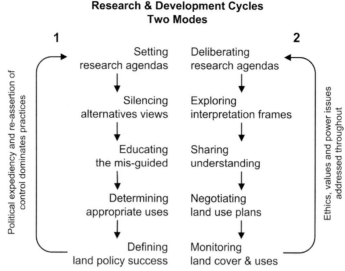

Figure 6.1. Integrated mission-directed research for upland development has had two modes.

obtained personal identification cards (showing Thai citizenship). This strengthened communities' interests in managing their land, but the problem of providing land-use permits or title remained unresolved during the project (Dirksen 2002, p. 352; Puginier 2002). Participatory land-use planning with state officials often breaks down because of the Thai state's forest and upland agriculture policies.

Another major concern with highland agriculture development is many new crops faced problems with pests or disease. Some crops introduced did not fit the local agro-climatic conditions. The commercial viability of other cash crops was dubious. Ms Alema – a Lisu woman in Doi Chang village, Doi Wawi subdistrict, Mae Suay district, Chiang Rai province interviewed by one of the authors (RD) in the mid-90's – described the project that came to the Doi Wawi area in 1982–83. 'The good outcome of the TG project was that they supported the planting of perennial fruit trees. But the main problem with the project was they did not buy the produce. So the village people had to find their own markets. We would rent a vehicle and travel down to the city market in Chiang Mai and, later, in Chiang Rai to sell the produce.' Other problems she'd noted were heavy use of pesticides and other chemicals and debt. 'In some years, if the yield is good, we would get a good income. But sometimes we do not have money to rent the vehicle to travel to the market or we do not know where to sell the crop, so the produce would go to waste' (Watershed 2000).

Farmers would have benefited from more on-farm research and development on pests, diseases and weeds. For more inaccessible areas, help was needed to explore alternative income-generation opportunities. More information was needed about agroforestry, non-wood forest products and livestock, or tourism promotion (Elawat 1997; Dirksen 2002).

A 1995 review of the TH-HDP admitted that the longer term success of sustainable goal achievement depended on the *'political willingness of the central government to relinquish power on the one hand, and on the Royal Thai Government's commitment to capacitate relevant formal institutions to fulfil their new role and functions effectively, on the other'* (Schoepf 1995).

Empowering evidence

Overall, it has proven unusually difficult to get the best science available into national or other higher level watershed-management policies (Tomich *et al.* 2004). Regulation and land-use planning have not succeeded and there has been insufficient experience with incentive-based systems, such as payment for environmental services, to draw strong policy conclusions (Tomich *et al.* 2004). Decisions about upland development in northern Thailand have often been made with little reference to evidence and science.

ICRAF's influence has been diffuse, important and consistent with its mission: strengthening evidence-based reasoning and deliberation. David Thomas, head of the ICRAF effort told us *'It was not up to us as a research organization to say what was right and what was wrong but we were saying that this is the evidence of what is, what has been, and what's going on. Now go compare this to what people say and make your own judgments'*. And: *'one cannot have all forests, and no agriculture with chemical use, and all the people moved to permanent fields given the systems that are available for them today and this was shown by our evidence'*.

This latter point is highly salient in the northern Thai context where discourses of integration of conservation and poverty alleviation have repeatedly produced false hopes and unrealistic expectations about land uses at the plot-level while ignoring landscape issues and livelihood impacts. *'We always had as part of our hope that the mapping information could help provide the basis for some kind of official recognition of land-use that could then be negotiated* (David Thomas, *pers. comm.*)'. The land use could be accepted informally but not at official forestry level because it had no legal standing. Despite the huge and historical ideological barriers, the ICRAF-ASB project has been able to get information and understanding into the official system.

David Thomas, the head of ICRAF office in Chiang Mai, has played an important role in bringing land-use change science to the attention of policy in the Ministry of Natural Resources and the Environment. First in promoting, and then showing, how to use evidence, for example, to understand and negotiate land and water use in sub-basins (Thomas 2005, 2006a), and also ways to monitor and evaluate management (Thomas 2006b). Much of this work has been supported by the World Bank. In other cases, researchers at ICRAF have analysed information and co-written articles with government researchers and officials (e.g. Suraswadi *et al.* 2005).

'*We showed that the whole basis for land-use was that people needed to negotiate among themselves the upstream-downstream issues; we showed that the sub-watershed unit was a very useful management unit at the local level – a lot of local names are based on the streams at the sub-watershed level*'. At present, the sub-basin group in MC is made up of at least 25 local sub-watershed networks that merged together and we helped them to put the information together. '*ICRAF played an important role in putting the maps and data and time series on the table; lifting the standard of debate*'.

ICRAF has also developed and demonstrated the use of participatory science- or evidence-based methods for monitoring the effectiveness and impacts of watershed management (Thomas *et al.* 2004; Saipothong *et al.* 2006; Thomas 2006b).

Despite these efforts, it has also been frustrating – even with some support for evidence-based approaches within the RFD. Others such as nature conservation groups or foresters refuse to accept the science and knowledge where it doesn't fit with their preconceptions and interests; because they are powerful, they can still influence how forests and upland areas are managed. Moreover, there is still no legal basis for using such information as ICRAF's in state land-use planning.

Each of the programs we explored had significant impacts. Influence on understanding, decisions and practices varied more or less according to where each program's capacities were. The notion of targeting programs to population areas that may capture donor interests also has the side-effect of disempowering missions that may be located elsewhere. Issues of scale are significant where the responsibility for research regarding development in the uplands requires shifting the subjects of inquiry and scrutiny elsewhere, such as to the corridors of key bureaucracies, aid agencies and science funding.

CONCLUSION

In the uplands of northern Thailand, the idea or consultation or engagement 'burnout' is becoming all too familiar; whether it is the fly-in expert from the multi-lateral agency attempting to find ideas, or the latest state-led project that attempts to transform the landscape and end poverty. Villagers have grown weary and wary.

Research programs that have engaged the development opportunities and challenges faced by people living in the uplands have, likewise, learnt to be more sceptical of development rhetoric. But it is only when researchers for development really take notice of local knowledge and opinions that integrated mission-directed research becomes effective. The main conclusions that we can make from these studies includes the following:

(1) The identification of problems is a critical ongoing negotiation in which it pays to be understandable to as wide a range of stakeholders as possible.
(2) The effectiveness of engagement by researchers with narrowly defined stakeholder groups or a wider public in their dealings with public policy issues is contingent on the sensibility they bring with them.
(3) Mission-directed research – because it can be very influential – carries with it ethical responsibilities that may not apply so strongly or frequently as in other kinds of research.

ENDNOTES

1 In the early 1990s the Thai government's Doi Sam Muen project was seen as a benchmark site for watershed planning that captured both forest and agriculture issues.

REFERENCES

Anonymous (1998) Solutions for a water-short world. *Population Reports* **26,** Johns Hopkins School of Public Health, Maryland, USA.

Clark WC and Tomich T (2007) 'Global knowledge for local actions: CGIAR alternatives to slash and burn programme as a model knowledge system'. KSSD Working Paper. Harvard University, Cambridge MA.

Dirksen H (2002) '18 years of Thai-German Highland Development Programme: has it been a success?' Deutsche Gesellschaft für Technische Zusammenarbeit (GTZ), Eschborn, Germany.

Elawat C (1997) Sociocultural and environmental impact of economic development on hill tribes. In: *Development or Domestication? Indigenous Peoples of Southeast Asia.* (Eds D McCaskill and K Kampe) pp. 83–96. Silkworm Books, Chiang Mai, Thailand.

Forsyth T (1998) Mountain myths revisited: integrating natural and social environmental science. *Mountain Research and Development* **18**, 126–139.

Forsyth T (2003) *Critical Political Ecology: The Politics of Environmental Science*. Routledge, London.

Hirsch P (Ed.) (1997) *Seeing Forests for Trees: Environment and Environmentalism in Thailand*. Silkworm Books, Chiang Mai, Thailand.

ICRAF (International Centre for Research in Agroforestry) (2007) <http://www.mekonginfo.org/partners/icraf/index.htm>, accessed 20 August 2007.

Laungaramsri P (2002a) *On the Politics of Nature Conservation in Thailand. Issue 1. Kyoto Review of Southeast Asia*. October 2002, Centre for Southeast Asian Studies, Kyoto University, Kyoto, Japan. <http://kyotoreview.cseas.kyoto-u.ac.jp/issue/issue1/article_168.html>

Laungaramsri P (2002b) *Redefining Nature: Karen Ecological Knowledge and the Challenge to the Modern Conservation Paradigm*. Earthworm Books, Chennai, India.

Lebel L, Contreras A, Pasong S and Garden P (2004) Nobody knows best: alternative perspectives on forest management and governance in Southeast Asia: politics, law and economics. *International Environment Agreements* **4**, 111–127.

McCaskill D and Kampe KE (1997) *Development or Domestication: Indigenous Peoples of Southeast Asia*. Silkworm Books, Chiang Mai, Thailand.

Missingham BD (2003) *The Assembly of the Poor in Thailand: From Local Struggles to National Protest Movement*. Silkworm Books, Chiang Mai, Thailand.

Neef A, Chamsai L and Sangkapitux C (2006) Water tenure in highland watersheds of northern Thailand: managing legal pluralism and stakeholder complexity. In: *Institutional Dynamics and Stasis: How Crises Alter the Way Common Pool Resources Are Perceived*. (Eds L Lebel, X Jianchu and A Contreras). Regional Centre for Social Science and Sustainable Development (RCSD), Chiang Mai University, Chiang Mai, Thailand.

Neef A and Heidhues F (2005) Getting priorities right: balancing farmers' and scientists' perspectives in participatory agricultural research. In: *Participatory Approaches for Sustainable Land Use in Southeast Asia*. (Ed. A Neef) pp. 99–115. White Lotus Co. Ltd, Bangkok, Thailand.

Prasong Jantakad and Carson S (1998) Community based natural resource management from villages to inter-village network: a case study of

Pang Ma Pha district, Mae Hong Son province, northern Thailand. In: *Papers presented at a World Bank Community Based Natural Resource Management Workshop.* p. 14. World Bank, Washington DC.

Puginier O (1999) Land use planning in transition from shifting cultivation to permanent agriculture in Mae Hong Son, Thailand. In: *Proceedings of the Conference on Tropical and Subtropical Agricultural and Natural Resource Management (Deutscher Tropentag), Berlin.* <http://www.tropentag.de/index.php?menu=1>

Puginier O (2002) *Planning, Participation and Policy – Hilltribes Overcoming the Dichotomy Between Agriculture and Forest Preservation in Northern Thailand.* Deutsche Gesellschaft für Technische Zusammenarbeit (GTZ), Eschborn, Germany. <http://www.iapad.org/publications/ppgis/TOEB_Planning_Participation_and_Policy_in_Thailand.pdf>

Renard RD (2001) *Opium Reduction in Thailand 1970–2000: A Thirty Year Journey.* Silkworm Books for United Nations International Drug Control Programme, Chiang Mai, Thailand.

Saipothong P, Kojornrungrot W and Thomas DE (2005) Comparative study of participatory mapping processes in northern Thailand. In: *Mapping Communities: Ethics, Values, Practice.* (Eds J Fox, K Suryanata and P Hershock) pp. 11–28. East-West Center, Honolulu, Hawaii.

Saipothong P, Preechapanya P, Promduang T, Kaewpoka N and Thomas DE (2006) Community-based watershed monitoring and management in northern Thailand. *Mountain Research and Development* **26**, 289–291.

Saipothong P and Thomas D (2007) Spatial information tools for land use management networks in montane mainland Southeast Asia. *Information Development* **23**, 129–136.

Sato J (2003) Public land for the people: the institutional basis of community forestry in Thailand. *Journal of Southeast Asian Studies* **34**, 329–346.

Schoepf F (1995) 'Internal Paper No. 195, Project Progress Report 1995'. Deutsche Gesellschaft fur Technische Zusammenarbeit (GTZ) GmbH, Thai-German Highland Development Programme (TG-HDP), Chiang Mai, Thailand.

Suraswadi P, Thomas DE, Pragtong K, Preechapanya P and Wyerhaeuser H (2005) Northern Thailand: changing smallholder land use patterns. In: *Slash-and-Burn Agriculture: The Search for Alternatives.* (Eds CA Palm, SA Vosti, PA Sanchez and PJ Eriksen). pp. 355–384. Columbia University Press, New York.

Tapp N (1986) 'The Hmong of Thailand: opium people of the Golden Triangle'. Indigenous Peoples and Development Series Report No. 4.

Anti-Slavery Society and Cultural Survival, Inc.., London and Cambridge, MA.

TG-HDP (1991) Thai-German Highland Development Programme (TG-HDP). Office of the Narcotics Control Board (ONCB), Deutsche Gesellschaft fur Technische Zusammenarbeit (GTZ) GmbH. Eschborn, Germany

Thomas DE (2005) 'Participatory watershed management in upper northern region of Thailand'. ICRAF, Chiang Mai, Thailand.

Thomas DE (2006a) 'Participatory watershed management for the Ping River Basin'. Final Project Report. Office of Natural Resources and Environmental Policy and Planning, Ministry of Natural Resources and Environment, Bangkok, Thailand.

Thomas DE (2006b) 'Results measurement framework for pilot sub-basins'. Office of Natural Resources and Environment Policy and Planning, Ministry of Natural Resources and Environment, Bangkok, Thailand.

Thomas DE, Preechapanya P and Saipothong P (2004) 'Developing science-based tools for participatory watershed management in montane mainland Southeast Asia: final report to the Rockefeller Foundation for Grant No. 2000 GI 086'. World Agroforestry Centre (ICRAF), Chiang Mai, Thailand.

Tomich TP, Thomas DE and van Noordwijk M (2004) Environmental services and land use change in Southeast Asia: from recognition to regulation or reward? *Agriculture, Ecosystems and Environment* **104**, 229–244.

Uplands Program (2006) Sonderforschungsbereich 564. Zweite Folgeantrag, Stuttgart, Germany.

van Kerkhoff L (2005) Integrated research: concepts of connection in environmental science and policy. *Environmental Science and Policy* **8**, 439–463.

van Kerkhoff L and Lebel L (2006) Linking knowledge and action for sustainable development. *Annual Review of Environment and Resources* **31**, 445–477.

Vandergeest P and Peluso NL (1995) Territorialization and state power in Thailand. *Theory and Society* **24**, 385–426.

Walker A (2003) Agricultural transformation and the politics of hydrology in northern Thailand. *Development and Change* **34**, 941–964.

Watershed (2000) Interview with Ms Alema, ethnic Lisu woman in Doi Chang village, Doi Wawi subdistrict, Mae Suay district. *Watershed* **5**(3) March–June, 46–47.

Winichakul T (1994) *Siam Mapped: A History of the Geo-body of a Nation*. Silkworm Books, Chiang Mai, Thailand.

Chapter 7

A sociological analysis of the participatory application of agricultural decision-support systems

Emma Jakku and Peter Thorburn

ABSTRACT

Technologies are important mediators of relationships in integrated mission-directed research. Scientists have attempted to make agricultural systems science more accessible and useful for industry stakeholders through decision-support systems (DSSs). However, the poor uptake of agricultural DSSs by intended users has lead to critical reflection on the way in which these technologies are developed and applied. The current shift towards participatory research, development and application approaches recognises the benefits of fostering collaborative and mutually beneficial relationships between scientists and their stakeholders, but lacks a detailed analysis of the interaction between the multiple parties involved in DSS application. To address this gap, we have analysed the participatory application of DSSs, using concepts from science and technology studies, through a project examining the application of knowledge intensive technologies in the Australian sugar industry.

In this chapter, we outline a theoretical framework for understanding the role of technologies in interactions between scientists and practice communities. The framework focuses on the phases of participatory DSS application, and the likely outcomes of this process. The framework is based on three concepts from science and technology studies: namely interpretative flexibility, technological frames and boundary objects. We reflect on how this framework contributes to understanding the challenges and benefits of integrated, mission-directed research, including the challenges of problem definition and role definition and the potential benefit of generating new knowledge and insights. We argue that participatory DSS application must begin with negotiation of the different perspectives of the scientist and other stakeholders involved in DSS application, with an emphasis on co-learning between experts and local people.

INTRODUCTION

Technologies often act as intermediaries that facilitate interaction between scientists and practice communities in integrated mission-directed research. Participatory approaches are becoming common in this type of research and the shift towards the participatory development and/or application of technologies requires new ways of thinking about the process of designing and implementing technologies. The interaction between people and technology is the focus of science and technology studies. Thus it is likely that concepts from science and technology studies may contribute to new ways of thinking about the process of designing and implementing technologies.

An example of the use of technologies as intermediaries between scientists and practice communities is the application of decision-support systems (DSSs) to improve management of farming systems. DSSs are software applications that are based on simulation or other quantitative analysis. Issues such as declining profitability of agriculture, climate variability and increasing concerns over the environmental impacts of farming pose complex challenges to the management of farming systems. DSSs are seen as a means of making scientific knowledge available to agricultural practice communities to guide changes to management. However, DSS developers have generally viewed the success of these endeavours as limited (Hayman 2004; Stone and Hochman 2004). Much of the activity has been directed at participatory development of the DSS, assuming subsequent use by practitioners, although there are examples of participatory application (Cash 2001). In practice, the two processes, development and application, are often complimentary. Participatory DSS development and application is underpinned by adult learning principles and focuses on local stakeholders and researchers cooperating as active co-experimenters engaged in joint learning (Ridley 2004). Walker (2002) maintains that participatory research can ensure that DSS development integrates researchers', developers' and users' perspectives in order to clarify objectives and foster co-learning. Moreover, Douthwaite *et al.* (2001) observe that as the complexity and knowledge intensiveness of technological innovations increases, so does the need for participatory research to ensure the relevance and effectiveness of the new technology.

We have used three concepts from science and technology studies to develop a framework to provide an analytical structure for examining the social context and process of participatory DSS application. The framework also allows clearer definition of the possible outcomes of the participatory development/application process. After outlining the framework, we illustrate the application of this framework through two case studies.

SOCIOLOGICAL CONCEPTS FOR UNDERSTANDING PARTICIPATORY DSS APPLICATION

Science and technology studies demonstrate that 'scientific knowledge is not the passive product of nature but an actively negotiated, social product of human inquiry' (Cozzens and Woodhouse 1995, p. 534) and that technology is 'a social product, patterned by the conditions of its creation and use' (Williams and Edge 1996, p. 866). The concepts of interpretative flexibility and technological frames from science and technology studies describe the way in which scientists and/or practice communities view and interpret technologies. The concept of boundary objects describes a process that can facilitate the forms of social interaction that shape technology development. These concepts can be combined to form a framework (Figure 7.1) that describes and explains the possible processes of participatory DSS application, and identifies the potential outcomes of the process. The overall structure of Figure 7.1 was inspired by Pahl-Wostl and Hare's (2004, p. 194) model of social learning.

The background of the framework emphasises that participatory DSS application is conditioned by its external social, political, economic and environmental context. The contextual factors that can influence participatory DSS application range from macro-level economic and political factors, such as world markets, through to micro-level social and cultural factors, such as individuals' educational and generational backgrounds, farming styles and traditions, and attitudes towards risk (Doorman 1991;

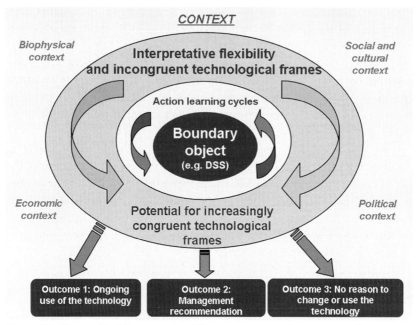

Figure 7.1. Theoretical framework of the processes and outcomes of participatory DSS application, which are embedded within a social, cultural, political, economic and biophysical context and shaped by interpretative flexibility and technological frames.

Ang *et al.* 2001). The outer circle in the framework focuses on how the concepts of interpretative flexibility and technological frames can help us to understand the social context of participatory DSS development. Interpretative flexibility means that any object can mean different things to different people, depending on contextual factors (Hess 1997). Thus, a specific technology can be interpreted in diverse ways by different social groups (Pinch and Bijker 1987; Bijker 1995). When applied to technologies such as DSSs, the concept emphasises that a DSS will mean different things to the various people involved its development. For instance, the scientists, extension officers and farmers involved in developing a DSS will have different interpretations of the meaning of that DSS and even of the issue that it is designed to address.

Interpretative flexibility also affects how technologies are designed:

> … there is flexibility in how people think of or interpret artifacts but also that there is flexibility in how artifacts are designed. There is not just one possible way or one best way of designing an artifact (Pinch and Bijker 1987, p. 40).

The interpretation of particular technologies depends on the problem that the technology is designed to address, which is shaped by the way in which different groups of people can define a problem in different ways (Bruun and Hukkinen 2003). Interpretative flexibility also recognises the way in which different technologies have 'different degrees of interpretative flexibility' (Orlikowski 1992, p. 421):

> … *there is flexibility in how people design, interpret, and use technology, but that this flexibility is a function of the material components comprising the artifact, the institutional context in which a technology is developed and used, and the power, knowledge, and interests of human actors …* (Orlikowski 1992, p. 421).

Interpretative flexibility therefore emphasises the way in which the design and implementation of technologies is not solely a technical issue, because there are a range of social factors that influence the choices made in this process (Williams and Edge 1996). The concept of interpretative flexibility emphasises that in order to understand the social context of participatory DSS application, it is important to recognise that a DSS and its capability will mean different things to the various people involved their development.

Technological frames are the assumptions, beliefs and expectations that groups of people hold about a specific technology, which in turn influence the design and use of that technology:

> *Technological frames provide the goals, the ideas, and the tools needed for action. They guide thinking and interaction. A technological frame offers both the central problems and the related strategies for solving them* (Bijker 1995, pp. 191–192).

The concept of technological frames draws on the concept of 'schema' from cognitive psychology (Bartlett 1932; Neisser 1976). A technological frame is therefore a kind of 'mental model', which consists of cognitive elements such as 'current theories, goals, problem-solving strategies, and practices of use' (Bijker 1987, p. 171). Technological frames are also shaped by the interaction between various groups of people and so evolve and change through time: a technological frame 'is built up when interaction 'around' an artifact starts and continues' (Bijker 1987, p. 173). Thus, the concept of technological frames reveals the 'dynamic character of technological development' (Bijker 1987, p. 174).

Orlikowski and Gash's (1994, p. 175) 'socio-cognitive approach toward information technology' complements Bijker's (1987) approach. Orlikowski and Gash (1994) show how Bijker's concept of technological frames can be applied to complex information technologies by identifying three important dimensions of technological frames:

(1) **nature of technology**, which refers to people's perceptions and understanding of the technology
(2) **technology strategy**, which refers to people's views of why their organisation acquired and implemented the technology
(3) **technology in use**, which refers to people's understanding of how the technology will be used and the likely or actual conditions and consequences associated with such use.

Analysis of these three dimensions of technological frames provides a useful platform for examining how people interpret the meaning and value of a particular technology, their views on whether it should be implemented and, if so, why it should be implemented and how it can be used to create a change in behaviour and practice.

The concept of technological frames is particularly concerned with examining whether people hold similar or different technological frames. Members of a particular social group will hold similar technological frames because they share common relationships and experiences (Sahay and Robey 1996). In the context of agricultural research, farmers and scientists hold different technological frames, reflecting their background and experiences. However, technological frames can also be different within social groups. For example, the soils and/or climatic condition on one farm may be different from others, shaping the technological frame of that farmer, while scientists from different disciplines may have different technological frames.

Orlikowski and Gash (1994, p. 180) refer to holding similar technological frames as congruence, which refers to 'the alignment of frames on key elements or categories'. Congruence in technological frames occurs when members of social groups share similar expectations about the nature of the technology and the use that it serves. Incongruence in technological frames occurs when members of different social groups hold differing expectations or assumptions about some important aspects of the technology. For instance, developers and/or advanced users of a DSS may hold quite different convictions and expectations to practitioners about what that technology can deliver, because their interactions with the DSS differ, they come from different social positions or backgrounds and have different needs and interests (Sahay and Robey 1996). Orlikowski and Gash

(1994) argue that incongruence in technological frames can create difficulties for the development and implementation of technology, because incongruence can lead to conflicts over the use and value of the technology, and so a key attribute in the participatory application of technologies is gaining increasingly congruent technological frames.

The inner circle in the framework focuses on the processes involved in the participatory application of DSS. The concept of a boundary object provides a novel perspective on the role of technology as an intermediary between scientists and practice communities in technology development. Star and Griesemer (1989) developed the concept of boundary objects in their study of the early years of the Museum of Vertebrate Zoology at the University of California, Berkeley. They define boundary objects as:

> … objects which are plastic enough to adapt to local needs and constraints of the several parties employing them, yet robust enough to maintain a common identity across sites (Star and Griesemer 1989, p. 393).

In their case study of the Museum of Vertebrate Zoology, Star and Griesemer (1989, p. 408) found that a variety of actors, such as sponsors of the museum, scientists and natural history amateurs were able to use items such as specimens of mammals and birds, field notes and maps of particular territories as boundary objects, because these were 'simultaneously concrete and abstract, specific and general, conventionalised and customized'. Star and Griesemer (1989, p. 393) argue that the:

> … creation and management of boundary objects is a key process in developing and maintaining coherence across intersecting social worlds.

Other studies have applied and developed Star and Griesemer's (1989) concept of boundary objects. Harvey and Chrisman (1998) examine how Geographic Information System (GIS) technology can act as a boundary object. Harvey and Chrisman (1998, p. 1683) argue that the concept of boundary objects:

> … articulates the process through which technology becomes part of different social groups, and how technology successfully connects multiple, even opposing, perspectives.

By mediating differences and providing a common point of reference, boundary objects facilitate cooperation between different groups of people. Harvey and Chrisman (1998, p. 1693) use the concept of boundary objects to understand how GIS technology 'exists as part of an intricate web of social relations', through which the diverse interest of scientists, policy specialists, various institutions and concerned citizens are linked.

Cash (2001) explored the way in which scientific models can act as boundary objects in agricultural extension, highlighting the potential for different kinds of models (including cropping, hydro-geologic and economic models) to serve as boundary objects:

> ... *models themselves can act as boundary objects, dependent on both the participation of farmers to get inputs that reflect reality and outputs that are useful, as well as on scientists who incorporate basic research on the systems under study and the technical capacity to guide the endeavor* (Cash 2001, p. 441).

Cash (2001, p. 441) used an example of a model of aquifer management to illustrate the way in which a model can facilitate interaction between scientists, farmers and water managers:

> ... *farmers and water managers were able to test different management scenarios they viewed as credible, and scientists were able to produce scientific outputs that were policy relevant and robust with respect to local data.*

This case study further illustrates the way in which boundary objects can facilitate cooperation between diverse groups of people, which in turn can provide mutually beneficial outcomes.

Acknowledgment of the potential of technologies to act as boundary objects addresses the challenge of how to manage interpretative flexibility and differences in technological frames in participatory DSS application, by drawing attention to the action learning cycles, negotiation and co-learning that are essential for participatory DSS application. A DSS is a boundary object when it means different things to different people yet still maintains a common identity, thus allowing for negotiation, cooperation and co-learning among the various people that are involved in its development. This highlights the way in which the participatory DSS application can encourage a more equitable balance between scientific and local knowledge systems, which in turns facilitates the integration of these knowledge systems. Through this process of action learning, the different social groups involved in the participatory DSS application may arrive at an increasingly similar or complementary understanding of the problem, which works towards increasingly congruent technological frames.

The framework also highlights the different outcomes possible from participatory DSS application. The complexity of the problem that is addressed is a key factor that influences the outcomes of the application process. DSSs that address complex problems are more likely to go through a longer phase of acting as a boundary object to facilitate the cycles of negotiation and co-learning that are required to form an increasingly shared understanding of the problem between the people involved in this process. The outcome may be the acceptance that the DSS needs to be used on an ongoing basis to determine the optimum management practice. Then further cycles of negotiation and co-learning may be necessary to further develop and/or modify the DSS (e.g. through making the software more user-friendly) for this routine role. Once the DSS is being routinely used, it ceases to act as a boundary object. This leads to Outcome 1, whereby a DSS may be able to influence industry stakeholders' management decisions through its continued role in problem solving; that is, optimising management practice.

In contrast, the cycles of negotiation and co-learning that occur through participatory DSS application may lead to a better understanding of the problem and its context. This may allow for simplification of the problem within the specific management and/or biophysical context and result in the discovery of a new and widely applicable management practice with ongoing relevance that can be applied without ongoing use of the DSS (Outcome 2 in the framework, Figure 7.1). This outcome is really the development of a knowledge-embedded management recommendation, which can be routinely used by industry stakeholders. It highlights the well-recognised trend of industry stakeholders learning and developing their own management practices after using a DSS, either in participation with scientists or by themselves (Hearn and Bange 2002; McCown 2002; Stone and Hochman 2004; Thorburn *et al.* 2006).

The framework also recognises that through the process of applying the DSS, the parties involved may find that there is no reason to change current practice or decision-making processes. This third outcome may occur because the participatory DSS application leads to a better understanding of the problem and its context and an acceptance that there is no need or opportunity for further optimisation of current management practice. It may also occur if the parties involved believe that the DSS will not provide a sufficient advantage necessary to justify its use.

CASE STUDIES OF THE APPLICATION OF AGRICULTURAL DSSS

The case studies in this section are drawn from projects using knowledge-intensive technologies to improve the profitability of the value chain of the Australian sugar industry. Two issues were studied: the application seasonal climate forecasting systems to improve management across the sugar value chain; and the exploration of opportunities for diversifying products from the sugar value chain.

Seasonal climate forecasting systems for the Australian sugar industry

As part of a broader research project on the adoption of knowledge-intensive technologies, an industry case study group consisting of sugarcane growers, harvesters, millers, extension officers and other industry representatives was established in Tully, North Queensland to explore in a participatory manner the opportunities for, and possible benefits of, using seasonal climate forecasting to improve decision in the farming, harvesting and milling sectors of the value chain (Everingham *et al.* 2006). The initial meetings between the researchers and the case study group focused on developing the group's understanding of climate forecasting terminology, in order to build understanding within the group of the strengths and limitations of seasonal climate forecasting. An important focus of these early meetings related to clarifying the difference between weather forecasting and seasonal climate forecasting. This difference illustrates the interpretative flexibility that shaped participants' initial reactions to seasonal climate forecasting and the interactions between the scientists and the industry participants. Another significant phase of the early meetings involved identifying when seasonal climate forecasting might be able to assist industry decision making. This process was necessary because some of the growers, harvesters, millers, extension officers and scientists initially had different perceptions about when seasonal climate forecasting information might be useful and how this information should be delivered. These differences illustrate the different technological frames held by those involved in the case study group. However, after a series of discussions, the case study group reached a level of consensus about the definition of seasonal climate forecasting and its ability to assist decisions relating to fertiliser regimes, harvesting, planting and herbicide applications (Everingham *et al.* 2006). This consensus illustrates the way in which a participatory process can facilitate the development of congruent technological frames.

The interaction between local and expert knowledge in the case study group is also worth noting here. In the initial meetings, where the emphasis was on clarifying the difference between weather forecasting and climate forecasting and building the industry participants' understanding of climate forecasting terminology, the expert knowledge of the scientists was the dominant feature. However, when the discussions shifted to considering the relevance and impact of seasonal climate forecasting on industry decision making, the industry participant's local knowledge became dominant. This illustrates the way in which participatory DSS development and application needs to be based on an interaction between local and expert knowledge as complementary knowledge systems, which can each make valuable contributions to a broader process of co-learning for all participants.

Discussions with the industry participants about how to extend the use of seasonal climate forecasting systems beyond the case study group initially focused on the development of a DSS called RainForecaster. This DSS was designed to be used by the case study group coordinator and local extension staff to produce climate updates that were tailored to the Tully region. Outputs from RainForecaster were to be placed on the local grower website and were displayed as a graph familiar to the case study group participants. RainForecaster was designed in consultation with the case study group, so that the outputs were relevant to, and able to be interpreted by, the industry participants (Everingham *et al.* 2006). This illustrates the negotiation and cooperation that underpinned the action learning cycles between the scientists and industry participants during the application of seasonal climate forecasting for the Tully region. It also emphasises the way in which participatory DSS development and application allows for the recognition and exploration of the different perspectives that people hold. This can improve the design and development of technologies, by combining different knowledge systems, such as scientific and local knowledge – a point already recognised by many DSS developers (e.g. Carberry *et al.* 2002; Foale *et al.* 2004). This open recognition and negotiation of the various perspectives can facilitate the development of trust and ownership that many DSS developers have recognised as critical for successful DSS development and application (Hearn and Bange 2002; Foale *et al.* 2004).

Attention within the case study group then turned to identifying other ways in which seasonal climate forecasting might reach a larger audience in the Tully sugar industry. As part of a brainstorming session on this issue, the idea of summarising the recommended management reactions to different RainForecaster outputs onto a refrigerator magnet was suggested. This illustrates a move towards Outcome 2 identified by the framework, whereby participatory iterations between scientists and industry participants result in the simplification of the problem, which in turn allows for the identification of a 'rule of thumb' that can act as a management recommendation with ongoing relevance. This 'rule of thumb' can then be distributed through appropriate extension processes, including information packages such as refrigerator magnets.

Product diversification in the Australian sugar industry

A contrasting example comes from efforts to improve profitability of the sugar industry in a region in Queensland, Australia through diversification of products from the raw sugar value chain. This supply chain is complex and diversification will necessitate substantial changes to the chain. The impacts and net benefits of diversification will be difficult to predict *a priori*, and so assessment of diversification options will be aided by quantitative analysis of the options. An industry case study group consisting of representatives from each sector of the value chain (growers, harvesters and millers) and scientists specialising in the technology of the different sectors of the chain was established in Maryborough, South Queensland to explore in a participatory manner diversification options in that region (Thorburn *et al.* 2006).

Initially, the value chain in the region was qualitatively mapped by the case study group at a workshop. This process allowed expression of the details of each sector – from both an operational and technical perspective – and highlighted interactions between sectors. It allowed participants to explore the interests and perspectives held by different industry sectors and, in doing so, provided an opportunity to express their technological frames and gain insights into others' frames. It also facilitated a common learning experience: the beginning of making the technological frames of the group members more congruent.

Subsequently, a quantitative model of the whole value chain was developed that reflected the attributes and linkages initially mapped. The model was then used as a DSS to examine the impacts of a diversification option that was being considered in the region: maximising the co-generation of electricity at the local sugar mill through harvesting the whole crop (i.e. leaves as well as cane stem). In this scenario, additional income from electricity sales had to be weighed against not only the costs of constructing and operating the co-generation facility, but also the costs associated with: (1) loss of crop residues from the field; (2) harvesting and transporting to the mill the additional material; and (3) the negative impact of the changes on sugar mill operations. The DSS acted as a boundary object, as scientists presented outcomes of various assumptions of the scenario, allowing stakeholders to gain better understanding of the operation of their value chain and the consequences of different potential operational strategies. Different strategies were investigated by the group in an effort to identify one that would be profitable for the region. After all strategies were explored, the group came to a unanimous decision regarding the attractiveness of the venture (it would not be profitable) and so the DSS ceased to be useful. Thus the group reached Outcome 3 of the framework (Figure 7.1).

However, during the cycles of negotiation and exploration, several opportunities for improving operations within the current value chain were identified. One of these – optimising transport of the harvested crop from farms to the sugar mill – has subsequently been investigated further. It will require the participatory application of a transport scheduling DSS (based on the model of Higgins 2006), with a vision that it will be routine operated by mill staff (i.e. reaching Outcome 1 of the framework).

Overall, the predicted impacts of the diversification option were different from those anticipated by stakeholders. The analysis provided both the stakeholders and the scientists with a more complete understanding of the possible impacts of whole-crop harvesting than previously available, or than would have been be obtained using more traditional assessments, and allowed them to evaluate the viability of venture. The analysis also increased stakeholders' understanding of the sugar supply chain in their region, leading to short-term benefits, such as improving harvesting and transport logistics.

DISCUSSION

The shift towards participatory development and application of agricultural DSSs has prompted critical reflection on the way in which these knowledge-intensive technologies are developed and implemented. Although most previous examples of the development and application of agricultural DSSs centre on efforts to improve farm management, the principles are equally applicable to other problems within the whole agricultural value chain. In this chapter we provide a theoretical framework for analysing the social processes that are at the core of the current debate over the value and impact of participatory DSS application. The framework also identifies some of the key challenges and benefits of integrated mission-directed research. For instance, the challenge of problem definition underpins the framework's focus on the need to begin participatory application of DSSs with the recognition and negotiation of the different interests and perspectives of those involved in this process. The framework's emphasis on co-learning between experts and lay people relates to the challenge of role definition. In particular, the concepts of interpretative flexibility and technological frames reinforce the importance of acknowledging the different perspectives that are held by people involved in participatory DSS application and then working towards a shared understanding between these people, which are key strategies for successful problem and role definition.

The framework also illustrates a potential benefit of integrated mission-directed research by pointing to the way in which participatory approaches to DSS application can break down the barriers between the developers and potential users of DSSs. Participatory approaches recognise the value of involving potential users early in the development process, rather than treating them as passive recipients of knowledge (Kloppenburg 1991; Massey *et al.* 2006). One of the key benefits of participatory DSS application is that it allows developers and potential users to work together to build new knowledge and insights. This resonates with Bammer's (2005) work on integration and implementation science, which identifies participatory methods and recognition of the need to value the diverse ways in which people understand the world as two key principles of integrated mission-directed science. Bammer (2005, p. 6) argues that participatory approaches allow researchers and practitioners to 'learn together about problems of common interests' and 'combine their perspectives to build new concepts, insights and/or practical innovations, which they could not produce alone.'

The concept of a boundary object reinforces the value of participatory DSS application for encouraging co-learning between the different groups involved in this process. The idea that a DSS can act as a boundary object and encourage dialogue and collaboration between industry participants and scientists supports the calls for a shift in thinking about the role of agricultural DSSs made previously (Leeuwis 1993; Carberry *et al.* 2002; Hayman and Easdown 2002; Loevinsohn *et al.* 2002; Walker 2002; Stone and Hochman 2004). Although they do not use the term boundary object, Hearn and Bange (2002, pp. 53–54) recognise the way in which development of DSSs 'has facilitated communication between farmers and scientists …' by providing a 'meeting point where farmers and scientists can explore' questions related to farm management. Similarly, Stone and Hochman (2004, p. 11) emphasise the importance of the relationship between scientists and farmers in the development and application of DSSs and highlight the value of DSSs in terms of 'providing a focal point and form for communication between farmers and scientists rather than the main basis of the relationship.' Moreover, Walker's (2002) call for a reappraisal of the role of DSSs is based on recognition of the value of DSSs for fostering learning and co-learning. Thus, appreciating the way in which a DSS can act as a boundary object involves appreciating the ways in which cooperation and co-learning among the various people involved in DSS development and application can occur, despite the fact that these people can hold diverse perceptions of a DSS or the issue it is designed to address. Instead of seeing the application of a DSS that develops into a tool to be used by industry stakeholders in a routine manner as the primary goal, we suggest that the participatory application of a DSS can be a valuable process in itself. The process can create a space for improved communication and co-learning between industry stakeholders and scientists and, as a result, can contribute to developing more useful knowledge and achieving greater impact. Even if the process does not result in further development and ongoing use of the DSS by industry stakeholders, there may be positive outcomes for participants in simply being part of the research and development process. This, in turn, emphasises the value and importance of the intangible positive outcomes of participatory DSS application, which goes beyond seeing participatory methods purely as a means for facilitating increased adoption of DSSs – a common goal among DSS developers (Hayman 2004; Stone and Hochman 2004).

The framework proposed in this chapter identifies three different scenarios for successful DSS development and, in doing so, provides a novel approach to evaluating the outcomes of agricultural DSS applications. Ongoing and routine use of a DSS, which we have characterised as Outcome 1 of Figure 7.1, is the traditional definition of success for many DSS developers (Hayman 2004; Stone and Hochman 2004). However, as illustrated by our case study examples, Outcome 2 (Figure 7.1) suggests that a DSS may become redundant once it has fulfilled its function as a tool for co-learning – the cycles of action learning and negotiation result in the development of a clearer understanding of the problem by all, and a subsequent management recommendation, based on this understanding. Outcome 3 suggests that the processes of co-learning may result in an informed decision that no change to management is justified or required and, in which case, the DSS serves no further purpose. This raises the important question of whether the duration of use of a DSS is the most appropriate definition of a successful DSS application process. In defining Outcomes 2 and 3 of the participatory DSS development process, we are clearly supporting previous calls for the need to rethink the way in which we define success of DSS application (Cox 1996; Walker 2002; Hayman 2004; Stone and Hochman 2004). Successful DSS application should be viewed as a participatory process leading to practice change, which in turn results in improved farm or value chain management, irrespective of whether or not this involves ongoing DSS use.

CONCLUSION

We argue that our framework is a useful tool for reflecting on the role of technologies in integrated mission-directed research and the key challenges and potential benefits associated with this research approach. Our framework addresses the challenges of problem definition and role definition by characterising participatory DSS application as a mutual learning process between actors with complementary contributions, which in turn places expert and local knowledge on a more equal footing and acts as a catalyst for new knowledge and insights. The framework also clarifies the range of potential outcomes of participatory DSS application and emphasises the way in which successful DSS application can be defined in terms of achieving impact through practice change, rather than solely being based on the ongoing use of a DSS. Although these themes are already evident in the literature on DSSs and participatory technology development and application, the use of concepts from science and technology studies sheds new light on these issues. The theoretical framework presented in this chapter demonstrates the way in which science and technology studies can facilitate reflection on the core principles for improving the role of technologies in interactions between scientists and practice communities in the context of integrated mission-directed research. We hope that our framework provides researchers and practitioners involved in integrated mission-directed research with some new conceptual tools to reflect on the social dimensions of their work and evaluate the outcomes of their practice and, in doing so, contributes to enabling more effective and efficient participatory technology application.

ACKNOWLEDGEMENTS

This study was supported by funds from the Australian sugar industry and Australian Government through Sugar Research and Development Corporation, which are gratefully acknowledged. The authors would like to thank Drs Bob McCown and Toni Darbas (CSIRO Sustainable Ecosystems) for their constructive comments on earlier drafts of this chapter.

REFERENCES

Ang C, Davies M and Finlay P (2001) An empirical model of IT usage in the Malaysian public sector. *Journal of Strategic Information Systems* **10**(2), 159–174.

Bammer G (2005) Integration and implementation sciences: building a new specialization. *Ecology and Society* **10**(2), 6.

Bartlett F (1932) *Remembering: A Study in Experimental and Social Psychology.* Cambridge University Press, London.

Bijker W (1987) The social construction of Bakelite: towards a theory of invention. In: *The Social Construction of Technological Systems.* (Eds W Bijker, T Hughes and T Pinch) pp. 159–187. Massachusetts Institute of Technology Press, Cambridge, MA.

Bijker W (1995) *Of Bicycles, Bakelites, and Bulbs: Toward a Theory of Sociotechnical Change.* Massachusetts Institute of Technology Press, Cambridge, MA.

Bruun H and Hukkinen A (2003) Crossing boundaries: an integrative framework for studying technological change. *Social Studies of Science* **33**(1), 95–116.

Carberry P, Hochman Z, McCown R, Dalgliesh N, Foale M, Poulton P, Hargreaves J, Hargreaves D, Cawthray S, Hillcoat N and Robertson M (2002) The FARMSCAPE approach to decision support: Farmers', Advisers', Researchers' Monitoring, Simulation, Communication and Performance Evaluation. *Agricultural Systems* **74**, 141–177.

Cash D (2001) In order to aid in diffusing useful and practical information': agricultural extension and boundary organizations. *Science Technology and Human Values* **26**(4), 431–453.

Cox PG (1996) Some issues in the design of agricultural decision support systems. *Agricultural Systems* **52**(2–3), 355–381.

Cozzens S and Woodhouse E (1995) Science, government, and the politics of knowledge. In: *Handbook of Science and Technology Studies.* (Eds S Jasanoff, G Markle, J Petersen and T Pinch) pp. 533–553. SAGE Publications, London.

Doorman F (1991) A framework for the rapid appraisal of factors that influence the adoption and impact of new agricultural technology. *Human Organization* **50**(3), 235–244.

Douthwaite B, Keating J and Park J (2001) Why promising technologies fail: the neglected role of user innovation during adoption. *Research Policy* **30**(5), 819–836.

Everingham Y, Jakku E, Inman-Bamber G, Thorburn P, Webster T, Attard S and Antony G (2006) Understanding the adoption of knowledge intensive technologies in the Australian sugar industry: a pilot study. *Proceedings of Australian Society Sugar Cane Technologists* **28**, 76–85.

Foale M, Probert M, Carberry P, Lack D, Yeates S, Brimblecombe D, Shaw R and Crocker M (2004) Participatory research in dryland cropping systems – monitoring and simulation of soil water and nitrogen in farmers' paddocks in Central Queensland. *Australian Journal of Experimental Agriculture* **44**(3), 321–331.

Harvey F and Chrisman N (1998) Boundary objects and the social construction of GIS technology. *Environment and Planning A.* **30**, 1683–1694.

Hayman P (2004) Decision support systems in Australian dryland farming: A promising past, a disappointing present and an uncertain future. New directions for a diverse planet: *Proceedings of the 4th International Crop Science Congress*. Brisbane, 26 September–1 October 2004, URL: <www.cropscience.org.au>.

Hayman P and Easdown W (2002) An ecology of a DSS: reflections on managing wheat crops in the northern Australian grains regions with WHEATMAN. *Agricultural Systems* **74**(1), 57–77.

Hearn A and Bange M (2002) SIRATAC and CottonLOGIC: persevering with DSSs in the Australian cotton industry. *Agricultural Systems* **74**(1), 27–56.

Hess D (1997) *Science Studies: An Advanced Introduction*. New York University Press, NY.

Higgins A (2006) Scheduling of road vehicles in Sugarcane transport: a case study at an Australian sugar mill. *European Journal of Operations Research* **170**, 987–1000.

Kloppenburg K (1991) Social theory and the de/reconstruction of agricultural science: local knowledge for an alternative agriculture. *Rural Sociology* **56**, 519–548.

Leeuwis C (1993) *Of computers myths and modelling. The social construction of diversity, knowledge, information and communication technologies in Dutch horticulture and agricultural extension.* Department of Communication and Innovation Studies, Wageningen Agricultural University, Wageningen, Netherlands.

Loevinsohn M, Berdegué J and Guijt I (2002) Deepening the basis of rural resource management: learning processes and decision support. *Agricultural Systems* **73**(1), 3–22.

Massey C, Alpass F, Flett R, Lewis K, Morriss S and Sligo F (2006) Crossing fields: the case of a multi-disciplinary research team. *Qualitative Research* **6**(2), 131–149.

McCown R (2002) Changing systems for supporting farmers' decisions: problems, paradigms, and prospects. *Agricultural Systems* **74**(1), 179–220.

Neisser U (1976) *Cognition and Reality: Principles and Implications of Cognitive Psychology.* W. H. Freeman and Co., San Francisco, CA.

Orlikowski W (1992) The duality of technology: rethinking the concept of technology in organizations. *Organization Science* **3**(3), 398–427.

Orlikowski W and Gash D (1994) Technological frames: making sense of information technology in organizations. *ACM Transactions on Information Systems* **12**, 174–207.

Pahl-Wostl C and Hare M (2004) Processes of social learning in integrated resources management. *Journal of Community and Applied Social Psychology* **14**, 193–206.

Pinch T and Bijker W (1987) The social construction of facts and artifacts: or how the sociology of science and the sociology of technology might benefit each other. In: *The Social Construction of Technological Systems.* (Eds W Bijker, T Hughes and T Pinch) pp. 17–50. Massachusetts Institute of Technology Press, Cambridge, MA.

Ridley A (2004) The role of applied science in helping farmers to make decisions about environmental sustainability. *Australian Journal of Experimental Agriculture* **44**, 959–968.

Sahay S and Robey D (1996) Organizational context, social interpretation, and the implementation and consequences of Geographic Information Systems. *Accounting, Management and Information Technology* **6**(4), 255–282.

Star S and Griesemer J (1989) Institutional ecology, 'translations', and boundary objects: amateurs and professionals in Berkeley's Museum of Vertebrate Zoology 1907–1939. *Social Studies of Science* **19**, 387–420.

Stone P and Hochman Z (2004) If interactive decision support systems are the answer, have we been asking the right questions? New directions for a diverse planet: *Proceedings of the 4th International Crop Science Congress.* Brisbane, 26 September–1 October 2004, URL: <www.cropscience.org.au>.

Thorburn P, Archer a, Hobson p, Higgins a, sandell g, prestwidge d, Andrew B, Antony G, mcdonald l, Downs P and Juffs R (2006) Value chain analyses of whole crop harvesting to maximize co-generation. *Proceedings of Australian Society Sugar Cane Technologists* **28**, 37–48.

Walker D (2002) Decision support, learning and rural resource management. *Agricultural Systems* **73**(1), 113–127.

Williams R and Edge D (1996) The social shaping of technology. *Research Policy* **25**, 865–899.

Chapter 8

Modelling and learning about coastal development and sustainability

Russell Gorddard and Gail Kelly

ABSTRACT

Managing change is an essential ingredient for sustainable development and requires new approaches to understanding regions and systems. Science for sustainability is increasingly using participatory approaches in combination with quantitative modelling. We report on two recently completed projects that used a regional development framework based on systems thinking in two Australian coastal regions facing intense development pressures. The two regions– the Augusta-Margaret River Shire in Western Australia and the Central Coast in NSW – face similar development pressures but are at opposite ends of the development process. An important component of both projects involved the development of regional-scale simulation models of selected sustainability issues in order to investigate development options. The aim of these models was to produce integrated and logically consistent scenarios of future development in order to stimulate and clarify debate about possible future issues. We discuss the lessons learned from these projects for both the modelling methods and the social learning process in which they were embedded.

INTRODUCTION

The concept of sustainability has evolved over time with the term 'sustainable development' now widely being accepted as referring to achieving a sustainable quality of life through the integration of social, economic and environmental activities, outcomes and impacts (Eckersley 1997). Managing change is an essential ingredient of sustainability and, when addressing issues of both structural and relational change, there is a need to look beyond the change in one aspect of a system, and examine the links between the economic, social and environmental sub-systems (Hart 2006). This requires new ways of thinking about systems and communities and, in response, participatory or collaborative approaches are increasingly being included in research for sustainability (Kates *et al.* 2001).

Governments are increasingly recognising that regions are an important scale for the coordinated management of sustainability issues. Consequently, a variety of approaches to regional sustainability issues have been developed, ranging from qualitative modelling approaches (e.g. Pahl-Wostl and Hare 2004) to modular multidisciplinary long-term quantitative simulation modelling projects (e.g. Waddell 2002). The scope of these approaches is from single resource issues (e.g. managing the water system) to integrated assessments across all biophysical sustainability issues within a region (Carmichael *et al.* 2004). Implicit in these approaches are a range of pathways through which the modelling work is intended to support sustainability efforts. Thus, the modelling tools are being developed to integrate with traditional decision-making mechanisms for land use and social planning, and are more frequently including local knowledge and local participation processes in their development.

This chapter reports on two research projects that used a collaborative systems-thinking framework (Senge 1990) and system-dynamics modelling to engage with regional stakeholders to address regional-level sustainability issues. Regional sustainability issues, almost by definition, tend to be emerging and poorly defined. It is unclear who is affected, what feasible solutions may look like and who should implement them. The projects therefore were broadly defined. The geographic region and the broad concept of sustainability define the scope of issues, and we sought participation from a wide range of groups on a wide range of issues. The solution pathways for poorly defined problems also cannot be specified in advance. The projects therefore aimed to build a shared understanding of issues and options among regional groups as the basis for future initiatives.

We argue that research using participatory approaches, coupled with quantitative methodology designed to integrate and systematically evaluate social, economic and environmental issues, is particularly important to address the range of sustainability issues emerging from increasing development pressure. This analysis leads us to focus on two issues that are important to the success of this kind of research:

- What methodological tools can researchers use to help address the sustainability issues surrounding regional development?
- What processes should be used to ensure that these tools are effectively applied?

In order to address these questions, we compare the two regional systems and characterise the regional development process and the nature of the resulting sustainability issues. Key features identified include greater connectivity and complexity of the regional social-environmental system at later stages of development, changes in the nature and causes of uncertainties with the stage of development, and the emergence of novel issues throughout the development process. We argue that the modelling approach should be selected in order to address these issues. Therefore a region's stage of development should influence the modelling approach. This framework is used to suggest how modelling approaches may be matched to the requirements of regions.

In analysing how to improve the impact of modelling based research, we highlight three aspects of a region's adaptation to population pressure: discovering values, learning about the system and decision making. We believe these are distinct processes that require different research approaches. We argue that modelling should focus on assisting learning; however, model design in research projects needs to be informed by the values and decision-making processes highlighted during collaboration. In contrast with traditional systems thinking approaches (Senge, 1990), which place systems modelling at the centre of a process to develop a shared mental model, we advocate a less centralised approach, where both the model and the modeller are viewed as participants in a social learning process. Finally, we provide a brief review of the literature on learning, including recent insights from neuroscience, that suggests ways in which models and modelling processes can be improved to better support the learning process.

CASE STUDIES OF SYSTEMS APPROACHES TO REGIONAL SUSTAINABILITY RESEARCH

The two case study regions were the Central Coast, consisting of Wyong and Gosford local government areas situated north of Sydney in New South

Wales, and the Augusta–Margaret River Shire in the south-west of Western Australia. These two regions are both under strong development and migration pressure owing to their coastal location, proximity to large cities and attractive natural environments. Gurran *et al.* (2005) propose a topology of coastal communities to describe variations in many of these regions. It includes five 'ideal' types – coastal commuters, coastal getaways, coastal cities, coastal lifestyle destinations and coastal hamlets – largely based on population size and distance from capital cities. The application of this topology suggests that our two case studies are at opposite ends of the development spectrum. Augusta–Margaret River (AMR) is essentially a rural area with a population of around 12 000 people, but with rapidly growing visitor populations and absentee owners – so, according to Gurran *et al.*'s description, it is a coastal hamlet. The Central Coast region has over 300 000 people and is increasingly becoming integrated with Sydney. For instance, over 25% of workers spend up to 4 hours per day commuting to and from Sydney (NSW Department of Planning 2006). The Central Coast is best described as a coastal commuter community, which is developing into a coastal city.

The research projects investigated regional sustainability issues using systems-thinking techniques and system-dynamics modelling in combination with a variety of participatory approaches. A guide to regional sustainability, referred to as the Regional Development Futures (RDF) framework, was developed and applied by a multi-discipline research team. The RDF framework outlines four phases and a series of modules to guide a participative research process. There are a number of important assumptions underpinning the framework including:

- The region is a key scale at which to address sustainability issues.
- Many of the social, economic and environmental issues that regions face are interdependent and related, and need to be addressed together. Thus, viewing a region as a system provides the appropriate starting point for defining and exploring regional-scale sustainability issues.
- Systems thinking and system modelling provide an inclusive and rigorous basis for addressing these issues.
- A collaborative research partnership that includes a broad range of stakeholders within the region is crucial to identify the relevant sustainability issues and help develop the capacity of key decision makers (e.g. local councillors and strategic planners) to proactively manage change. The capacity of the researchers in terms of

integration of different types of knowledge and tool development is also enhanced.

A brief overview of the projects focusing on the issues addressed and the specification of the models is provided below.

Augusta–Margaret River overview

The AMR model consists of several modules – or themes – that represent key biophysical, economic and social characteristics of the Shire. These characteristics were identified during a 12-month period that applied a range of processes (e.g. oral histories, systems workshops and a community reference group) to engage the broad community in identifying the key drivers and issues related to the sustainability of the local system. Although the model does not fully represent all the issues identified (e.g. decline in sense of community was not included in the model), the modules provide a fair representation of the outcomes of the participatory processes (illustrated in Figure 8.1).

The three central modules – population and demographics, agricultural land use, and tourism and absentee ownership – were identified as drivers of change in the AMR system.

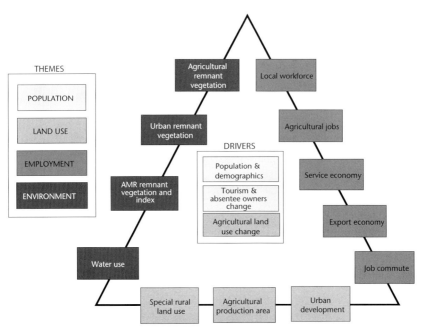

Figure 8.1. AMR Sustainable Future Model overview.

Two examples of scenario analysis using the AMR model illustrate its scope. We developed scenarios with key Council staff (e.g. strategic planners) with the key theme that the scenarios would address – the impact of development on the environment – being based on the earlier participatory research work where the community identified this as their major concern for the future. The scenarios investigated contrasting future development pathways over a 30-year time period. The first explored variations of a lifestyle and amenity options, epitomised by continued growth in tourism and related service industries, and an increasing number of properties owned by non-permanent residents. The second scenario illustrated the impact of strong growth in agriculture, particularly increased intensification and corporate ownership of enterprises. The scenarios differed in the strength of the key drivers, population (including absentee owner settlement), tourist numbers and agricultural land-use change. The natural environment and access to natural resources was important for both scenario options, and the implications for each scenario related to:

- remnant vegetation – loss of area, type and possible long-term condition
- water use for both urban development and agriculture, including the time taken to reach upper limits of sustainable use
- employment across a number of relevant sectors
- potential job commuting in and out of the region
- the time taken to reach current population planning limits in urban centres. For instance, scenario runs used different rates of growth and housing density options to identify how long it would take to exhaust the currently available cleared agricultural land for urban development.

The model was designed to allow its user (e.g. planner, community representative or researcher) to develop and explore other scenario options by being able to vary a range of factors, such as population and tourism growth, or by imposing management and policy options (e.g. fencing remnant vegetation).

The collaboration and model-building process indicated that AMR was a region in rapid transition, with increasingly diverse and competing values about how the region should develop into the future. In the planning process, uncertainty was mainly related to unknown time lags, local government financial shortfalls, and vulnerability to exogenous shocks (e.g. tourism trends, petrol rises and agricultural returns, such as for wine).

Central Coast case study overview

A partnership between local and state governments and the CSIRO researchers resulted in a similar participatory approach involving local planners, councillors and community leaders being used to develop a modelling tool for the Central Coast region. Figure 8.2 provides an overview of the resulting futures simulation model. This overview describes the relationships between the policy levers (on the left) for the main sustainability issues and drivers of regional land use and development identified by the local participants and researchers during the study.

The key findings from the Central Coast modelling component are described as follows:

- Land-use pressures and patterns are central to many of the social and environmental issues this region faces, and many of these issues (e.g. transport) cannot be modelled outside of their spatial context.
- Much of the population and policy debate in the region has focused on exogenous population pressure and on the role of the NSW State

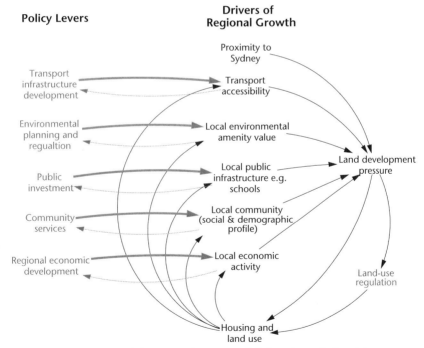

Figure 8.2. Overview of the Central Cost Model showing relationships between policy levers, sectors, drivers and feedbacks.

Government in controlling and allocating Sydney's population growth via land-use planning. The model development led us to emphasise the influence that the region's characteristics have on the attractiveness of the region to individuals and businesses, and the subsequent development pathway.

- How people value different outcomes, and how these values translate into behaviour such as household formation and location choices, and employment and transport decisions, are key uncertainties for the future of the region.
- The dashed feedback loops to the control levers in Figure 8.2 indicate there are limits to how policy levers can be adjusted. For example, traffic congestion beyond a politically acceptable threshold will trigger road infrastructure development, and this may limit the use of road infrastructure development as a means to influence future land-use pressure. The limitations of each of the controls highlight the need for an integrated policy approach.
- Time lags and spatial distance between the choice of policy interventions and their effects on the system means that a coordinated approach to using the policy levers is difficult to implement. Significantly, the indirect effects of policy decisions frequently operate by influencing people's values and behaviour (e.g. location decisions). These indirect behavioural effects are difficult to observe and quantify. They are therefore easily forgotten in the decision-making process.

In summary, outcomes from the Central Coast modelling process highlighted interactions across decision-making silos, and areas of key uncertainties (e.g. human behaviour). They also indicated ways in which issues (e.g. population growth) need to be reframed to account for the indirect and flow-on effects of policy decisions.

Lessons from the case studies

Based on our experience from the case studies, we concluded that many of the assumptions underpinning the RDF framework were important and substantially correct. However, a more sophisticated view of the regional development process is required to enable researchers to engage with, and address, regional sustainability issues. In particular:

- Although 'the region' is a key scale at which to address sustainability issues, links to both the larger and smaller scales are important.[1]
- Viewing a region as a system to address social, economic and environmental issues and their interactions is important, but being able

to link this analysis to the day-to-day life of a region remains a difficult challenge.

- Systems-thinking and system-dynamic modelling were useful methods to address regional sustainability by bringing rigour and quantitative analyses to bear on these issues. Although we believe modelling is essential to understanding scenarios for complex regional systems, the purpose of the model, how the model is developed and used, and the type of model developed, need to be appropriate for the characteristics of the region and the capacity of its constituents.

- Using a collaborative research partnership approach that involves a broad range of regional stakeholders is crucial to identify and scope emerging issues. However, the level and type of involvement that is required is not always clear, and the pathway from engagement to sustainability outcomes is highly uncertain and frequently outside the domain of the research project. Engagement can therefore be unsatisfying for regional participants and an improved framework for regional engagement is required.

With these lessons in mind, the remainder of the chapter focuses on developing a framework to address matters related to the application of appropriate modelling approaches and, more generally, on the role of modelling in addressing regional sustainability issues in regions facing population growth pressure.

CHARACTERISING REGIONAL DEVELOPMENT

Increased development and migration pressure have been the primary drivers of sustainability issues in coastal Australian regions in recent years (Salt 2001). Based on the two case studies, Figure 8.3 identifies some of the key issues for understanding sustainable regional development and how they change across the development spectrum.

Transition trends described in Figure 8.3 result from demands on the natural system nearing or reaching their limit. Consequently, resource use constraints emerge or start to bind. Individuals and businesses who could once operate with limited consideration of others, now find that their actions have greater connectivity to, and have an impact on, others in the region. Furthermore, with each additional emerging issue, they must operate in an increasingly complex environment. Conversely, a wider range of stakeholders and competing values become involved in addressing any given resource-management issue. As people begin to dominate the system, human actions become a more important driver of the behaviour of the

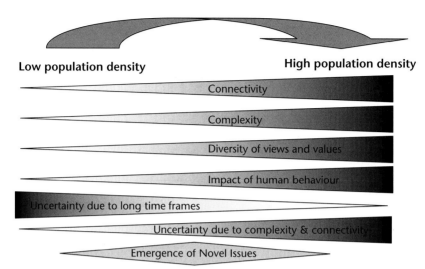

Figure 8.3 Changing characteristics of developing regions.

system. The uncertainty of how the system will respond increases owing to greater connectivity and complexity in regions with higher population density. However, in less densely populated regions, uncertainties about the future stem more from the fact that many key developments have not yet occurred. For instance, in AMR, many of the key issues are *if* and *when* certain resource limits will be reached – and the unknown conditions and potential impact of macro economic and social systems when those limits are reached.

This characterisation has several implications for how regional sustainability issues need to be addressed, and highlights the need for any approach to be tailored to the state of development of the region. We believe that *values*, *learning* and *decision making* are three key elements of the sustainability adaptation and management process and argue that they have implications for how regions and regional researchers should address sustainability issues. The implications of development pressure for these three adaptation processes are discussed below.

Values

As development pressures increase, the range of values that are relevant to any given resource-management decision increases, as do the number and diversity of people in the region who hold those different values. This causes novel issues and circumstances to emerge and there will not necessarily be a collective and established value system in place. That is, people will be engaged in the process of discovering, learning and articulating both individual and collective values. For example, as water resources become fully allocated, what was traditionally an engineering problem focused on meeting residential requirements may now involve households needing to consider their values around different household water uses. At the other end of the water supply chain, increasing and competing potential land-use options for water catchment areas undoubtedly lead to greater conflict and require new formal and informal mechanisms to negotiate collective outcomes.

New people relocating to a region arrive with a different value set. In our case study regions, migration tended to occur in waves, with each new wave of migrants having similar life circumstances and values to each other, but different from those who settled in the region before them. For example, in AMR, government settlement schemes in the 1920s brought lower socioeconomic migrants from England, with a strong work ethic and desire to build a new life; their values were in sharp contrast to the wave of immigrants in the 1960s seeking a place to 'drop out' of society and find alternative ways to live. Not only do the new waves of migrants bring different values, they may also value different attributes of the region to the existing population and will not always agree with suggested development options. A further factor is that the connectivity of the region to other regions tends to increase as the population density grows. For instance, in both our coastal case study regions, increases in absentee land ownership and tourism further spread the range and type of values that need to be considered. A key challenge for regional sustainability is to understand and incorporate this emerging and widening set of values.

Learning

We characterise regional development pressure as creating novel issues as well as exacerbating and spreading the domain of existing resource-use tensions. Addressing these issues therefore requires institutional and personal learning. Collaborative learning processes are therefore important. We argue below that a key role for integrative research is to underpin and facilitate these learning processes. From a research perspective, the emergence of new issues implies a need for an ongoing reductionist research program, while the increase in connectivity with development also increases the importance of a systemic approach to research. Researchers who are interested in understanding regional-scale systemic implications of development pressure will work in an environment where values about new issues are poorly understood and difficult to translate into clear objectives with measurable outcomes: the institutional system is not designed to address the new issues; data and knowledge is lacking; and there is a wide range of differing views about what the important issues are and how they may best be solved. There is also a need to coordinate the reductionist and integrative research programs. These represent significant challenges. The ability of regions to support and interact with these research agendas varies.

Decision making

The emergence of novel situations and increasing connectivity between issues has implications for decision-making processes. First, the emergence of new resource use issues requires that the existing decision-making structures and mechanisms need to adapt to incorporate and negotiate these issues. Second, there are stronger links between the factors that need to be considered in the decision-making process requiring a greater coordination between a range of policy decisions. Third, as stated previously, migration brings people with different values and needs to the region and this requires the evolution of new decision-making processes, or changes to existing processes in order to accommodate the greater diversity of values. The resulting decision problems will have many of the characteristics of messy (Vennix 1999) and wicked problems. That is, they will have different and uncertain boundaries because of novel links and lack information about what links may be significant. There will be disagreement over (a) if there actually a problem and (b) what the nature of the problem is. The different groups of decision makers will also bring a range of values, perspectives and possible solutions to these uncertain issues.

Regions and communities are dynamic and always in transition, and many of the coastal regions typified by Gurran *et al.* (2005) evolved over time. By taking an historical overview, it is possible to see how the decision-making structures and processes have also evolved in order to accommodate development. For instance, the Central Coast was once a coastal get away, but it is now classified as a coastal commuter and is more likely to be identified as a coastal city within a relatively short period of time. The local government structure common in rural shires throughout Australia tends to consist of five to seven councillors with a focus on 'roads, rates and rubbish'. With development, the structure evolves to engage skills to enable sophisticated decisions to be made about complex environmental, social and economic planning issues. However, there are numerous examples throughout Australia where these structures have become inflexible and unable to change to accommodate necessary processes and mechanisms to avoid conflict and social fragmentation (the AMR local government was dismissed and placed in administration in 2000 because of a failure of its decision-making processes to manage competing values and rapid rates of change).

ANALYTICAL METHODS FOR REGIONAL SUSTAINABILITY

Our interest in using quantitative models for the analysis of regional sustainability issues stems from several potential benefits. First, modelling provides a way to help systematically catalogue and articulate the knowledge that is currently available about how the region works. That is, it provides the methodology to attempt a comprehensive and logical analysis of regional systems. Second, modelling provides a method to attempt integrated analysis of different, but frequently interacting, issues. Integration across these different issues is usually difficult because stakeholder groups' issues are often about different aspects or perspectives on the same system, as opposed to separate but loosely linked systems. Integration therefore, requires reconciling a variety of interpretations about the same social-ecological system, and usually requires a broader theoretical framework in which to nest different world views together with careful analysis of the meaning of common terms and relationships.

Given these interests, the strengths and weaknesses of the system dynamic modelling approach used in the case studies is discussed below. We also consider how a range of similar models could be matched to regions at different stages of development and also be applied to different tasks. Figure 8.3 identifies the main issues that appeared to determine the value of the modelling in our case studies. Their implications are discussed next.

Complexity and connectivity

The ability of system dynamic models to track a large number of interactions, including their feedbacks into the system, was valuable for the more highly developed Central Coast region. In contrast, in AMR many of the resource-use issues were relatively unconnected and could be dealt with separately. For example, urban growth does not yet impinge significantly on rural land, and the transport systems are not congested. The system dynamic model in this instance was still very useful in painting integrated future scenarios of possible development pathways, but the systemic feedbacks were not as significant and the model tended to behave in a relatively linear and predictable way compared with the Central Coast. In comparison, the increased complexity and connectivity characterised by the Central Coast suggests that system dynamic modelling has greater applicability to these types of regions.

Uncertainty

The nature of the uncertainty varied between the case study regions. In AMR, many of the key sustainability issues were uncertain because they will occur in the distant future, and although current policy decisions will undoubtedly influence how they will play out, the time lag means that the particulars of how this will occur remains uncertain. A review of the past development of the Central Coast suggested that this early phase is important (Fenner 2004). For instance, the spatial layout of townships and road systems based on past planning decisions can limit the options for improving the current and future transport systems, although the impact of many of these infrastructure developments was difficult to predict or manage at the time of their planning and implementation.

In contrast, the uncertainty facing the future of highly developed regions such as the Central Coast is more to do with the behaviour of a complicated system due to multiple pressures and interactions. As the region develops, the number of potential interactions across issues grows and the uncertainty about which ones may be important increases. System dynamic modelling can help sort through this, and this proved to be one of the main strengths of the Central Coast system model.

Human behaviour

In more highly developed regions, the impact of human behaviour is greater and can affect more aspects of the system. There is, therefore, a greater need to learn about motivations for decisions and the behaviour of people. For instance, the behaviour of a congested transport system depends on transport-use decisions. Knowing how people will behave in response to new developments is difficult, and becomes one of the main irreducible uncertainties in a system dynamic model.

The increasing impact of human behaviour with development also means that modelling government decision making and policy becomes more significant. Many of the important system feedbacks occur via the unintended and unforseen influence of policy on human behaviour. These are often the result of the specifics of the policy tool used, rather than the broad intent of the policy, and such issues are difficult to model in future-orientated scenarios based on broad strategies alone. Furthermore, political considerations limit the degree of control over many planning issues. Examples include the public resistance to closing schools, the imperative to build transport infrastructure to address traffic congestion and the ability of development pressure (and developers) to influence land-use zonings. Limited controllability of aspects of the system reinforces the need for an integrated approach to policy, and analysis of these within a modelling framework is extremely valuable.

In contrast, in the less densely populated AMR, understanding the biophysical system and the direct impacts of humans on it was a more important focus than human behaviour *per se*. Essentially, human behaviour in these systems is less constrained and can be treated as relatively exogenous.

Novelty

In our case studies, novel issues appeared to continue to emerge with development pressure in both low-population-density and highly developed areas. As well as creating new problems that are not well understood, novel issues present a challenge for modelling and understanding regional systems more generally. Predicting the emergence of new issues is difficult and quantitative modelling will not, in general, flag the emergence of novel constraints of a qualitatively different kind.

Implications for the appropriate scope of modelling

When considering analytical methods for regional sustainability research, the focus of the project is an important issue. Because of the emergence of novel issues in the system, the focus of the modelling project is unlikely to be specified in advance. The boundaries of the problem, across economic sectors, government departments and spatial areas, are also likely to be poorly specified. For these reasons, a broad focus is desirable, although a defined purpose greatly simplifies the modelling task. In addition, a clearly defined purpose makes motivation, management of expectations and communication within the collaborative process much easier. Although it is vital to incorporate all significant and relevant values, this is unlikely to occur if the models' scope is specified at the outset, given the existence of ill-defined values and decision-making institutions that are not designed to address the emerging issues.

In our case study regions, a series of mental mapping exercises engaging a wide cross section of constituents provided an appropriate broad and qualitative starting point. The extent to which the quantitative modelling was, and should be, applied depends on development stage of the region. In AMR, an integrated-assessment model was valuable, not because of the strength of the connections across sectors, but because it helped in the articulation of values about a wide range of issues. In the Central Coast project, an integrated model highlighted the need for coordination across sectors and helped frame some of the important issues, such as the central role of transport in the regional development process. The complexity of the system and technical nature of many of the issues this region faces, together with the need for a technical understanding of many issues, means that other models that focus on specific resource issues, such as native vegetation or water supply and use, or some key decision points, would also be valuable.

Alternative modelling approaches

Figure 8.4 illustrates how an analysis of regional characteristics can help match modelling approaches and objectives to regions. We briefly discuss how some of the modelling and conceptual approaches we are aware of may fill these niches. In regions like AMR, which are at an early stage of development, approaches such as Resilience Theory (Walker and Salt 2006), which identify broad principles of maintaining a functioning system in the face of uncertainty, hold promise. Such approaches might, for example, focus on developing land-use strategies that maintain flexibility in future use options across the region, or identify areas where future land use might be uncertain and certain types of development may lock the region into particular development pathways.

For regions and issues where the complexity of the system is such that robust empirical models cannot be developed, complex systems modelling approaches, such as network theory, may help to identify generic results about the behaviour of these systems and hopefully guide, if not directly inform, policy. Qualitative systems approaches may help to address the issue of emerging novelty, whereas approaches such as resilience or complex

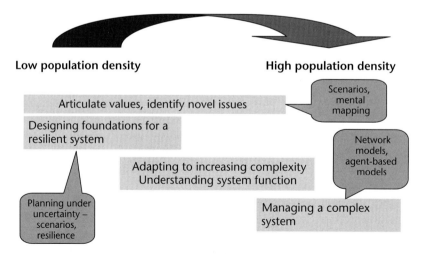

Figure 8.4 Matching modelling approaches to regional development stage and tasks.

systems science may help develop strategies to address the unknown. Case studies of similar regions with higher density development may provide the best option to identify which new issues are likely to emerge.

In summary, the role of the model and the appropriate modelling method depends on the stage of development of the region. In less developed regions (e.g. AMR), the modelling process can identify key knowledge gaps and paint scenarios of possible future development that help to articulate characteristics of the region that are highly valued and are potentially threatened by future development. In more developed regions, where the connectivity is greater (e.g. the Central Coast), system dynamic models can help people comprehend the volume of information and ensure a balanced view of issues. These types of models are also useful to identify potentially important system-level interactions, and highlight where coordination across sectors is required. Future systemic research on regional sustainability issues should be tailored to take account of the different complexity and uncertainty of issues that arise at the different stages of development.

LEARNING AND THE PROCESS OF MODEL DEVELOPMENT AND USE

In this section we discuss some of the issues for the process of engaging communities in a regional-scale sustainability modelling exercise. As we have argued, sustainability requires an integrated and holistic systems approach. Addressing these issues requires institutional and personal transformation in understanding and practice; thus, it relies on enhancing social capital and the collective capacity to respond positively to sustainability challenges (Blackstock *et al.* 2007). As a result, practitioners of 'sustainability science' (Kates *et al.* 2001) are increasingly advocating participatory and collaborative approaches to environmental decision making.

Our characterisation of regional development suggests that novelty, uncertainty and increasing complexity occur with greater development. It also suggests that values and decision-making processes are continually evolving and will not therefore provide strong guidance and support for the learning process. To make an effective contribution to the management of regional sustainability issues related to development pressure, we argue that regional-scale modelling should focus on learning, rather than decision making. Furthermore, the processes for developing the model need to be designed to accommodate the shifting values and decision-making systems that are inherent in sustainability issues. The argument for a focus on learning is based on the nature of the information generated by a modelling project. That is, separation from the decision-making process is required because the projects are likely to reframe existing problems and raise new issues, rather than provide quantitative analysis of predefined problems. In addition, existing decision-making structures in developing regions are likely to be under significant pressure to change in order to address the issues effectively. Engaging with this moving target has proved difficult.

Social learning and modelling

Participatory research processes imply collaboration to problem solve and to produce new knowledge in a self-reflective community of inquiry (Wallerstein 1999). An assumption is that participation promotes social learning – the interplay between individual and situational factors in generating human understanding (Maarleveld and Dangbégnon 1999). Given the complexity of the sustainability issues, and the wide range of backgrounds and professional view points of those involved, knowledge about sustainability is not a discrete well-defined commodity; rather it is highly contextual and person-dependent. Learning involving models, therefore, is more than a simple knowledge transfer of the information generated from the models. Rather, it is part of a participatory and social learning process.

Vennix (1999) notes the difficulty in finding a sound social theoretical basis for attempts to use system models to promote social learning and address messy problems. He argues that although systems thinking emphasises that people are not good at understanding the implications of feedbacks for system behaviour, there are also a range of other social learning problems. Key issues include the extreme diversity in views and the difficulty in bridging the 'soft-system, hard-system' divide. In addition, there are a wide range of issues for social learning processes, which are independent of the modelling contribution. Vennix also ponders the possible demise of hard-systems models in social processes, suggesting that, in many cases, proceeding beyond a soft-systems understanding is difficult and may even be misleading. Although these issues are relevant, the regional scale sustainability decision-making environment is substantially different to the business management environment that system dynamics usually addresses, and different approaches are needed.

Keen and Mahanty (2006) argue that there are three important concepts for learning in NRM: systems orientation, negotiation and dialogue, and reflection. Our project methodology used systems-thinking techniques in a forum that required dialogue about the relationships between attributes of the system, and we believe the system models aided the process of reflection. In recognising that dealing with sustainability issues involves dealing with an uncertain future, the project design focused on developing processes to set in place continuous learning about the system. These processes involved developing hypotheses about system interactions, testing them (Lee 1993) and feeding into decision-making processes – thus revising actions. In this way, the projects set out to enhance the adaptive capacity of the region to deal with uncertainty. Figure 8.5 illustrates how researchers and the region would ideally relate through a 'learning laboratory'. This involved researchers and regional stakeholders interacting in a series of systems-thinking workshops, the outcomes of which formed the basis of the system-dynamics models. The benefits can be two-fold: researchers can use this experience to help guide their research agenda (including model development), while for regional stakeholders the process complements their experiential learning process. All stakeholders, including the researchers, have a view of the world or mental model about how the world works, and learning can be thought of as the process of updating this mental model.

The view of learning shown in Figure 8.5 contrasts with the system modelling view of Vennix (1999) and others in which the system dynamic model sits at the centre of a social-learning process. In our approach, the model exists as part of a research agenda, and the model and modellers become participants, rather than drivers, of the social learning process. The model is designed to provide benefits to both the researchers and to the regional participants.

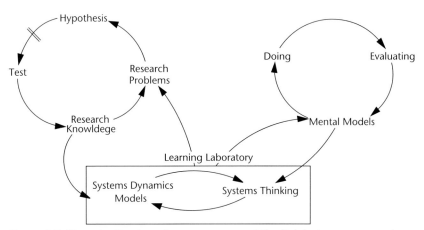

Figure 8.5. The adaptive learning processes and the link between research and regional stakeholders underpinning the model development process.

Defining the modelling role in this way addresses several issues. Regional systems are complicated, and a substantive effort is required to usefully model their biophysical and social characteristics. An ongoing research agenda that is separate from the role of the model as a regional learning tool is therefore needed. A related challenge is the time needed to develop and modify models – this process occurs at a far slower rate than the decision-making cycle and should not limit the social-learning process. Defining a modelling research agenda that is separate from, but interactive with, the social learning process fundamentally changes the relationship between the model and the learning process. It suggests less ownership of the model, and less congruence between the individual or shared mental models of the stakeholders and the system dynamic model. For complex models, identifying the model with the modeller(s) occurs naturally. Learning *with a modeller*, rather than directly from a model, may be a more viable option.

The problems of an incorrect and misleading system model are also addressed by the processes shown in Figure 8.5. Firstly, it allows an adaptive process of modelling to correct problems as they arise and, secondly, the researcher becomes the spokesperson for the model and the information can be framed to address the issue in a way that is not misleading. In our case studies, we found people are better able to assess the value and credibility of information when it is expressed by a modeller, and there was a heavy reliance on the modellers to explain and qualify the model results. This structure implies that the modeller is seen as simply another participant in the social-learning process, with their own mental model – albeit one that is supported by a formal model. That is, developing a shared mental model, based on the quantitative model, is not the aim of the project. Instead, the model and the modeller become another source of information to enable stakeholders to adapt their world views to incorporate other aspects of the system as required. This process also highlights the importance of the modeller being able to communicate effectively with a broad range of stakeholders.

Distributed and centralised knowledge

An additional complication for collective learning in regions when compared with the business environments considered by Vennix (1999) is a reduced amount of top-down control and less centralisation of knowledge. Social learning and systems approaches generally aim for centralised holistic learning or shared learning. This may not be possible nor sufficient for effective coordination and change in a regional context where knowledge and decision making is typically and efficiently dispersed across individuals and organisations (Norgaard 2004). As the complexity of the system grows, the importance of effectively linked and distributed knowledge and learning increases. That is, there is a need to learn both about the system, and also to develop a system that learns and adapts to sustainability issues. Developing a shared understanding will provide support for this, but may not be sufficient to achieve an effective learning network, or even to help establish an effective decentralised decision-making network.

Individual learning and modelling

Vennix (1999) notes that there are numerous barriers to learning about systems: both group learning barriers and some that relate to individual learning. This section briefly reviews some relevant literature to identify impediments to individual learning that may help structure regional sustainability modelling projects in order to overcome these obstacles. Malcolm Knowles (reviewed in Smith 2002) argues that adult learning is self-directed, goal-oriented, relevancy-oriented and practical. This view is consistent with the observation that mental models of regional decision makers are practical and specialised, and differ depending on their roles. The goal-oriented nature of adult learning is also an issue for learning for regional sustainability because the goals are frequently unclear. Many specialists are trained to solve problems in a specific way, which involves viewing problems in a certain way in order to find a particular type of solution. Examples include engineers, lawyers, policy makers and land planners. This practical orientation causes divergent mental models about how the system works. It also means that when changing circumstances require a different type of solution (e.g. an engineering solution for what was previously a legal problem), the people, and therefore the region, may be slow to adapt.

The education literature suggests there are a number of factors related to why people fail to learn, including a lack of motivation, and the financial, time and psychological costs of the learning process (Atherton 2008). Atherton (2008) also makes the distinction between 'supplantive' learning and simple additive learning. Supplantive learning calls into question previous ways of acting or prior knowledge and replaces them. Atherton (2008) claims that supplantive learning is difficult, even when under the learner's control. It is problematic if it is demanded, or if there is significant emotional investment in previous beliefs or ways of acting. In addition, 'down time' is required for adjustment because supplantive learning occurs as a process of destabilisation, disorientation (including a loss of competence) and reorientation. This is clearly relevant to regional sustainability issues, which require new ways of viewing and solving problems. The people who we engaged with during our case study projects typically needed to function as high-level decision makers on development and resource-use issues on a daily basis, and the cost of an adjustment process as part of supplantive learning are therefore high. Their working mental models are sophisticated and complex, and optimised to allow them to work effectively within the brief of their job. Many of these jobs also fit within organisations and institutions that have evolved a particular way of functioning – making wholesale change difficult.

Rieber (2008) found that, even for simple mechanical problems that are well represented by simulation models, people are unable to learn from simulations without some guidance or structure. We have found that although there is stated demand for decision-support tools, people are generally uncomfortable using them. This may be partly because the computer model does not structure the problem as they see it (this can surprise many people). As discussed earlier, having a human face (modeller) to the computer system is important to enable people to relate to the outputs. There may be several reasons for this, such as the ability of the modeller to frame the question and required information in a relevant way, or the capacity to answer queries about the underlying assumptions and logic. People also appear to be better able to judge and use information that is presented by a person rather than a computer.

Cognitive science and neuroeconomics may also provide insights into how learning about messy problems and learning with models might best be structured. Reviews of relevant literature by Camerer et al. (2004) and Sanfey et al. (2006) provide the following pertinent findings:

- Humans have both hard-wired (automatic) and deliberative (controlled) decision-making pathways. There is limited capacity to use deliberative pathways and, in general, they account for a small amount of behaviour.
- The human brain is basically a mammalian brain with a larger cortex. Thus, human behaviour will generally be a compromise between highly evolved animal emotions and instincts, and more recently evolved human deliberation and foresight.
- Brains are modular and decision making involves interactions among multiple subsystems that may be governed by different principles.
- Most complex behaviour requires communication among the different modules of the brain.[2]

- Brains tend to process information in a 'top-down' manner. That is, our process of making sense of the world is highly dependent on expectations, and we can quite literally be blind to novelty.
- The human brain is similar to that of a monkey, with the equivalent of a cortical press secretary (interpreter) who can provide glib explanations for behaviour.
- The interpreter is not necessarily privy to why a module will respond in a certain way. It simply takes this information at face value and attempts to fit it into a mental schema.

This emerging picture of cognitive processes suggests several reasons why learning about regional sustainability issues may be difficult, and also points to possible improvements in our regional processes.

In our case studies, model development and use involved describing future scenarios that represented alternative development pathways about critical sustainability concerns. This information was then used to help to specify the system dynamic model. Generally, people described the process as hard work and struggled to develop meaningful and rich scenarios. Specifically we found that:

- The scenarios were typically dominated by a single theme, sector or issue and focused only on part of the picture.
- The scenarios tended to overlook the links across sectors, or to only emphasis the positive or negative links.
- Where policy choice was part of the scenarios, only the direct and intended consequences were considered.

Scenarios do not appear to be a natural way for people to think about sustainability issues. This is consistent with the view of human thinking from cognitive science, which suggests that people do not think about problems by mentally running a simulation or any other formal model. The expectation that there will be congruent mapping between an individual or group mental model, and a computer model is therefore unrealistic. Scenarios are explicit, which suits computer models (which need to be literal); however, they are processor hungry and not particularly suited to human minds. This does not imply that scenario exercises are not valuable; indeed, it points to the value of using computers to help underpin scenario development. However, we may want to think about other methods for exploring these issues that more closely aligned with people's thought processes. People may also have specific ways to think about the complexity, uncertainty and ambiguity that do not correspond to formal modelling approaches (e.g. Hsu *et al.* 2005). Understanding these mechanisms may also help us represent uncertainty in more meaningful ways.

Finding ways to overcome the blindness to novelty caused by top-down processing would appear to be important in research for regional sustainability. It could be argued that the mental mapping exercises may uncover some of the hidden assumptions in people's automatic processing, and communicate different mental schemas that can potentially go some way to overcoming 'change blindness'. The modular nature of our brains, combined with the 'glib cortical press secretary', may also explain the difficulty people often have in reconciling two different perspectives on the world. This phenomenon seems to be a key part of the integration problem. One valuable role for the use of models is to uncover these internal inconsistencies and hidden assumptions.

Automatic processing would appear to be a key reason for locking in our existing behaviour. Newell (2005) argues that while simple fast and frugal algorithms of human cognition may be an over-simplified view of how people learn and acquire information to make decisions, an adjustable spanner analogy, in which people devote variable resources to decision-making problems, may be valid. Increasing the deliberative effort used to address sustainability issues would appear to require a combination of personal motivation and institutional factors. As already argued, separating learning process from decision-making processes may be a key institutional requirement. The cognitive science research suggests that participatory decision making and negotiation involves a combination of emotion and reasoning, and this may limit the ability to engage deliberative cognitive processes. Funding for time and cognitive space to learn, and removing the immediate pressure for decision making, appears to be an important requirement for the supplantive learning required to address regional sustainability issues.

DISCUSSION AND CONCLUSIONS

A range of formal modelling approaches can be valuable in researching complex regional sustainability issues related to development pressure. The process of relating this research to the region is vital to both the quality of the research and its ability to help address the issues. We argue that novelty and increasing connectivity and complexity are features of sustainability issues in developing areas, and that consideration of these features should influence the choice of modelling approach and the process for engaging with the region.

We summarise our finding in relation to three of the themes of this book.

Technical integration

A wide range of modelling approaches based on systems thinking and complex systems science may be valuable for participatory modelling research. The modelling approach needs to match the development stage of the region, and the resulting nature of the uncertainties and level of connectivity that exists. A broad modelling focus is argued for, on the basis that emerging issues and changing values are part of the sustainability challenge for developing regions. For more developed regions, models focused on particular resource issues may also be valuable. An important aspect of a modelling effort is to build on, and contribute to, a systematic collection of data and information and link to research on specific issues – guiding and being guided by them.

Role definition

Three elements of the region's response to growth pressures and sustainability issues are identified: articulating values, learning and decision making. We argue that the best role for modelling is to focus on supporting learning, both by researchers and as part of a social learning process in the region. We question the value of structuring the regional learning process around the modelling process, as suggested by a system dynamics approach. Instead, we argue that a distinct research program (focused on sustainability modelling) should be strongly linked to the regional social learning process but viewed as a separate stakeholder in the process. This, in turn, raises unaddressed questions about how these social learning processes should be structured.

Adaptive capacity

We note that there are a number of barriers to learning about sustainability issues and to the use of formal models for learning at the individual and collective levels. However, our analysis also suggests that participative modelling processes provide a sound basis for improving the adaptive capacity of a region. Cognitive science offers insights into the learning and decision-making processes that may help inform the appropriate process for engaging with models and the ways in which models can help improve learning and decision-making processes for regional sustainability.

ENDNOTES

1   This is in line with approaches to understand the resilience of regions; for example, see Walker and Salt 2006.

2   It is still unknown if higher-level deliberative processes rely on a single tightly linked mechanism or on multiple mechanisms (Sanfey *et al.* 2006)

REFERENCES

Atherton JS (2008) *Learning as Loss* (web page). <http://www.doceo.co.uk/original/learnloss_1.htm>

Blackstock KL, Kelly GJ and Horsey BL (2007) Developing and applying a framework to evaluate participatory research for sustainability. *Ecological Economics* **60**, 726–742.

Camerer CF, Loewenstein G and Prelec D (2004) Neuroeconomics: why economics needs brains. *Scandinavian Journal of Economics* **106**, 555–579.

Carmichael J, Tansey J and Robinson J (2004) An integrated assessment modeling tool. *Global Environmental Change* **14**, 171–183.

Eckersley R (1997) 'Perspectives of progress: is life getting better?' Working Paper Series 97/27. CSIRO Wildlife and Ecology, Canberra.

Fenner R (2004) *In hindsight: Reflections on past planning and development on the Central Coast.* CSIRO Sustainable Ecosystems, Canberra.

Gurran N, Squire C and Blakely E (2005) 'Meeting the sea change challenge'. Report No. 2, for the National Sea Change Task Force. Planning Research Centre, University of Sydney.

Hart M (2006) *Sustainable measures* (web page). Sustainable Measures, West Hartford, CT. <http//:www.sustainablemeasures.com/Sustainability/index.html>.

Hsu M, Bhatt M, Adolphs R, Tranel D and Camerer CF (2005) Neural systems responding to degrees of uncertainty in human decision-making. *Science* **310**, 1680–1683.

Kates RW, Clark W, Corell R, Hall J, Jaeger C, Lowe I, McCarthy J, Schellnhuber H, Bolin B, Dickson N, Faucheux S, Gallopin G, Grübler A, Huntley B, Jäger J, Jodha N, Kasperson R, Mabogunje A, Matson P, Mooney H, Moore I and O'Riordan T (2001) Sustainability science. *Science* **292**, 641–642.

Keen M and Mahanty S (2006) Learning in sustainable natural resource management: challenges and opportunities in the Pacific. *Society and Natural Resources* **19**, 497–513.

Lee KN (1993) *Compass and Gyroscope: Integrating Science and Politics for the Environment*. Island Press, Washington DC.

Maarleveld M and Dabgbégnon C (1999) Managing natural resources: a social learning perspective. *Agriculture and Human Values* **16**, 267–280.

Newell BR (2005) Re-visions of rationality? *Trends in Cognitive Sciences* **9**, 11–15.

Norgaard RB (2004) Learning and knowing collectively. *Ecological Economics* **49**, 231–241.

NSW Department of Planning (2006) *Draft Central Coast Regional Strategy*. NSW Department of Planning, Sydney.

Pahl-Wostl C and Hare M (2004) Processes of social learning in integrated resources management. *Journal of Community & Applied Social Psychology* **14**, 193–206.

Rieber LP (2009) Supporting discovery-based learning within simulations. In: *Cognitive Effects of Multimedia Learning*. (Ed. R Zheng) pp. 217–236. International Science Reference Hersey, New York.

Salt B (2001) *The Big Shift: Welcome to the Third Australian Culture, The Bernard Salt Report*. Hardie Grant Books, Melbourne.

Sanfey AG, Loewenstein G, Mcclure SM and Cohen JD (2006) Neuroeconomics: cross-currents in research on decision-making. *Trends in Cognitive Sciences* **10**, 108–116.

Senge PM (1990) *The Fifth Discipline: The Art and Practice of the Learning Organization*. Doubleday, New York.

Smith MK (2002) Malcolm Knowles, informal adult education, self-direction and anadragogy (web page). Infed, YMCA George Williams College, London. <www.infed.org/thinkers/et-knowl.htm>

Vennix JAM (1999) Group model-building: tackling messy problems. *System Dynamics Review* **15**, 379–401.

Waddell P (2002) Urbansim: modeling urban development for land use, transportation and environmental planning. *Journal of the American Planning Association* **68**, 297–314.

Walker B and Salt D (2006) *Resilience Thinking: Sustaining Ecosystems and People in a Changing World*. Island Press, Washington DC.

Wallerstein N (1999) Power between evaluator and community: research relationships within New Mexico's healthier communities. *Social Science & Medicine* **49**, 39–53.

Part 3

Supporting policy development and decision making

Chapter 9

Integrating science within the West Australian Rural Towns Liquid Assets project

Olga Barron, Jeffrey Turner, Anthony Barr, Trevor Smales, Mark Pridham, Michael Burton and Jo Pluske

ABSTRACT

The RTLA project aims to develop a Water Management Plan (WMP) for Western Australian towns that will be used by decision makers to improve the rural town water cycle and supply. To facilitate development of an adequate WMP, the project has adopted a systematic approach to acquiring biophysical data that in itself is essential, but also necessary for subsequent engineering and economic analyses. The approach that was developed enabled a 'paradigm shift' from addressing a biophysical problem (water table and salinity effects on infrastructure and natural resources) to the social and economic advancement of the rural town (conservation of biodiversity, reduced water imports from external sources, and economic opportunities from increased supplies of treated, fit-for-purpose water and from products extracted during water treatment). Accordingly, a conceptual system model was designed that integrated all these aspects and required inputs from numerous disciplines, agencies, professions and manufacturing industries. This chapter demonstrates the application of the systems approach in a case study for Wagin, one of the Western Australian towns. It shows that all proposed water management options (groundwater abstraction and disposal to the salt lake, groundwater abstraction, water desalination, permeate sale and brine disposal to the salt lake or evaporation pond) provide benefits for the town site, but to a varying extent, with the greater economic benefit from groundwater abstraction and disposal to the salt lake. Furthermore, to account for town community expectations, technical management considerations and potential uses of desalinated water, the final water management plan should be completed in consultation with the town community.

INTRODUCTION

The mission for CSIRO's National Flagship *Water for a Healthy Country* is to achieve a ten-fold increase in the social, economic and environmental benefits from water by 2025. The Flagship's program within south-west Western Australia aims to increase water benefits from farms, towns and catchments, as well as metropolitan Perth. More specifically, the Rural Town Water Management research project aims to help solve pressing problems facing country towns in the wheat-belt area of Western Australia such as salinity, waterlogging and declining populations.

In 2004–05, this project merged with the bigger Rural Towns Liquid Assets (RTLA) project to form a partnership involving the Department of Agriculture and Food Western Australia, the School of Agricultural and Resource Economics and the Centre for Water Research (both at the University of Western Australia), the Cooperative Research Centre for Landscape Evolution and Mineral Exploration (CRC LEME), the Western Australia Chemistry Centre, Wheatbelt Enterprise Technologies, four regional Natural Resources Management (NRM) Councils and 16 wheat-belt shires. The project is also supported by the National Action Plan for Salinity and Water Quality (NAP). The main outcome of this project is to demonstrate improved water resource management at a local scale and provide the capacity for rural communities in Western Australia to solve environmental and socioeconomic problems facing their towns.

The RTLA project undertook to develop a Water Management Plan (WMP) for each of the 16 towns to be used by decision makers within a town to improve the rural town water cycle and supply. In addition, the project will generate integrated Water Management Pilot Schemes for four of the selected towns and develop models of best management practices for water resources that can be applied to other towns across Western Australia's agricultural region and beyond.

To facilitate the development of an adequate WMP, the project has adopted a systematic approach to acquiring biophysical data that in itself is essential, but also necessary for subsequent engineering and economic analyses. The approach that was used enabled a 'paradigm shift' from addressing a biophysical problem (waterlogging and salinity effects on infrastructure and natural resources) to the social and economic advancement of the rural town (conservation of biodiversity, reduced water imports from external sources, and economic opportunities from increased supplies of treated, fit-for-purpose water and from products extracted during water treatment). Accordingly, a conceptual system model was designed that integrated all these aspects and required inputs from numerous disciplines (hydrology, hydrogeology, hydrochemistry, urban water management, economics, social science, livestock science and mineral processing); agencies (agricultural and water authorities); professions (water engineering); and manufacturing industries (desalination). This conceptual system model underpins the Rural Towns Liquid Assets (RTLA) project and is a major contribution to the knowledge platform for catchment management for rural towns. The project involved 30 researchers and required continuous nurturing of productive collaboration within such a large, diverse and multi-disciplinary team.

For the purpose of this chapter, some elements of the systems approach will be demonstrated in a case study for Wagin – one of the above-mentioned pilot towns. The study uses a comprehensive database that is constantly being expanded as further research results are generated. Currently, the conclusions drawn for Wagin are considered as indicative and open to review.

In the following section the integration process that has evolved throughout the RTLA project is explained. Following that, a section describes how, as a result of integration, a system approach to research could be put in place. An overview of the Wagin case study and key findings are then provided, with the final section reflecting on how integration of the social and biophysical sciences have contributed to achieving the designated mission and, more specifically, the influence this research will have on local government policy.

THE INTEGRATION PROCESS

What does integration mean in the context of this project? As suggested by Bammer's (2005) work on integration and implementation of scientific research, it appears that the process of research integration can be formally structured. However, there has not been a great deal of work done in this area, especially in the public sector (van Kerkhoff 2005). In this context, the

RTLA approach was defined to meet the project objectives and, as such, can be considered as a starting point from which to mould integration processes that could be followed in future public research projects. The integration of the efforts by the multidisciplinary and multi-agency project team has been an ongoing process. Although our project was progressing, work was continuously being done to insure fruitful interdependency of the project activities and outcomes so that we could achieve integration at two levels.

Firstly there was integration of the research team. So that all disciplines had an opportunity to help shape the direction of the research, research plans and progress were monitored by a project research team and overseen by a project steering committee. A management committee and project leaders were responsible for making sure that timelines were in place and deadlines were met. As this team involved a diverse group of social and biophysical scientists, good communication was essential. Hence, internal and external protocols were established to ensure that research remained focused and data was available to all. Regular meetings also provided an opportunity for people working in different disciplines to ask questions and learn each other's 'language'. Although the integration of economic, social and other scientific research enabled richer outcomes to evolve, it was important that everyone involved with each discipline represented in the project respected those in the other disciplines to ensure that outputs could be generated for the benefit of the project and research overall. This was especially important with the multidisciplinary development of the systems model that is explained in later in this chapter.

The second level of integration in the RTLA project focuses on the integration of project findings in a water management plan, with the aim of influencing policy and management practice specifically at the local level. Working with interested parties within the relevant towns is essential throughout the project, as well as during the period when the plan is being written up and then presented to them. It is important that those on the ground have an adequate understanding of the science and economic implications if the findings are to influence policy associated with water management.

Having a defined framework in place is a good start to ensure that integration will produce effective outcomes. However, ensuring the process works often goes beyond the level of research expertise of the people involved. Other skills – as alluded to by Bammer (2005) – associated with general problem solving, thinking in systems and bridging any gaps between research and practice are all important, and are certainly being addressed in this project.

A SYSTEMS APPROACH

A systems approach for water management in rural towns involves integration at all levels. It must encompass both natural and human-made components that contribute to water balances and hence provide a wide understanding of the processes. In practice, the two components are interrelated because, for example, rainfall determines the amount of water available for harvesting in and around the town and the amount of rainfall determines how much scheme water – imported to the towns from the coastal water reservoirs – is applied to gardens, parks and playing fields. How much water is imported is also a function of the cost of the scheme water and hence should be incorporated into the economic modelling part of the system. The systems model and its application is discussed in the following sections to show how integration has worked in the RTLA project.

Improving town-site water management should reduce the impact of dryland salinity by establishing greater control of groundwater levels or surface water accumulations. Harvested and/or abstracted water resulting from salinity control measures may be available for re-use. These could result in social benefits from improvement of water management in rural towns. A conceptual model was designed to provide a systems framework for a water management plan (WMP) development, reflecting the concept of rural town water resource development. This views water as a potential asset, whereas currently it is considered as a threat. The model structure is given in Figure 9.1. The system analysis is built on the following concepts.

- Rural town water resources include groundwater, stormwater and imported potable water, which, under current water management practice, can cause waterlogging. Potable water is imported from coastal reservoirs to many wheat-belt towns, which are located several hundred kilometres inland, and this provides an additional source of groundwater recharge as well as leakage from water-storage reservoirs, wastewater facilities and also with town site irrigation systems. All this cause land salinisation, which greatly affects the rural town environment (including infrastructure), causing economic losses, social tensions and the general decline of the town.
- Water resources may be considered as a potentially valuable asset that can be harvested/abstracted, treated and re-used. Using these resources will allow control of waterlogging and salinity development: reducing infrastructure damage while adding value to the abstracted water. Surface water harvesting, desalination technologies, optimal

disposal facilities and potential mineral recovery will be evaluated, where appropriate.

- Water re-use may promote development of new industries or support existing enterprises. Options are likely to be influenced by the economic viability and social acceptance of such industries and/or enterprises.
- The quality to which water is treated will be determined by end use requirements (fit-for-purpose).
- The approach will also allow consideration of water-saving strategies on a regional scale, reducing the demands on the coastal water resources currently used for water supply to the inland towns.

The systems approach is based on a multidisciplinary evaluation of water management options and cost–benefit analyses with consideration for the triple bottom line (TBL) and multiple benefits for local communities. Barron *et al.* (2005) present a detailed outline of the system approach used in the RTLA project. Furthermore, to tailor this model to a specific town, Barron and Smales (2005) developed a comprehensive framework to prioritise water management options within a town. Therefore in this chapter we will present just a brief overview of some of the key considera-

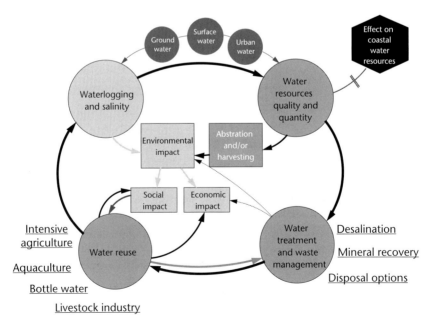

Figure 9.1. Conceptual systems model for rural town water management.

tions required for the model. More specifically, the overview will cover an assessment of the salinity impact on infrastructure, estimate the relevant infrastructure damage cost and evaluate water management options to control salinity and potentially generate additional water supply source for a town.

Infrastructure damage evaluation

Infrastructure damage in the area affected by waterlogging and salinity is related to various physical, chemical and biochemical processes that result in a different level of impact on various assets, such as roads, buildings, parks and gardens.

- Road damage is mainly related to waterlogging and, to a lesser extent, water salinity; the threshold depth to the groundwater that is damaging to the road structure is considered to be 0.5 metres below the road base.
- Damage to building materials (e.g. bricks or concrete) occurs as a result of their saturation with saline water. Construction material degradation depends on the salt content of soil water (both concentration and composition) and level of subsoil saturation. The latter defines water fluxes from soil to the walls and therefore the evaporation intensity from the wall surface, the rates of salt precipitation and material weathering.
- In Western Australia, waterlogging is the main cause of park and garden degradation. According to Nulsen (1981), salinity affects plant growth when groundwater levels reach a trigger level of 1.8 metres below the ground surface. However, the trigger depth may vary between soil types.

An estimation of current infrastructure damage is required as a baseline against which the cost-effectiveness of proposed management options is evaluated. Economic evaluation of the infrastructure damage associated with salinisation was based on the 'Urban Salinity Economic Analysis Package' (Rural Towns Management Committee 2001). This model provides an economic analysis tool that assesses strategies for controlling rising groundwater in urban areas by accounting for both control and damage costs. The control strategies include groundwater pumping and disposal, recharge reduction, tree planting and reduced household water use and discharge. Damage costs reflect the costs to infrastructure when various water management strategies are in place, which are dependent upon the depth to the water table and infrastructure type.

Within the RTLA project, USEAP was adopted to a GIS environment to provide a platform for integration between land-use data, hydrological and economic analyses, and proposed water management options. A spatial town-site infrastructure layer was built on a number of base datasets to fulfil the requirements of the USEAP model, providing identification by type of all relevant infrastructures within the town (USEAP data layer).

The complete spatial economic model integrates the USEAP data layer, USEAP economic algorithms and spatial layers identifying salinity risk. Infrastructure damage costs are calculated based on the simultaneous analysis of the salinity risk (as outputs of hydrogeological/hydrological modelling) and the USEAP data layer. The average salinity risk of each land parcel is determined, and damage is calculated using an algorithm adapted from the USEAP model. Each category included in the model has an assigned annual damage cost, derived from the USEAP value assuming a 100% impact (Table 9.1). Given the uncertainties in the modelling, and the impacts of discounting, a 20-year period was proposed as a sufficient timeframe for analysis.

The advantage of this approach is that it allows the evaluation of proposed water management options on infrastructure damage by individual properties, or collectively on a district or town basis, analysing spatial distributions of benefits derived from water management alterations. This maps the type of infrastructure and salinity risk against costs over time, spatially and in proportion to the salinity risk. More importantly, costs are aggregated for each year and then discounted to give a net present value over a period of time. Finally, the calculations give the change in damage costs associated with various water management actions.

The key component of the infrastructure damage analysis is definition of the salinity risk and its spatial distribution in a town.

Table 9.1. USEAP annual damage cost.

Name	Quantity	Cost ($)
Residential building	per/household	563
Commercial building	per/1000 sq m	663
Oval	per/hectare	1900
Open space	per/hectare	685
Sealed road	per/1000 m	400
Unsealed road	per/1000 m	200

Source: USEAP model (URS 2001)

Plate 1

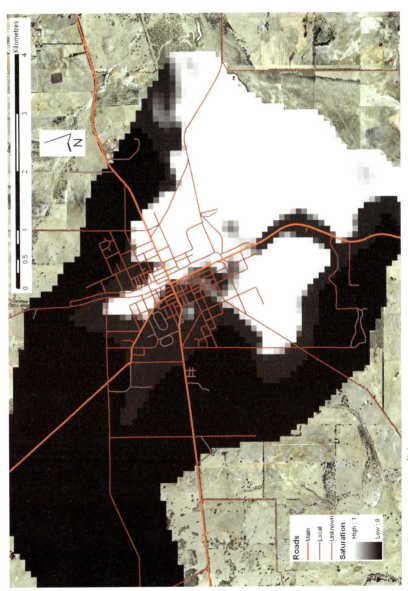

Plate 1. Salinity risk: current conditions.

Plate 2

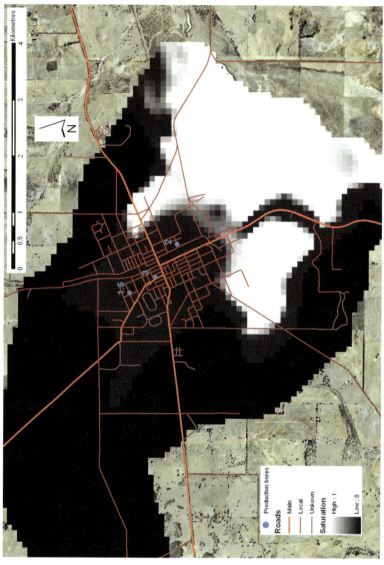

Plate 2. Salinity risk after 20 years pumping from three production bores (2, 3 and 15) with abstraction rates of 1.5, 3 and 2 L/s respectively.

Plate 3

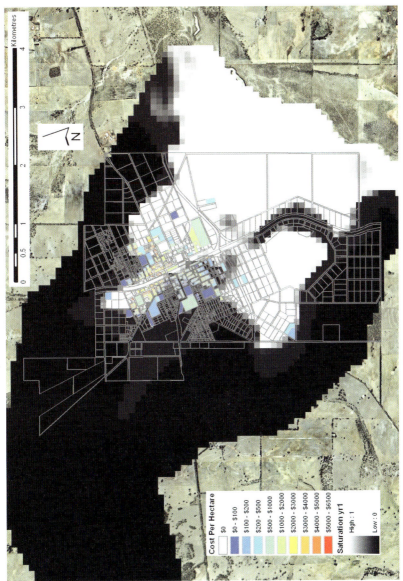

Cost Per Hectare

- $0
- $0 - $100
- $100 - $200
- $200 - $500
- $500 - $1000
- $1000 - $2000
- $2000 - $3000
- $3000 - $4000
- $4000 - $5000
- $5000 - $6500

Saturation yr1

High : 1

Low : 0

Plate 3. Infrastructure damage under current conditions.

Plate 4

Plate 4. Infrastructure damage after 20 years pumping from production bores.

Salinity risk assessment

The assessment of salinity risk to infrastructure was based on an evaluation of soil saturation levels at a given depth below the ground surface. Soil saturation at the level of the groundwater table is 100%, which reduces upwards in the absence of a perched water table. When soil saturation is considered at a given depth (e.g. 1 metre below the surface), the saturation level becomes a function of the depth to groundwater table, the soil material, land use and the history of precipitation. In a general case, the deeper the groundwater table, the lesser would be the soil saturation at the considered depth.

This approach was employed in this project so that adaptation of the USEAP model was possible. This model evaluates the infrastructure damage cost for a situation when the groundwater table is at 0.5 metres and 3 metres below the surface (URS 2001). Because the USEAP framework does not define the groundwater regime, for the purpose of developing a link between hydrogeological information and economic analysis, a number of assumptions were made in this project.

The first assumption suggested that the critical depth to the groundwater table applicable for infrastructure damage evaluation was taken as 1 metre below ground level. Actual research on the ground in the towns allowed for adaptation of the outcomes from groundwater modelling to be linked with USEAP algorithms – both spatially and in time – incorporating the GIS town infrastructure/damage model.

Secondly it was assumed that infrastructure damage is proportional to soil saturation at a critical depth to the groundwater table (1 metre below the ground level). In addition, damage costs are assumed to be proportional to the salinity risk. In an area where the salinity risk is one (e.g. groundwater table is at a trigger level or above, hence the soil saturation is 100%), the damage cost is evaluated as 100%. In areas where the salinity risk is less than one, the damage cost is reduced in accordance with salinity risk reduction. For a sufficiently deep groundwater table, the infrastructure damage cost is close to zero. Salinity risk is considered minimal when soil saturation is less than 10%, because the residual moisture content in the soil does not affect urban infrastructure. Adoption of various water management options resulting in groundwater table drawdown will reduce soil saturation and, consequently, salinity risk and infrastructure damage.

Quantification of the processes leading to a rise in the groundwater table was undertaken by hydrological and hydrogeological investigations in town catchments as explained by Barr (2005a). These investigations were then extended by Barr (2005b) to develop urban groundwater models. The application of modelling allows definition of the depths to the groundwater table and spatial variation within the town-sites and prediction of groundwater table fluctuations under various water management options.

For instance, MODFLOW groundwater modelling was used in the Wagin case study to define the long-term groundwater table depth and drawdown under proposed pumping regimes. Outcomes include estimated groundwater abstraction volumes required in order to mitigate salinity and waterlogging in towns, and predictions of water quality trends in the pumped groundwater. The WAVES model (Zhang and Dawes 1998) – a one-dimensional (vertical) simulation model that incorporates vegetation evapotranspiration – was used to simulate the unsaturated zone in Wagin and its catchment.

Evaluation of water management options

In the project, town-site water management is considered in terms of a complete system rather than its individual technical or engineering components. The specifics of groundwater pumping and/or surface water management for a town-site are obtained from the simultaneous analysis of the hydrology and hydrogeology and town infrastructure and damage models. This, in turn, provides information on the quality and quantity of abstracted water and requirement for water treatment to achieve 'fit-for-purposes' qualities. This information can then be directly used for economic evaluation of water abstraction and treatment.

Because water quality can also be identified, the most efficient water treatment option can be selected based on demand for the product water. If, in the process, reject water is produced, the method of disposal or re-use is also determined. By obtaining costs and benefits for each stage of the water abstraction and treatment process, the net benefits from various management options can be calculated.

The technical aspects of water management options were further informed by socioeconomic analyses. This was important for ensuring that the options were relevant for, and endorsed by, the local community. Field visits and telephone surveys were conducted with a range of stakeholder groups in each town (Johnston et al. 2005) to gain an overview of local attitudes, values and aims associated with water use, management and supply in the town.

The system approach is further demonstrated in the Wagin case-study below, where groundwater abstraction was proposed for salinity control in the town-site.

THE WAGIN CASE STUDY

Wagin is located 225 km south-east of Perth (Figure 9.2) and has a population of approximately 1400 residents. Town-site salinity affects the central business area and south-eastern town district, although participants in a preliminary survey done by Johnston *et al.* (2005) did not have a high awareness of these salinity affects. This survey was part of the

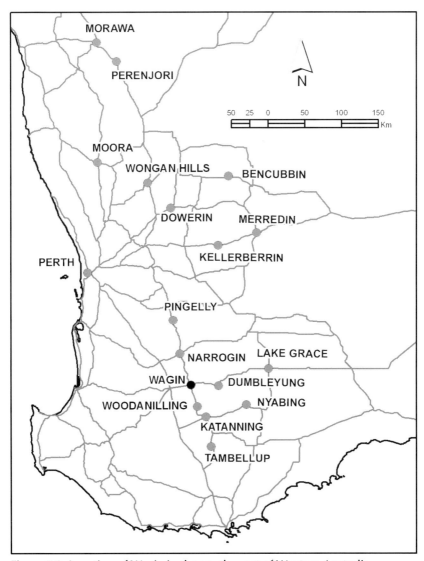

Figure 9.2. Location of Wagin in the south-west of Western Australia.

socioeconomic component of the research and was designed to gain an overview of local attitudes associated with water use, management and supply in the town. Twenty people, representing a range of community interests, were personally interviewed to gain local input to the research. To develop a background understanding of the town's social context, general information was firstly elicited as to perceptions of the town's major challenges and future opportunities and aspirations. Overall, there was a sense of attachment to, and pride in, the town, and positive hopes for the future. With respect to local views about salinity and water specifically, it was found that people did not tend to see a link between salinity and water management or use in the town. Salinity was typically perceived of as a 'farming problem', but most participants noted rising groundwater levels in the town, and even associated impacts on infrastructure such as the local hotel. Further findings of importance for the research project were widespread support for water harvesting and extraction for the town's benefit, and for rigorous and comprehensive analysis before any decision making.

This work provided a positive first step to integrated research by gaining local input to the project. Moreover, in addition to helping to develop community support for the project, the knowledge about local values and aspirations for water management in their town was a consideration in decision making in further aspects of the research in Wagin. As part of continued collaboration, the project aims and progress were reported to decision makers within the town, with meetings also being held on a regular basis.

To understand where water is being distributed within Wagin over time, Grant and Sharma (2005) completed a water balance model for Wagin. They found that for significant improvements in water management to be achieved, stormwater collection, groundwater extraction and use should be considered. As a part of the town-site hydrogeological system characterisation, the salinity and waterlogging processes in the town-site is largely defined by the catchment groundwater systems (Barr 2005b). Groundwater abstraction was identified as an effective water management option for salinity control in the town-site (Barr 2005b).

Wagin salinity risk map

The groundwater model using the simulation package MODFLOW created for Wagin (Barr 2005b) incorporates the surface water catchment, which coincided with the groundwater catchment, and consists of two layers: an upper layer representing the clay and superficial deposits; and a lower layer representing the saprolite grits that act as the main lateral groundwater flow channel (aquifer). Simulations of pre-clearing and post-clearing vegetation scenarios indicated that the water table has risen to the current levels observed within the town, and is presently in a steady state stage (Barr 2005b). Simulations have also been used to predict the effects of pumping on the water table, showing a significant fall in water tables within the town for three existing pumps operating at a combined rate of 6.5 litres per second over a period of 10 years. The water quality within the town has also been modelled for the pumping simulation (Barr 2005b).

Application of the WAVES model (Zhang and Dawes 1998) was used for estimation of the saturation above the water table. Using the groundwater model outcome as a water table depth for each model cell, the saturation at a depth of 1 metre was interpolated from the previously calculated unsaturated zone solutions. This enabled development of the salinity risk maps for the current conditions and for groundwater abstraction from three production bores. Colour plates 1 and 2 show how the area rated as a high salinity risk area (white colour on the maps) is reduced if groundwater abstraction is implemented.

Infrastructure damage

A GIS database for Wagin has been developed to provide a spatial context to the town infrastructure/damage model (Barron *et al.* 2005). The database includes a number of datasets to meet the requirements of the USEAP model. These included: Spatial Cadastral Database; Local Authority Town Planning Scheme (TPS); Property Sales Data; Western Australian Generic Road Centreline Network; and Aerial Photography.

Infrastructure damage costs were calculated based on the simultaneous analysis of the salinity risk and the USEAP data layer. The average salinity risk and associated damage cost for each land parcel was calculated using an algorithm adapted from the USEAP model. The outcomes of the infrastructure model are displayed spatially in colour plates 3 and 4. The cost could be expressed in a damage cost per land parcel per area unit (e.g. per hectare or per square metre). The infrastructure damage was zero where there was no infrastructure within the considered area.

Evaluation of the proposed water management option

The water management options evaluated and presented in this report is limited to groundwater pumping, abstracted water disposal and/or treatment. A cost–benefit analysis was undertaken for each of the options outlined below. The costs associated with the implementation of the water management option were estimated (KBR 2004).

Do-nothing option

Within the 'do-nothing' option, the economic analysis is based on the assumption that the current water management plan in the town remains unchanged and the shire and community bear the damage costs to local infrastructure. For Wagin, the net present value of the damage costs, over a 20 year horizon, was estimated at $1.125 million. This is a relatively minor cost, but in line with values produced elsewhere using the USEAP methodology. It appears that the most significant cost is associated with salinity impacts on residential and industrial properties (Barron *et al.* 2005).

The outcome of the damage cost evaluation within the 'do-nothing' option represents the baseline for the cost–benefit analysis of water management options proposed for town-site salinity control.

Effect of groundwater abstraction on town-site salinity damage

As identified earlier in this report, groundwater abstraction is required to control the shallow water table in the Wagin town-site. The prediction of groundwater pumping on the groundwater table was based on a simulation, run with three production bores generating 6.5 litres per second (Barr 2005b). The location of the bores has not been optimised, nor calibrated against observed groundwater drawdown at this time, but it is based on existing test bores and their yield. Running the simulation of this pumping regime generates an alternative time profile of salinity risk and hence an alternative profile of infrastructure costs. Over a 20-year pumping simulation (which is assumed to be at equilibrium), the cost of infrastructure damage is reduced to just $0.283 million and the overall saving to the infrastructure amounts to about $0.842 million. The greatest reduction in damage cost relates to the residential properties (Barron *et al.* 2005).

Implementation cost (groundwater abstraction, treatment and disposal)

Overall, four options were considered, with variations related to abstracted water re-use and disposal: a direct disposal to the existing salt lake; direct disposal to an evaporation pond; abstracted groundwater desalination and re-use with brine disposal to the existing salt lake; or abstracted groundwater desalination and re-use with brine disposal to an evaporation pond.

The cost of implementing these options includes capital and an operation and maintenance (O&M) component.

Groundwater desalination technologies were considered to increase the value of abstracted water. A reverse osmosis desalination plant will treat abstracted groundwater generated by three production bores at the rate of 6.5 litres per second. The recovery rate (65 %) and plant specifications were based on groundwater quality in Wagin. Presence of silica (about 70 mg/L) is the main limitation on the recovery rate. The plant production rate is 365 kilolitres per day permeate, with 196.5 kilolitres per day in a reject stream (KBR 2005). Groundwater or brine disposal bears an extremely high cost. The cost of installing an evaporation pond varies depending on the technology adopted, but it is likely to be in the range of $7 to $15 per square metre. Other limitations are related to local climatic conditions (Wagin has an average annual rainfall of 428 mm and an average pan evaporation of 1607 mm). According to the engineering evaluation undertaken by KBR (2005), the cost for an evaporation pond for brine disposal in Wagin is $2.1 million (−20% +30% cost variances). Net benefits resulting from the introduction of an option were estimated as a difference between the cost of the option implemented and the reduction in the infrastructure damage cost (as a result of the groundwater table lowering). In this preliminary analysis, groundwater/brine disposal into the existing salt lake presents a more desirable alternative (Table 9.2). While this option seems to considerably reduce the implementation costs, environmental impacts need to be considered and costed, and this has not been undertaken at this stage.

The groundwater desalination option with brine disposal to the salt lake appears to be within the boundary of breaking even assuming that the permeate sale is based on $0.78 per kilolitre (Table 9.2). However, introduction of desalination technologies deliver additional benefits by also allowing production of fresh water. Potential government support to implement a desalination scheme may also increase the viability of the option. If capital costs or water pricing components are subsidised within the Community Service Obligation scheme, desalination may be the most beneficial option for water management for the Wagin community. There is also an opportunity to reduce the capital costs if the desalination plant is optimally sited. However, the work required to facilitate this option is currently outside the scope of this project.

Applying a systems approach to water management in Wagin provides a demonstration of the approach given the current constraints. It shows that

Table 9.2. Economic parameters and results for groundwater management options (over a 20-year period).

	Pumping/disposal		Pumping/desalination/ brine disposal	
	Evaporation pond	Salt lake	Evaporation pond	Salt lake
Costs (× $1000)				
Capital cost	7890	240	3275	586
O&M cost (NPV)	55	55	1254	1254
Total cost of the option	7945	295	4529	1840
Benefits (× $1000)				
Damage cost saving	843	842	842	842
Water sale (NPV)	0	0	1075[1] or 1254[2]	1075[1] or 1254[2]
Net benefits (× $1000)				
Total	−7102	547	−2612 or −2433	−77 or 256
CSO subsidies (investment in desalination scheme)	*−3071*	*185*	*303 or 583*	*303 or 583*

1 As a revenue from water sale applying the current water price ($0.78/kL)
2 As a revenue from water sales under the condition that the water sale covers operation and maintenance costs

all proposed options (groundwater abstraction and disposal to the salt lake, groundwater abstraction, water desalination, permeate sale and brine disposal to the salt lake or evaporation pond) provide benefits for the townsite, but to a varying extent, with the greater economic benefit from groundwater abstraction and disposal to the salt lake. Furthermore, to account for town community expectations, technical management considerations and potential uses of desalinated water, the final water management plan should be completed in consultation with the town community.

Further development of the systems approach will be related to water-use options. The approach may enable a balance between water supply and water demand by various industrial enterprises. If the quantity of water required by an enterprise is greater than that supplied, then it has the option of using water from another source as well. This means that all treated water will be used if additional water is available and if the benefits of running the enterprise outweigh the costs. Intensive animal industries, such as beef production (Pluske and Schlink 2005) and aquaculture, are potential options for use of this water (Pluske et al. 2006a). There is also the option that water with sufficiently low levels of salt could be used for irrigation purposes or on salt-tolerant grasses without any prior treatment (Pluske *et al.* 2006a).

REFLECTION ON THE INTEGRATION PROCESS AND POLICY OUTCOMES

An integrated approach has been developed in the RTLA project to support a decision-making process for water management in rural towns affected by salinity. A systems framework provides a basis for salinity risk evaluation and estimation of acquired infrastructure damage costs. Within this framework, effectiveness of the water management options in salinity risk reduction can be tested, and cost–benefit analyses of the options can be undertaken to guide future policy decisions. This process is extensively discussed in Pluske *et al.* (2006b). It is important to remember that the values captured should encompass all changes that are appropriate. In addition, the system should be defined to incorporate all aspects that may change as a result of management. It is also important that the technical information is available to enable changes to be evaluated.

Combining the results into a water management plan is essential for delivering the research findings to local government and communities in towns involved in the RTLA project. The social analysis was important for helping to identify how this plan could be relevant for the town and supported by the local community. It was also important for identifying gaps between the reality of the scope of town-site salinity problems, and associated options, and the perceptions of the community. This is vital for managing expectations, between researchers and people in the town, and between local government and its citizens. For example, in the case of Wagin, the water management plan can help the Shire place emphasis on water re-use aspects in line with previously expressed local aspirations. Acknowledging such issues, and hence structuring the water management plans to focus on the most relevant aspects, is important. Furthermore, because local communities are not generally familiar with the scientific and economics associated with water management in rural Australia, researchers need to take extra care when delivering the results to local decision makers to ensure that results are communicated in a way that can be readily understood by the 'lay community'.

The final question for this chapter is to consider how integration has contributed to achieving the mission for CSIRO National Flagship *Water for a Healthy Country* and, more specifically, how this research has influenced local government policy. In addressing the latter, the RTLA project is just half way through its life and already on-ground work is occurring in a number of West Australian rural towns. It would certainly seem that study findings will not stop at the research institution level but will be implemented in practice. Finally, with regard to 'the mission', it is perhaps optimistic to think that the RTLA project will achieve a 10-fold increase in the social, economic and environmental benefits from water by 2025 for each town. Nevertheless, through integration, significant water benefits at each of the three levels should be realised for each town involved in this project.

REFERENCES

Bammer G (2005) Integration and implementation sciences: building a new specialization. *Ecology and Society* **10**(2), 6. <http://www.ecology-andsociety.org/vol10/iss2/art6/>

Barr A (2005a) 'Hydrogeological modeling of the first four towns: Lake Grace, Nyabing, Wagin and Woodanilling'. Interim Technical Report. CSIRO: Water for a Healthy Country National Research Flagship, Canberra.

Barr A (2005b) 'Hydrogeological modeling of Wagin'. Interim Technical Report. CSIRO: Water for a Healthy Country National Research Flagship, Canberra.

Barron O, Barr T, Smales T, Burton M and Pluske J (2005) 'Systems approach to rural town water management'. Interim Technical Report. CSIRO: Water for a Healthy Country National Research Flagship, Canberra.

Barron O and Smales T (2005) 'The framework for prioritisation of water management options in WA Rural towns'. Interim Technical Report. CSIRO: Water for a Healthy Country National Research Flagship, Canberra.

Grant A and Sharma A (2005) 'Water balance study of Lake Grace, Wagin, Nyabing and Woodanilling'. Technical Report CMIT(C)-2005-284. CSIRO: Water for a Healthy Country National Research Flagship, Canberra.

Johnston C, Green M and Helmert E (2005) 'Rural Towns-Liquid Assets: social scoping study for the town of Wagin;. Interim Technical Report. CSIRO: Water for a Healthy Country National Research Flagship, Canberra.

KBR (Kellogg Brown & Root Pty Ltd) (2004) Katanning Desalination Demonstration Plant: Business plan. Report to CSIRO Land and Water, Canberra, ACT, Australia. 2 July 2004.

Nulsen RA (1981) Critical depth to saline groundwater in non-irrigated situations. *Australian Journal of Soil Research* **19**, 83–86.

Pluske J, Burton M and Weersink A (2006b) 'New water: policy issues for Western Australian rural towns'. Interim Technical Report. CSIRO: Water for a Healthy Country National Research Flagship, Canberra.

Pluske J, Turner J and Pridham M (2006a) 'Options for water utilisation and reuse: Merredin, A Rural Towns Liquid Assets Report'. 31 May 2006, CSIRO: Water for a Healthy Country National Research Flagship, Canberra.

Rural Towns Management Committee, 2001, 'Economic impacts of salinity on townsite infrastructure', Western Australia Department Of Agriculture, Bulletin 4525, Perth WA. <http://www.agric.wa.gov.au/pls/portal30/docs/FOLDER/IKMP/LWE/SALIN/TOWNSAL/BULL4525.PDF>

Chapter 10

Integrated modelling of European agricultural land use scenarios

Wolfgang Reiher, Lutz Breuer, Patrick Sheridan, Thorsten Pohlert, Martin Bach, Stefan Gäth, Friedrich Kuhlmann and Hans-Georg Frede

ABSTRACT

A key aspect in integrated mission-directed research is to assist stakeholders and decision makers in evaluating their actions and policies by enabling the use of scientific assessment of different targets. The Integrated Tool for Economic and Ecological Modeling (ITE^{2}M) was developed to assess landscape services of different land-use options. ITE^{2}M is a network of several models addressing agro-economy, agricultural policy and environmental services with respect to soil, water, floral and faunal biodiversity. A central part of ITE^{2}M is a bio-economic simulation model that predicts economically optimal land-use distributions. Its site-specific outputs comprise land rent, land use and management information. These data form the basis for other ITE^{2}M models. In this chapter, the concept of ITE^{2}M is presented along with a case study that evaluates the current and former European Common Agricultural Policy with particular regards to the evaluation of soil- and water-related landscape services.

INTRODUCTION

Landscapes provide a wide range of services, including employment, economic income, habitat for fauna and flora, water supply and food production (Costanza *et al.* 1997). The evaluation of changes in land use or management systems should be considered concurrently with landscape services and their interactions. Integrated modelling approaches can be used to evaluate agricultural policy that leads to different land-use and management patterns in a landscape.

The European Common Agricultural Policy (CAP) has changed radically over the years. The MacSharry reforms of 1992 and the AGENDA 2000 package attempted to reduce the price support for single crops, even though the largest shares of subsidies were still directed towards produced volume. In 2003, European Union (EU) farm ministers adopted a fundamental reform of the CAP, with emphasis on direct payments to farmers (assumed to be the best way of guaranteeing farmer incomes), food safety and quality, and environmentally sustainable production. The frequency of reforms of the agricultural policy at the EU-level, and the dispersion of intentions at which they aim, demonstrate that there is a need for tools to predict both the economic and ecological consequences of agricultural policy strategies. One goal of integrated mission-directed research is to enable stakeholders and decision makers to evaluate their potential decisions before they become law. In this process, it is important to focus not only on a single target, such as water quality, but to get an idea of what may happen to other targets as well. In an analysis of a landscape, the impact of decisions and measures should be considered in an integrated view of the manifold landscape functions.

The Collaborative Research Center 'Land Use Options for Peripheral Regions' at the University of Giessen, Germany, develops integrated methodologies and tools towards the achievement and appraisal of economical and ecologically sustainable options for regional land use (see Box 10.1 for a short description). Different targets regarding economic, social and environmental issues are investigated and used for assessments of landscape services.

This study presents the conceptual design of the Integrated Tool for Economic and Ecological Modeling (ITE^{2}M). The conceptual description of the research approach of the SFB 299 is followed by an illustrative application of ITE^{2}M. Agricultural land-use and management options are assessed by means of characteristic model outputs describing economic production, soil quality, hydrological function and riverine nutrient export. Benefits and drawbacks of the concept are demonstrated and discussed. A more detailed reflection on the interaction of the different subprojects of the SFB 299, as well as a compilation of its publications, is given in Waldhardt (2007).

BOX 10.1. COLLABORATIVE RESEARCH CENTER 'LAND USE OPTIONS FOR PERIPHERAL REGIONS' (SFB 299) (WALDHARDT 2007)

The SFB 299 is a 12-year interdisciplinary project at the University of Giessen, Germany, which started in 1997 and is funded by the German Research Foundation (DFG). It comprises currently 16 subprojects arranged in five thematic blocks. The core of the project is the development of an integrated methodology towards the achievement and appraisal of economically and ecologically sustainable options for regional land use based on spatially explicit models (thematic block A: three subprojects) as part of the model network ITE^{2}M. The developed models have been tested and at least partially validated using data that result from research of the thematic blocks B (soil information and biotic data: five subprojects), C (agronomic data: four subprojects) and D (agricultural policy and political science: two subprojects). However, communication and data exchange are not limited within a thematic block, but are common in the interdisciplinary project as a whole. Furthermore, since around 2000, modelling has not been restricted to block A, but has become more and more important in several subprojects of block B. Meanwhile, 9 years after the project started, the research focus in both blocks has become the modelling of relations between land use and variables that indicate landscape functionality. In the first project phase (1997–1999), research in many subprojects focused on relations between land use and dependent variables at the patch or field scale. Thereafter, and continuing today, research on broader scales has characterised the SFB 299. In general, most of the subprojects have involved basic as well as applied research.

MODEL NETWORK ITE^{2}M

ITE^{2}M comprises several models addressing agro-economy (ProLand), cost and benefit evaluation (CHOICE), faunal (GEPARD), floral (ProF) and general biodiversity (ANIMO), and environmental services with respect to soil quality (ATOMIS) and water quantity and quality (SWAT) (Figure 10.1).

As the core of the project, the bio-economic model ProLand predicts site-specific land-use maps. These maps and further model-specific information form the basis for all ITE^{2}M component models to simulate economic and ecological landscape services. Trade-offs and win–win situations between these landscape services are calculated and evaluated within the ITE^{2}M network (e.g. Frede *et al.* 2002). In principle, the network is open to the inclusion of additional models simulating targets for

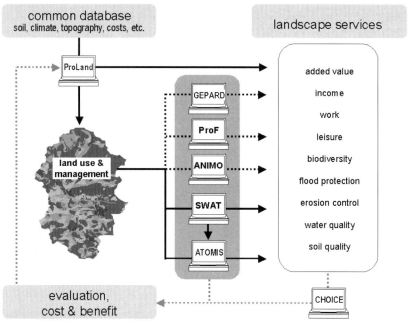

Figure 10.1. The ITE²M-model-network setup. The continuous black lines indicate data flows and results that are described in detail in this chapter. Dotted lines indicate additional pathways of data exchange, predicted landscape services and evaluation, as well as back-coupling mechanisms that are not further described here. For more information readers should refer to the literature cited in the text.

the evaluation of further landscape services, such as quantifying carbon sequestration, emission of trace gases, tourism or genetic diversity (Breuer *et al.* 2007; Waldhardt 2007).

One of the key aspects of integrated modelling within ITE²M is the inter-model data exchange. Apart from the fact that ProLand provides land-use maps, which are used by all other models, there is additional data exchange and back-coupling between the models (Reiher *et al.* 2006b). This holds true especially for questions of model outputs regarding agricultural management that are addressed by ATOMIS and SWAT in view of potential heavy metal enrichment in soils and calculation of nutrient output of a landscape. The work presented here focused on the interaction of these three models by investigating economic and ecological effects of the former ('AGENDA 2000') and current ('CAP') European Common Agricultural Policy in the low mountainous Dill catchment, Germany. We then discuss the conceptual integration of models with different temporal and spatial scale into one modelling network. Further information on the biodiversity models associated with ITE^{2}M, and results referring to biodiversity, can be found in Steiner and Köhler (2003), Waldhardt *et al.* (2004), Waldhardt (2007), Gottschalk *et al.* (2007).

The bio-economic model ProLand

The bio-economic simulation model ProLand (Prognosis of Land Use) is a comparative static model predicting the spatially explicit allocation of land-use systems (Kuhlmann *et al.* 2002; Möller *et al.* 2002). The basic assumption of the model is that land users select the agricultural or silvicultural land-use systems that are expected to generate the highest possible lend rent on a decision unit (Kuhlmann *et al.* 2002; Weinmann *et al.* 2006). Land rent is defined as the sum of monetary yields on a decision unit, including all subsidies, minus all costs except those of land. Decision units in ProLand are either based on pixels (grid mode) or field boundaries (vector mode).

The land rent is calculated in several steps (Weinmann 2002). First, ProLand estimates the site-specific maximum realisable yield for a given set of agricultural production systems. A production system is a predefined production process including all sub-processes in crop and animal production, such as seedbed preparation, plant protection or milking. Site-specific data, such as soil properties, accumulated temperature and long-term mean annual precipitation in growing season, are used as inputs to determine yield. The second step is the calculation of the production costs, which are adjusted for site conditions such as slope, field size and soil tillage resistance. Using these calculations, the land rent is estimated for every decision unit. In the last step, the land-use system that maximises the land rent is selected for each decision unit.

The output of ProLand includes a set of economic key indicators, as well as maps of land use with site-specific management information (e.g. crop rotation or fertiliser application). The spatial resolution of the derived land-use maps depends on the resolution of the data (here 25 × 25 m). A detailed description of the ProLand concept (in its vector based mode) and the basic assumptions used in the design of our AGENDA 2000 and CAP scenarios is presented in Weinmann *et al.* (2006).

The Soil Water Assessment Tool (SWAT)

SWAT (Arnold *et al.* 1998) is a semi-distributed eco-hydrological model that combines conceptual and process-orientated approaches. Based on a digital elevation model, a catchment is partitioned into a number of subbasins with a spatially explicit location. Water is routed between the subbasins with a kinematic wave approach. A further subdivision of the subbasins into hydrological response units (HRU) is based on land use and soil information. An HRU does not have a spatially explicit location within a subbasin; it is a lumped land area comprised of a unique combination of land use and soil type. For the calculation of hydrological fluxes we used SWAT-G: a model version adapted for application in low mountainous catchments with its typical shallow rock aquifers and a high portion of interflow (Eckhardt *et al.* 2002).

Beside run-off prediction, SWAT is used within the ITE^{2}M framework to calculate river N- and P-concentration. It has a stand-alone crop growth simulation module that requires detailed management information on nutrient supply. ProLand provides this information by estimating site explicit N and P demands. The demands are used to estimate average N and P fertilisation rates for the SWAT simulations. The most prevailing crop rotation and pasture system as predicted by ProLand were assumed to cover the entire agricultural and pasture land, respectively. To improve N simulation mineralisation and nitrification, routines from the biogeochemical DNDC model (Li *et al.* 1992) and denitrification algorithms from the Crop-Syst model (Stöckle *et al.* 2003) were implemented (Pohlert *et al.* 2007b).

In this study, SWAT simulations were used to generate long-term average annual data on seepage water and evapotranspiration used by ATOMIS. Because SWAT is a semi-distributed hydrologic model, the relocation of HRUs is done in a spatially explicit way by their known aggregation of information on soil type, land-use and sub-basin affiliation, following the approach developed by Haverkamp *et al.* (2005). Figure 10.2 gives an example for the redistributed hydrologic information provided by SWAT.

The Assessment Tool for Metals in Soils (ATOMIS)

In terms of soil quality, the heavy metal status of soils is a major indicator for evaluating sustainable land management. Heavy metal enrichment in soils should be avoided owing to their potential toxicity. At a minimum, precautionary values – especially if legally defined – should not be exceeded. Agricultural heavy metal input into soils is mainly dependent on type (e.g. sewage sludge, animal manure or mineral fertiliser) and amount of fertiliser applied (Nicholson *et al.* 2003), with the latter dependent on crop rotation and potential yield. The fate of heavy metals – that is, whether they are adsorbed, taken up by plants or leached out – depends on soil adsorption characteristics, which are either stable (such as texture and clay content) or

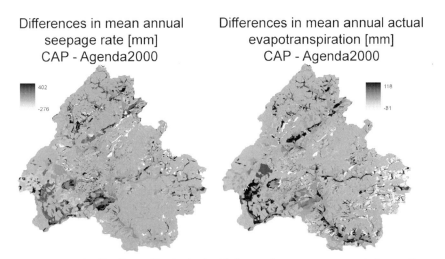

Differences in mean annual seepage rate [mm] CAP - Agenda2000

402
-276

Differences in mean annual actual evapotranspiration [mm] CAP - Agenda2000

118
-81

Figure 10.2. Redistributed hydrological information on seepage rate beneath the top soil and actual evapotranspiration rate provided by SWAT: differences between CAP and AGENDA 2000 scenario; positive values indicate higher, and negative values indicate lower rates in the CAP scenario compared with the AGENDA 2000 scenario.

labile (such as pH-value and soil organic carbon content (SOC)). Labile soil properties in particular are dependent on land use and management.

ATOMIS (Reiher *et al.* 2004; Reiher 2008) predicts site-specific, dynamic long-term development of heavy metal concentrations in topsoils. The metal input stemming from land-management practices was derived from ProLand P-fertilising data using average heavy metal contents in different P-fertilisers. Metal input by atmospheric deposition was taken from a representative monitoring station. Pedotransfer functions (PTF) derived from adsorption experiments (Horn *et al.* 2004; Horn *et al.* 2006; Reiher 2008) and from extraction data were used to estimate the element concentrations in soil solution that can be removed from the topsoil by leaching and plant uptake. Leaching and actual evapotranspiration rates used to calculate plant uptake were provided by SWAT. According to Wohlrab *et al.* (1992), actual evapotranspiration data was corrected by factors for arable land, grassland and forest to estimate the transpiration rate. PTFs are parameterised by soil adsorption characteristics (e.g. pH, SOC and clay content) and heavy metal background value (LABO 2003). ATOMIS identifies areas where the geologic background, site characteristics, such as soil properties and seepage water, and agricultural land-use and management systems may lead to problematic enrichment of heavy metals in soil. Sustainability of land-use and management options is assessed by comparing the projected total metal concentrations in topsoils to legally specified threshold values after a defined period of time. For this study, the German precautionary values (BBodSchV 1999) for Copper (Cu) and Zinc (Zn) in soils were used as the sustainability criteria. Cu- and Zn-inputs on agricultural fields are mainly affected by land management through the amount and type of applied fertiliser. The target value was the percentage of agricultural land exceeding the precautionary values within 100 years under assumed constant land management and site conditions.

ProLand assumes site-specific adjusted land management production systems. Based on this, ATOMIS assigns land use and soil texture dependent pH-target-values (Fürchtenicht *et al.* 1993) to each site. Additionally, three classes of SOC were applied that separate agricultural land from forest and arable land from grassland. Phosphorus demand is calculated from algorithms estimating the maximum realisable yield for each decision unit by ProLand. In ATOMIS, the type of added P-fertiliser is allocated to each site depending on the site-specific production system. The prevailing crop rotation simulated by ProLand for both scenarios is maize silage / maize silage / winter wheat. Where animal husbandry is profitable, indoor stock keeping of cattle during the entire year – pre-processed by a plant production system producing cattle forage – is calculated by ProLand to be most effective economically. If cattle are not grazing on meadows, they are fed with mineral dietary supplements, which are supplemented with Cu and Zn. Cattle manure is only applied to sites of cattle forage production. These production sites include grassland as well as arable land with crop rotations that include the production of cattle fodder as silage maize and clover–grass. As there is a P-export out of the agricultural system via milk and meat, it is assumed by ATOMIS that the site-related difference between P-removal and P-input by cattle manure is substituted by mineral P-fertiliser. All sites without cattle forage production are completely fertilised by mineral P-fertiliser in the model.

Study area

The results presented here are obtained from the first test area of ITE^{2}M: the low mountainous area of the Lahn-Dill Highlands in the central part of Germany. Because a hydrological model is part of ITE^{2}M, the boundary of the region for which the model network can be applied to is restricted to river catchments. Here, the Dill river catchment (693 km^2, Figure 10.3) north-west of Frankfurt was chosen because of its rural landscape, which comes along with constraints for intensive agriculture, but exhibits rich biodiversity.

The catchment is characterised by shallow soils and a patchy field structure with average field sizes of 0.7 ha. Both of these characteristics lead to a low agricultural potential.

For this model application, SWAT-G was calibrated and successfully validated (Huisman *et al.* 2003; Pohlert *et al.* 2007a). Simulations for calculating nitrate loads in the river were conducted for the period 1 January 1980 to 31 December 1999, with the first 3 years acting as a warming up period for the hydrological cycle.

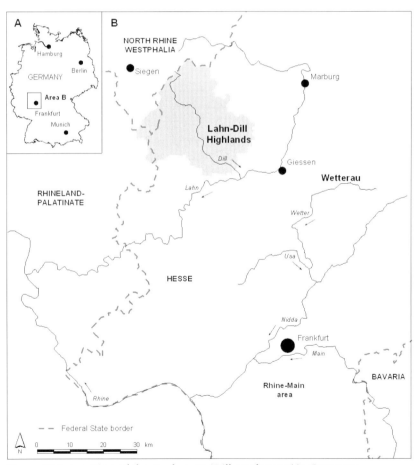

Figure 10.3. Location of the study area 'Dill catchment' in Germany.

RESULTS OF MODELLING EUROPEAN AGRICULTURAL LAND-USE SCENARIOS

Economic driven land use change

Land use distribution predicted by ProLand is significantly different between the former policy (AGENDA 2000 scenario) and the current Common Agricultural Policy (CAP scenario). The land use distribution is 9.6% (6687 ha) for arable land, 6.5% (4526 ha) for grassland, and 73.9% for forest in the AGENDA 2000 scenario and 0.5% (344 ha), 29.9% (20 716 ha), and 58.0% under CAP conditions, respectively (Table 10.1 and Figure 10.4). Urban area is not simulated by ProLand and thus was kept constant at 9.2%. The total agricultural land rent generated in the region is substantially higher in the CAP scenario, mainly due to higher amounts of transfer payments. A large share of the predicted forested area under the conditions of the AGENDA 2000 policy is predicted to be grassland under CAP. In addition, cropland almost disappears at the expense of permanent grassland. The latter can be explained by the change from a product-based subsidising system in AGENDA 2000 to a direct payment practice under CAP. Apart from the overall change in land use, a spatially differentiated analysis reveals an even more drastic alteration in certain areas. Individual sub-catchments in the western part of the Dill catchment show increases in pasture of more than 50 % of the total area (Fig. 10.4).

The economic evaluation of the land use scenarios confirms that the CAP reform removes the distorting effects of coupled transfer payments. All economic measures show increasing performance under the CAP conditions. The land rent increases from €12 Mio to €18 Mio and added value rises from €17 Mio to €25 Mio. The quantity of work demanded increased

Table 10.1. Land use distribution (%) for the AGENDA 2000 and the CAP scenario.

	AGENDA 2000	CAP
Arable land (%)	9.6	0.5
Grassland (%)	6.5	29.9
Forest (%)	73.9	58.0
Others (fallow, mulching*) (%)	0.5	2.1
Urban (%)	9.2	9.2
Surface waters (%)	0.3	0.3

* Mulching is a grassland land-use system funded according to the CAP reform. Here, management is restricted to cutting the grass once a year, with removal of the grass prohibited.

AGENDA 2000   CAP

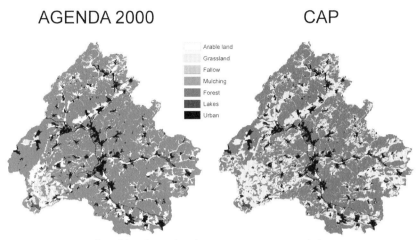

Arable land
Grassland
Fallow
Mulching
Forest
Lakes
Urban

Figure 10.4. Simulated land use for the AGENDA 2000 and the CAP scenario.

by almost 60%. Apart from the positive economic effects of changes in land use on the economy, effects on the environment were both positive and negative.

Ecosystem services

The predicted changes in water fluxes were low, with a decrease of annual discharge by 11 mm (–3%) and an increase of evapotranspiration of 9 mm (+2%) from the AGENDA 2000 to the CAP scenario. The results are similar to other investigations in the area (e.g. Fohrer *et al.* 2005; Weber *et al.* 2001). Nevertheless, for the Aar subcatchment within the study region, it was shown that even small changes in water flux components can be significant with respect to parameter uncertainty (Breuer *et al.* 2006). Beyond that, a recent model comparison project revealed that the direction of change for similar land-use change scenarios were in agreement for a variety of different model structures (Huisman *et al.* 2007).

The average annual nitrate loads as predicted by SWAT are 13.4 kg N ha^{-1} for the AGENDA 2000 and 11.6 kg N ha^{-1} for the CAP scenario, reflecting a reduction of 13% in nitrate load (Figure 10.5). Even though the portion of agricultural area is small, the differences in the overall N loads in the Dill river at the catchment's outlet are significant.

Due to the geogenic background, 13.0% (1459 ha) of agricultural land in the AGENDA 2000 scenario and 20.2% (4254 ha) in the CAP scenario exceed the precautionary value of Cu at the beginning of simulation and 41.3% (4626 ha) and 98.2% (20 687 ha) for Zn, respectively. After one

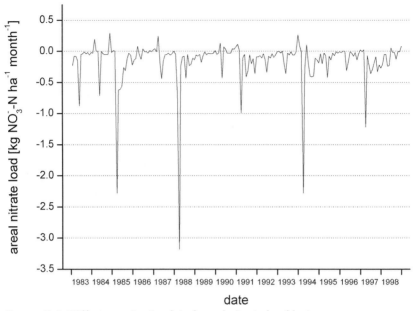

Figure 10.5. Differences in simulated areal nitrate load between AGENDA 2000 and CAP scenario. Negative values indicate lower nitrate loads in the CAP scenario compared with the AGENDA 2000 scenario.

century, the percentages increase to 48% (AGENDA 2000) and 99% (CAP) for Zn, whereas they remain stable for Cu with 13.0% and 20.4%. The increase of Zn for AGENDA 2000 can be explained by fertilisation inputs (estimated number of cattle is 8965 for AGENDA 2000 and 20 566 for CAP scenario) and a larger share of arable land. Arable land has higher P-demands and pH-values compared with grassland, which in turn increases the Zn-adsorption of topsoil. In contrast, the higher percentage of land exceeding the precautionary value for Zn under CAP is due to the definition of the precautionary value in the German Soil Protection Ordinance (BBodSchV 1999): the lower the pH, the lower the precautionary value has to be. A change from arable land to grassland leads to a drop of the pH-target-value due to reduced liming of grassland areas. As most of the agricultural area under the CAP scenario is pasture and the geogenic background concentration of Zn in the research area is relatively high, almost the entire agricultural land exceeds the precautionary value at the end of the simulation. Figure 10.6 shows a summary of the fate of Cu in topsoils of the Dill catchment as an example. The relatively poor site conditions for agricultural use are associated with relatively low input of fertiliser, and therefore the

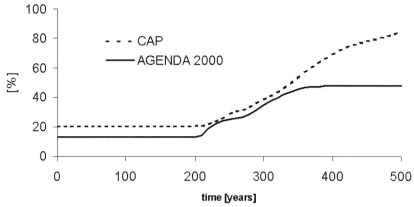

Figure 10.6. Percentage of agricultural land showing exceedance of precautionary value of Copper over 500 years. Constant management and site conditions are assumed.

percentage of agricultural area exceeding the precautionary values does not increase considerably within the first 200 years. Regarding Cu, both scenarios proved to be sustainable, because the exceedance of precautionary values within the first century was almost entirely caused by geogenic reasons and was hardly affected by land management (trend of both curves over the first hundred years in Figure 10.6). However, land use does affect the relative areas exceeding the precautionary values (difference of both curves in Figure 10. 6 at the beginning of simulation).

Trade offs and win–wins

In order to compare the results of the AGENDA 2000 and CAP scenarios, the different economic, soil and water related values predicted were standardised. We defined targets for each value and set these to 100%. For example, the higher quantity of work demanded in the CAP scenario was defined as the target, because it provides an opportunity to reduce unemployment rate in the region. The quantity of work demanded in the AGENDA 2000 was therefore calculated to be 37% less (Figure 10.7). In cases where lower targets are preferable to others, such as for nitrate loads, we calculated the inverse. The targets were defined as follows: *high* quantity of work demanded, land rent and added value as economic attractiveness; *low* percentage of exceedance of precautionary values of heavy metals for soil quality; and *low* discharge and evapotranspiration rates for water quantity. Economic, soil and water-related values were finally combined to create a picture of overall ecosystem services (Figure 10.7) as proposed by Foley *et al.*

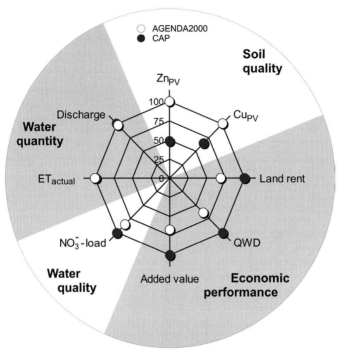

Figure 10.7. Ecosystem services for the CAP and AGENDA 2000 land-use scenario as derived by ITE^{2}M. Model outputs were standardised (best result of both scenarios = 100%), see text for details. QWD = Quanitity of work demanded; NO$_3^-$ load = riverine nitrate load at gauging station; ET$_{actual}$ = actual evapotranspiration; Cu$_{PV}$/Zn$_{PV}$ = Exceedance of precautionary value of Cu/Zn in per cent.

(2005). The main goal of the SFB 299 is to provide models for evaluating landscape services, not to define normative targets. Therefore, the combination of all model outputs was done without any weighting procedure, because the model outputs and the graphical output (Figure 10.7) should be used to assist stakeholders and decision makers rather than to draw conclusions that depend on normative definitions. The CAP scenario shows advantages in economic performance and water quality, whereas the AGENDA 2000 scenario is preferable with respect to soil quality. Both scenarios are similar in terms of hydrological-related ecosystem services.

The results of this study, and the tools used to develop them, are designed to lend support to the complicated decision-making processes regulating land use. However, it must be recognised that these results are limited to a supporting role in this process. The tools provide a more objective estimate of potential endpoints. The final selection of preferred ecosystem services and their weighting must still be defined by society's needs. An example of a methodology for developing such composite indicators can be obtained from Nardo *et al.* (2005). Within the ITE^{2}M modelling network, the evaluation framework CHOICE can be used to provide further advice for decision makers and is discussed by Borresch *et al.* (2005).

DISCUSSION OF THE APPLIED METHODOLOGY – ADVANCES AND LIMITATIONS

The key concept of ITE^{2}M is its integrated and spatially explicit modelling approach. A clear benefit for all modelling studies conducted in ITE^{2}M is that all landscape services predicted can be evaluated using economic measures derived by ProLand. Nevertheless, the ITE^{2}M concept also has drawbacks. Hence, we would like to discuss critically the underlying premises of the models used in the present study and the assets and drawbacks of the ITE^{2}M concept in general in the following sections.

Model philosophy and reality

ProLand has a central position in the ITE^{2}M concept because it provides both predictions of economic landscape services and spatially explicit land-use maps that are used by all other ITE^{2}M component models. The predictions of landscape services related to water, soils and biodiversity depend on these maps of the occurrence, spatial distribution and relation of land-use systems. One should therefore consider the inherent premises of ProLand when analysing the economic landscape services and land-use maps. The two most relevant basic assumptions of ProLand are (1) land rent maximising behaviour of all land users in a given region, and (2) that all resources for production, including capital, are unlimited and fully divisible. The assumptions can lead to a selection of a land-use system by ProLand that is only marginally superior in terms of financial benefits to other land uses also under consideration. In certain regions, this difference can be smaller than the results' variance associated with the inevitable uncertainty of model input. Also, several input parameter values that are assumed homogeneous throughout the region are, in reality, heterogeneously distributed. Examples are factor endowment and the associated opportunity costs of capital and labour. Therefore, the realised land-use system may deviate from the prognosis. Finally, land users may not behave in a land-rent-maximising manner because of tradition, beliefs or missing knowledge. This holds especially true for rural regions of middle European landscapes, where part time and small-scale farming is dominant. Consequently, simulated and *in situ* land use and management do differ in some cases. Additionally, as in all comparative static models, ProLand predicts endpoints of adaptation processes and therefore cannot generate development paths. This further implies that ProLand simulations cannot be calibrated with current land-use distributions derived by remote sensing or from land registers. Hence, only scenario-based modelling and analysis of potential bio-economic performances are feasible. We therefore suggest that, in a real evaluation process, scientists should assist stakeholders and policy makers in developing scenarios and interpreting them.

It has been shown that detailed knowledge of site-specific hydrological data is of importance for estimating element outputs of soils by leaching and plant uptake when calculating heavy metal balances. The usage of SWAT results in ATOMIS proved to be a useful application, even though SWAT is only a semi-distributed hydrological model and the HRU-concept implies conceptual simplifications. Despite the limited spatial accuracy of the SWAT model, we think that the approach is sufficient for scenario comparison presented here. Compared with other available digital data on seepage water (e.g. Duijnisveld *et al.* 2003) and evapotranspiration, the advantages of using SWAT in this study were that the same site characteristics, common spatial resolution, and detailed land use and management data were able to be used across all models. The approach of integrating hydrological information could be improved using a fully distributed hydrological model. However, such an approach also has drawbacks, such as an extended model run time and the necessity of a large number of model parameters, among others (e.g. Beven 2001; Perrin *et al.* 2001; Refsgaard 1997).

Feedback mechanisms

In most applications of ITE^{2}M, the ProLand model set the frame under which all other models predicted landscape services. However, the model framework is also capable of taking feedback mechanisms into account (shown as light grey dotted lines in Figure 10.1). For instance, back-coupling ATOMIS estimates to ProLand were used to calculate opportunity costs in terms of sustainable heavy metal criteria in soils as demonstrated by Reiher *et al.* (2006a). This way of data exchange demonstrates the potential of ITE^{2}M for evaluating legally defined threshold values and their economic assessment. Similarly, Weinmann *et al.* (2005) evaluated the economic performance of different pest management strategies in plant production. Thus, it is also possible to investigate and evaluate land-use distributions with ProLand developed by the use of other techniques, such as normative scenario development (Nassauer and Corry 2004).

Model transferability

Modelling spatially explicit decision units (i.e. grid cells or field polygons) proved to be a valuable approach in the ITE^{2}M concept. It is the only way that distributed models can make use of spatial land use and management information. Land users and decision makers are able to use such explicit information to identify and observe sensitive areas.

However, the ProLand approach reveals conceptual problems regarding the modelling of animal husbandry systems whose fodder production is spatially independent from the animal production, such as pig husbandry, intensive poultry farming and egg production. Even though this might not be relevant for the prediction of land use distribution, other ITE^{2}M component models might need information on such production systems. For example, ATOMIS and SWAT require information on the type of farmyard manure applied to a site, because different types of manure and fertiliser have considerably different compositions of heavy metals (Nicholson *et al.* 2003) and nutrients. Even though most of the breeding farms receive feed and other operation supplies from outside the region under investigation, waste material such as manure is disposed in the region itself. Disregarding such production systems might heavily influence model outputs in regions of intensive animal production. In consequence, current research is identifying the factors determining the optimal location of such production systems.

The extension of the developed model network to larger domains such as regions or countries is feasible, though there are some restrictions for using the ITE^{2}M network in its current form. The ProLand model currently considers agricultural and silvicultural production systems that are typical for the research area and potentially realisable. Applying the model to areas with different climates, cultivars and crop rotational systems would require yield functions, market prices and working costs applicable to the respective transfer region to be applied. In a recent study, ProLand was used to estimate economic potentials for farmers producing bioenergy and renewable resources and associated land-use changes in Germany (Nusser *et al.* 2006).

The SWAT model integrates several conceptual approaches in terms of the hydrological and biogeochemical process description, which need calibration for the study catchment. Depending on the catchment characteristics, the effort that has to be put into model calibration can be substantial

(Eckhardt and Arnold 2001). Long-term data for model calibration and verification have to be at hand, limiting the application of the model to gauged catchments. Finally, ATOMIS is limited to areas for which the model implemented PTFs were derived. The PTF concept may fail, especially in regions with alkaline soils and capillary rise. To summarise, all models have to be validated before being applied in areas with different boundary conditions. As part of this validation, the current ITE^{2}M network is now being tested in the intensive agrarian region of the Wetterau (Figure 10.3), Germany, where land use and management differs substantially from the peripheral region in which ITE^{2}M has been developed.

Recent applications of ITE^{2}M-tranferability focused on land-use distributions that depended on changes in bio-economic and political boundary conditions. Examples include the investigation of the effects of the European Common Agricultural Policy (Weinmann *et al.* 2006), the influence of land consolidation and its impact on field size distribution (Lenhart *et al.* 2003), the introduction of a grassland bonus to support extensive grazing systems (Weber *et al.* 2001) and the implementation of new extensive land-use systems such as suckler cow production (Breuer *et al.* 2006). In all these investigations, environmental boundary conditions remained fixed. Given recent estimates of future regional climate changes, ITE^{2}M provides an excellent framework for economic and ecological investigation of such effects. However, before the application of ITE^{2}M in such investigations, one has to carefully test the underlying validity of the model assumptions (e.g. effect of elevated CO_2 on plant growth, occurrence of plant and animal species under increased temperature). Only the SWAT model has been tested and applied under changing climatic conditions so far (Eckhardt and Ulbrich 2003; Rosenberg *et al.* 1999).

CONCLUSION

The SFB 299 developed an integrated methodology for the assessment of multifunctional landscapes by establishing the extensible model network ITE^{2}M based on an bio-economic land-use model. The model network is not implemented in a joint source code, but consists of independent models, which simplifies the affiliation of new models. ITE^{2}M aims to give decision support to land users and decision makers by stating results of agricultural policy measures in the light of of single ecosystem services, and not by calculating a set of indicators. Nevertheless, using a model network for an integrated evaluation of agricultural policy still requires an intensive cooperation of model developers, scientists and the target audience to avoid misinterpretation of model results. Similarly, setting up an integrated modelling network requires a strong collaboration of different model developers and experts. The developed methodology shows that site explicit modelling of land use and management provides a detailed basis for subsequent models to address environmental landscape services.

ACKNOWLEDGEMENT

This work is part of the Collaborative Research Center 'Land Use Options for Peripheral Regions' (SFB 299) supported by the German Research Foundation (DFG). We thank Birgit Reger for providing Figure 10.3. We thank Mindy Crandall for helpful comments on language and style of the text.

REFERENCES

Arnold JG, Srinivasan R, Muttiah RS and Williams JR (1998) Large area hydrologic modeling and assessment. Part I: Model development. *Journal of the American Water Resources Association* **34**, 73–88.

BBodSchV (1999) Bundes-Bodenschutz- und Altlastenverordnung (German ordinance on soil protection). BGBl. I, S. 502.

Beven KJ (2001) *Rainfall-runoff Modeling. The Primer.* John Wiley & Sons, Chichester, UK.

Borresch R, Schmitz K, Schmitz PM and Wronka TC (2005) CHOICE – Ein integriert ökonomisch-ökologisches Konzept zur Bewertung von Multifunktionalität. In: *Umwelt- und Produktqualität im Agrarbereich. Schriften der Gesellschaft für Wirtschafts- und Sozialwissenschaften des Landbaus e.V.*, **40**, 123–132.

Breuer L, Huisman JA and Frede H-G (2006) Monte Carlo assessment of uncertainty in the simulated hydrological response to land use change. *Environmental Modeling and Assessment* **11**, 209–218.

Breuer L, Reiher W, Pohlert T, Huisman JA, Weinmann B, Vaché K, Bach M, Gäth S and Frede H-G (2007) Integrated assessment of potential impacts on water and soil related ecosystem services due to the European Common Agricultural Policy. In: *Reducing the Vulnerability of Societies to Water related Risks at the Basin Scale.* (Eds A Schumann and M Pahlow) pp. 90–95. IAHS Press, Oxfordshire, UK.

Costanza R, d´Arge R, de Groot R, Farber S, Grasso M, Hannon B, Limburg K, Naeem S, O'Neill RV, Paruelo J, Raskin RG, Sutton P and van den Belt M (1997) The value of the world's ecosystem services and natural capital. *Nature* **387**, 253–260.

Duijnisveld W, Hennings V, Stolz W, Martin N, Richter A and Behrens J (2003) Mean annual rate of percolation from the soil. In: *Federal Ministry for the Environment, Nature Conservation and Nuclear Safety (BMU)*, Hydrological Atlas of Germany, Berlin, Germany.

Eckhardt K and Arnold JG (2001) Automatic calibration of a distributed catchment model. *Journal of Hydrology* **251**, 103–109.

Eckhardt K and Ulbrich U (2003) Potential impacts of climate change on groundwater recharge and streamflow in a central European low mountain range. *Journal of Hydrology* **284**, 244–252.

Eckhardt K, Haverkamp S, Fohrer N and Frede H-G (2002) SWAT-G, a version of SWAT99.2 modified for application to low mountain range catchments. *Physics and Chemistry of the Earth B* **27**, 641–644.

Fohrer N, Haverkamp S and Frede H-G (2005) Assessment of long-term effects of land use patterns on hydrologic landscape functions – sustainable land use concepts for low mountain range areas. *Hydrological Processes* **19**, 659–672.

Foley JA, DeFries R, Asner GP, Barford C, Bonan GB, Carpenter SR, Chapin III FS, Coe MT, Daily GC, Gibbs HK, Helkowski JH, Holloway T, Howard EA, Kucharik CJ, Monfreda C, Patz JA, Prentice IC, Ramankutty N and Snyder PK (2005) Global consequences of land use. *Science* **309**, 570–574.

Frede H-G, Bach M, Fohrer N and Breuer L (2002) Interdisciplinary modeling and the significance of soil functions. *Journal of Plant Nutrition and Soil Science* **165**, 460–467.

Fürchtenicht K, Heyn J, Kuhlmann H, Laurenz L and Müller S (1993) Pflanzenernährung und Düngung. In: *Faustzahlen für Landwirtschaft und Gartenbau*. (Ed. Hydro Agri Dülmen GmbH) pp. 254–295. Landwirtschaftsverlag: Münster-Hiltrup.

Gottschalk TK, Diekötter T, Ekschmitt K, Weinmann B, Kuhlmann F, Purtauf T, Dauber J and Wolters V (2007) Impact of agricultural subsidies on biodiversity at the landscape level. *Landscape Ecology* **22**, 643–656.

Haverkamp S, Fohrer N and Frede H-G (2005) Assessment of the effect of land use patterns on hydrologic landscape functions: a comprehensive GIS-based tool to minimize model uncertainty resulting from spatial aggregation. *Hydrological Processes* **19**, 715–727.

Horn AL, Düring RA and Gäth S (2004) Sorption of Cd in soils: pedotransfer functions for the parameters of the Freundlich sorption isotherm. *Water, Air, and Soil Pollution: Focus* **4**, 61–71.

Horn AL, Reiher W, Düring R-A and Gäth S (2006) Efficiency of pedotransfer functions describing Cadmium sorption in soils. *Water, Air, and Soil Pollution* **170**, 229–247.

Huisman JA, Breuer L, Eckhardt K and Frede H-G (2003) Spatial consistency of automatically calibrated SWAT simulations in the Dill catchment and three of its sub-catchments. In: *Proceedings of the 2nd SWAT Conference*, July 1–4 2003, Bari, Italy. (Eds R Srinivasan, JH Jacobs, R Jensen), TWRI Report 266, pp. 168-173, Texas Water Resources Institute, Tamu, TX, USA.

Huisman JA, Breuer L, Bormann H, Bronstert A, Croke B, Frede H-G, Gräff T, Hubrechts L, Jakeman AJ, Kite G, Lanini J, Leavesley G, Lettenmaier D, Lindström G, Seibert J, Sivaplan M, Viney N and Willems P (2009) Assessing the impact of land use change on hydrology by ensemble modeling (LUCHEM) III: Scenario analysis. *Advances in Water Resources* **32**(2), 159–170.

Kuhlmann F, Möller D and Weinmann B (2002) Modellierung der Landnutzung: Regionshöfe oder Raster-Landschaft? *Berichte über Landwirtschaft* **80**(3), 351–392.

LABO (2003) Bund-Länder-Arbeitsgemeinschaft Bodenschutz, Hintergrundwerte für anorganische Stoffe in Böden. Ministerium für Umwelt und Naturschutz, Landwirtschaft und Verbraucherschutz des Landes Nordrhein – Westfalen, Düsseldorf. <http://www.labo-deutschland.de/LABO-HGW-Anhang.pdf>

Lenhart T, Fohrer N and Frede H-G (2003) Effects of land use changes on the nutrient balance in mesoscale catchments. *Physics and Chemistry of the Earth* **28**, 1301–1309.

Li C, Frolking S and Frolking TA (1992) A model of nitrous oxide evolution from soil driven by rainfall events: 1. Model structure and sensitivity. *Journal of Geophysical Research* **97**, 9759–9776.

Möller D, Fohrer N and Steiner N (2002) Quantifizierung regionaler Multifunktionalität land- und forstwirtschaftlicher Nutzungssysteme. *Berichte über Landwirtschaft* **80**(3), 393–418.

Nardo M, Saisana M, Saltelli A, Tarantola S, Hoffman A and Giovannini E (2005) 'Handbook on constructing composite indicators: methodology and user guide'. OECD Statistics Working Paper JT00188147, STD/DOC(2005)3, OECD, Paris, France.

Nassauer JI and Corry RC (2004) Using normative scenarios in landscape ecology. *Landscape Ecology* **19**, 343–356.

Nicholson FA, Smith SR, Alloway BJ, Carlton-Smith C and Chambers BJ (2003) An inventory of heavy metals inputs to agricultural soils in England and Wales. *Science of the Total Environment* **311**, 205–219.

Nusser M, Seydel P, Sheridan P, Walz R and Wydra S (2007) 'Makroökonomische Effekte des Anbaus und der Nutzung von nachwachsenden Rohstoffen'. Report for the Bundesministerium für Ernährung,

Landwirtschaft und Verbraucherschutz, Fachagentur für nachwachsende Rohstoffe e.V., Gülzow.

Perrin C, Michel C and Andréassian V (2001) Does a large number of parameters enhance model performance? Comparative assessment of common catchment model structures on 429 catchments. *Journal of Hydrology* **242**, 275–301.

Pohlert T, Breuer L, Huisman JA and Frede H-G (2007a) Assessing the model performance of an integrated hydrological and biogeochemical model for discharge and nitrate load predictions. *Hydrology and Earth Systems Sciences* **11**, 997–1011.

Pohlert T, Huisman JA, Breuer L and Frede H-G (2007b) Integration of a detailed biogeochemical model into SWAT for improved nitrogen predictions – model development, sensitivity and uncertainty analysis. *Ecological Modelling* **203**, 215–228.

Refsgaard JC (1997) Parameterisation, calibration and validation of distributed hydrological models. *Journal of Hydrology* **198**, 67–97.

Reiher W (2008) Entwicklung eines regionalisierten Modells zur Projektion des landnutzungsabhängigen Schwermetallstatus von Oberböden. Boden und Landschaft 52, University of Giessen, Germany, PhD thesis.

Reiher W, Weinmann B, Düring R-A and Gäth S (2006a) Pricing opportunity costs to meet soil quality concepts in matters of heavy metal inputs into agricultural soils. In: 'Sustainable land use in intensively used agricultural regions, Landscape Europe'. Alterra report No. 1338 (Ed. BC Meyer), Wageningen, Netherlands.

Reiher W, Breuer L, Weinmann B, Pohlert T, Bach M, Düring R-A, Gäth S and Frede H-G (2006b) The integrated model network ITE^{2}M: model set-up and assessment of agricultural land use and management options. In: *Proceedings of the iEMSs Third Biennial Meeting*: '*Summit on* Environmental Modeling and Software'. (Eds A Voinov, A Jakeman and A Rizzoli). International Environmental Modelling and Software Society. Burlington, VT, USA, CD ROM. <http://www.iemss.org/iemss2006/sessions/all.html>.

Reiher W, Düring R-A and Gäth S (2004) Development of heavy metal contents in soils according to land use and management systems – a heavy metal balance approach. *Proceedings of the EUROSOIL 2004*. (Eds Wöhrle N, Scheurer M). Institut für Bodenkunde und Waldernährungslehre, Freiburg, Germany.

Rosenberg NJ, Epstein DJ, Wang D, Vail L, Srinivasan R and Arnold JG (1999) Possible impacts of global warming on the hydrology of the Ogallala aquifer region. *Climatic Change* **42**, 677–692.

SFB299 (Collaborative Research Center 'Land Use Options for Peripheral Regions'), www.sfb299.de, University of Giessen, Germany.

Steiner N and Köhler W (2003) Effects of landscape pattern on species richness – a modeling approach. *Agriculture, Ecosystems & Environment* **98**, 353–361.

Stöckle CO, Donatelli M and Nelson R (2003) CropSyst, a cropping systems simulation model. *European Journal of Agronomy* **18**, 289–307.

Waldhardt R (2007) The Collaborative Research Centre SFB 299: an example of landscape ecological research? *Colloquium Geographicum* **28**, 27–47.

Waldhardt R, Simmering D and Otte A (2004) Estimation and prediction of plant species richness in a mosaic landscape. *Landscape Ecology* **19**, 211–226.

Weber A, Fohrer N and Möller D (2001) Long-term land use changes in a mesoscale watershed due to socio-economic factors – effects on landscape and functions. *Ecological Modelling* **140**, 125–140.

Weinmann B, Schroers JO and Sheridan P (2006) Simulating the effects of decoupled transfer payments using the land use model ProLand. *Agrarwirtschaft* **55**(5/6), 248–256.

Weinmann B (2002) Mathematische Konzeption und Implementierung eines Modells zur Simulation regionaler Landnutzungsprogramme. PhD thesis, Agrarwirtschaft Sonderheft **174**, Agrimedia.

Weinmann B, Heier TJ, Kuhlmann F, Kogel K-H and Pons-Kühnemann J (2005) Nutzungspotenziale von Low-Input Pflanzenschutzverfahren und deren Auswirkung auf die Landnutzung. *Umwelt- und Produktqualität im Agrarbereich. Schriften der Gesellschaft für Wirtschafts- und Sozialwissenschaften des Landbaus e.V.*, **40**, 341–350.

Wohlrab B, Ernstberger H, Meuser A and Sokollek V (1992) *Landschaftswasserhaushalt*. Verlag Paul Parey, Hamburg.

Chapter 11

Accounting for multiple governance scales in integrated modelling and decision support

Alexander Smajgl

ABSTRACT

Integration summarises different approaches in research, from multi- or inter-disciplinary organisation of research projects (Parker *et al.* 2002) to the integration of stakeholders in the process of undertaking research (Jakeman and Letcher 2003). The need for integration across disciplines is widely accepted. This chapter argues that scales of decision making are a 'meta-level' for integration. In many cases, several decision makers that operate on different scales are relevant to the problem domain. For instance, the overuse of natural resources is rarely based on decisions made on a single scale. Instead, households make decisions on a micro scale, while concurrently regional or national authorities have a direct and indirect impact on resource use levels.

This chapter explains the relevance of multiple scales for research under the integration paradigm. It develops a multi-scale integration framework for applied research and demonstrates an implementation of such a framework in two examples: watershed management in the Great Barrier Reef region of Australia and forest management in East Kalimantan, Indonesia.

INTRODUCTION

Over the past two decades, *integration* – in the form of inter-disciplinary research or in the form of linking decision making and research – has significantly changed how research is organised and conducted. These changes cannot conceal the lack of real-world impact many research projects have. Seemingly, researchers have to distinguish between (a) improving the understanding of policy makers and (b) solving the real world problem. Obviously, the second paradigm does not occur without considering the decision-making process. Instead of focusing on one level of decision making, however, this chapter argues that the second paradigm involves multiple tiers of governance. Hence, the concept of integration has to be widened to include the distinction between multiple layers of decision making and their interaction. Such an approach to integrated research is based on the assumption that decision makers on different levels do not just respond to each other, they also (a) make assumptions on other decision makers' responses and (b) perceive the problem domain from a specific perspective.

This chapter assumes that this perspective varies according to the governance level. In other words, reality is perceived on some levels as a nearly linear system while on other levels real world problems are perceived as part of a non-linear system or even a chaotic system. Thus, the perceived degree of complexity depends on the decision-making level, so integrated research that aims to solve the problem through improved understanding of decision makers on multiple levels has to take the varying degree of complexity into account. Such an approach to integrated research requires a blend of methodologies, rather than developing one integrated tool that serves the need of one decision maker.

This chapter explains the relevance of multiple scales for research under the integration paradigm. It develops a multi-scale integration framework for applied research and demonstrates an implementation of such a framework in two examples: watershed management in the Great Barrier Reef region of Australia and forest management in East Kalimantan, Indonesia.

INTEGRATION: A MULTIDIMENSIONAL QUEST

The following step conceptualises integration in a decision-making-support context. This step reveals an additional dimension of integrated research, developed from the problem domain perspective and inherently linked to the decision makers' influence.

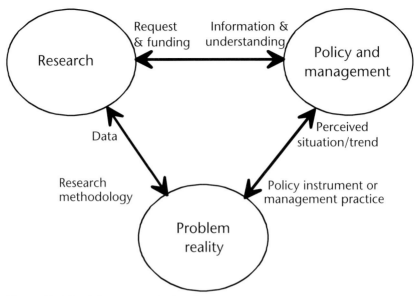

Figure 11.1. Decision-support triangle.

For simplicity, the applied decision-support context is reduced to three domains, shown in Figure 11.1: research, policy and management, and the problem reality. This process begins when researchers discover an existing or potential problem through investigation and analysis and carry this understanding to decision makers. It can also be initiated by policy makers and managers facing a problem and requiring advice from research.

Traditionally, different aspects of research were addressed by different individual research disciplines. This means that researchers from different disciplines subjectively analysed a given problem domain (Figure 11.2). This implies that methodologies are mainly developed according to disciplinary requirements. Such a traditional approach involves a 'weak' link between policy and research, characterised by aspects such as initial dialogues regarding expected project outcomes, funding and final presentation of research results. Policy or management is mostly represented by one stakeholder (or governance level), which perceives the problem domain in a manner based on available instruments and levers that translate directly into specifications of research projects. For research methodologies, the scale of information required by policy makers and the system boundaries of the analysis are crucial parameters. These vary across different levels of governance.

The introduction of the sustainability concept triggered substantial problems for research based on single disciplines, and the need for

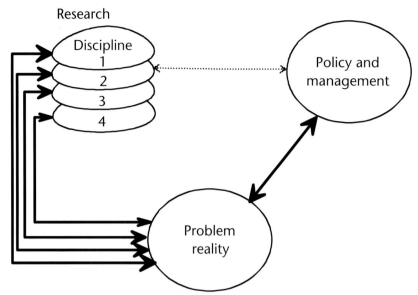

Figure 11.2. Decision-support triangle in a disciplinary view.

inter-disciplinary or multi-disciplinary research has become increasingly articulated. In such an integrated project design, various disciplines coordinate their research (Figure 11.3). The link to policy and management is designed in a way that requires more than one discipline to deliver answers or tools. This inter-disciplinary research approach is mostly meant by integration (Parker *et al.* 2002); the disciplinary integration in a holistic approach (type A integration). The second dimension within which integration operates is based on the link between policy and research (Jakeman and Letcher 2003). This dimension defines principles for stakeholder integration that require an ongoing communication of researchers and policy makers (type B integration).

   Both types of integration are likely to deliver substantial improvements compared with the traditional disciplinary approach. However, approaching such a conceptualisation from the perspective of the problem domain reveals an additional impediment for real-world impacts.

   Most real-world problems are actually linked to more than one governance level. For instance, in most areas, water quality levels are indirectly influenced by legislation and market incentives but are primarily determined by the actual behaviour of farm managers. Also, new fines on polluting water might not have any effect on water quality if monitoring and sanctioning do not trigger the behavioural effects that are required. Similarly, market incentives for reducing pollution loads might, theoretically,

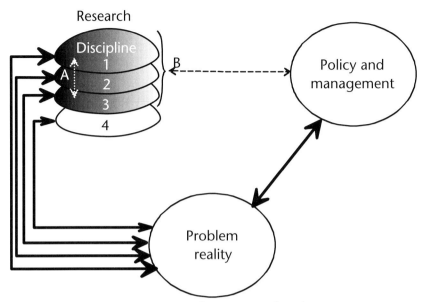

Figure 11.3. Decision-support triangle in an inter-disciplinary view.

lead to targeted water-quality levels, but land managers might perceive such incentives differently than higher governance levels assume and thereby cause targets to be missed.

Generally, research is defined (and funded) by one governance level. Each tier of governance requires information at a specific scale or resolution, which entails a specific level of data aggregation. Regional managers require indicators for whole regions (averages or totals) but are less interested in individual households within the region. Farm-scale managers are mainly interested in indicators that influence their farm and are crucial for effective land management decisions, such as water availability for each paddock. As research is mostly funded and directed by one tier of governance, a critical element is missing: lower governance levels adapt to perceived changes defined by higher governance levels. Figure 11.4 shows that a higher governance level might initiate a change (step a) aiming for an improved situation such as water quality. Lower governance levels perceive this change in the multitude of existing incentives (step b) and adapt (step c).

Therefore, decision support that advises the governance of, for example, natural resources, would have to consider these adaptation dynamics. This can happen to different degrees. Most effectively, research projects would aim for delivering an understanding for all crucial levels of governance linked to the relevant problem domain. If, for instance, quantitative modelling is involved, it would be insufficient to develop a model for the requirements one tier of governance as this would make implicit assumptions on other levels of governance. Understanding has to be improved consistently on the core levels of decision making on all tiers in order to target the problem domain effectively.

METHODOLOGICAL CONSTRAINTS IN A SOLUTION ORIENTED MULTI-SCALE ASSESSMENT

The ideas described above require a good understanding of decision-making processes in a given system. Each problem domain is likely to be affected by different decision makers. In order to allow further discussion, the focus of this chapter is limited to an environmental problem domain. Environmental problems are often classified geographically from hot-spot problems to global problems (UNCTAD 2001). This approach identifies *effects* as the main discriminator, while the *cause* is typically used to classify instruments impacting on perceived incentive systems.

Causing entities make resource decisions under given circumstances, which are mostly defined by other entities in a given governance system. For instance, a farmer decides to use fertiliser, which subsequently affects downstream nitrogen levels. Harm is not done per se because some species gain advantage while other slow-growing species may fall behind. This change in species composition can also include the loss of species. *Harm* is defined by other affected stakeholders perceiving the change as an unwelcomed observation (or expectation). The farmer acts within given parameters, some of which are defined by higher tiers of governance. Since the late 1970s, the call for internalising externalities has become louder, and research was requested (and often conducted) to improve our understanding of how changes triggered by higher tiers of governance might affect given environmental problems.

This creates a fallacy of integrated research: although most governance levels still perceive economic indicators as high priority, each level of decision making perceives the real-world system under a different degree of complexity. Some higher levels choose aggregate indicators such as GDP for successful or unsuccessful decision making. These indicators respond slowly because they aggregate multiple system variables. As a consequence, the decision maker observes a much more 'linear' behaving system than a decision maker who operates on a lower level with a higher resolution. At the lower level, system behaviour might be much more complex. What does this mean for developing research and integrated research?

Each level of decision maker makes assumptions based on the response of, and feedback from, other levels of decision making. The minister aggregates farmers into groups and assumes each group will respond or adapt in a certain way. Farmers have beliefs about governmental goals and intervention options and choose their strategies according to these assumptions. If research is focused on just one level of decision making – knowing that multiple levels of decision makers determine the environmental outcome – the caveat of potentially wrong assumptions is persistent because responses on other levels of decision making are exogenous to the research scope.

Thus, two steps have the potential to give applied research a greater real-world impact. Firstly, researchers must identify all levels of decision making that are critical for the environmental outcome and apply methodologies that serve the needs of each level. These requirements imply a certain level of complexity and aggregation of input and output data. Both are main drivers for choosing methods, not just in the domain of quantitative assessment.

Secondly, include design processes in the research that link real-world decision makers who operate on various levels. The likelihood of improving the environmental situation in a given context increases if systems understanding is developed on all levels of decision making that are critical to environmental conditions.

Both steps widen the current paradigm of integrated research, but require integration type A and B (see above). The additional design criteria for applied research define a meta-level for *integration* because they require the development and integration of multiple sub-projects and their effective linkage to the decision-making process of policy makers and managers. Apparently, such an approach requires significant resources and cannot be developed in all cases. Although this chapter advocates the need for this type of integrated project, it will not suit all research questions and will also require significant resources. In order to exemplify the idea of multi-scale assessment in a decision-support framework, and show how such an idea can be implemented, two case studies are described below.

CASE STUDY 1: THE GREAT BARRIER REEF REGION

Background

The condition of adjacent river systems has a significant impact on the marine ecosystems of the World Heritage-listed Great Barrier Reef ('GBR') region. Over 30 major catchments drain into the GBR lagoon.

Agricultural activities in the GBR region in particular contribute to declining water quality, which threatens tourism and other activities based on the condition of the GBR lagoon and its ecosystems. Recent economic data (Productivity Commission 2003) show that GBR-based tourism-related activities contribute $4,300 million to the regional economies, while agricultural activities contribute $3,200 million. In addition to its economic importance, the GBR is perceived as a cultural icon with high biodiversity and world significance, as well as a provider of ecosystems services to coastal communities.

The Australian and Queensland Governments recognised declining water quality as a threat to the GBR and established the Reef Water Quality Protection Plan ('Reef Plan') (Queensland Government 2003). The Reef Plan defines the mandate of '*halting and reversing the decline in water quality entering the Reef within 10 years*' through '*reducing the load of pollutants from diffuse sources in the water entering the Reef*' and '*rehabilitating and conserving areas of the reef catchment that have a role in removing water borne pollutants.*'

The multi-scale assessment approach

The Reef Plan proposes education and extension, economic incentives, planning for natural resource management and land use, regulatory frameworks, research and information sharing, partnerships, priorities and targets, as well as monitoring and evaluation. Following from these strategies, catchment authorities (natural resource management agencies) can be identified as core stakeholders for the realisation of the goals of the Reef Plan. The GBR Marine Park Authority and the state government can also be identified as decision makers for implementing listed strategies.

What would be a typical scenario? Research projects would be designed with regard to the information needs of these decision makers. Thus, information would be focused on indicators such as the total amount of sediment entering the GBR lagoon and the total amounts of nutrients entering streams within a catchment. *Integrated research* would include geo-hydrological, ecological, economic and social questions in order to develop a meaningful system representation that demands quantifying required indicators. As a result, quantitative models or qualitative approaches would help catchment authorities answer the question: which lever do we choose from in order to have the 'best' effect across the triple bottom line? It can be expected that such a process of organising research dominates integrated approaches. Often, researchers will attempt to include the decision makers in the process.

From a problem perspective – in this case mainly water quality issues – core decision makers are land managers who need to decide how much fertiliser to use, how much water for irrigation, and how much pesticide, fungicide and herbicide to apply. Clearly, catchment authorities and the state government are very likely to have an impact on land managers' decisions because their legislation and market-based incentives modify perceived incentives. The critical step of how such incentive changes are perceived by land managers and translated into behaviour is captured mainly in broad assumptions made by researchers and policy makers.

From a problem perspective, the perceptions of land managers and policy makers (catchment and state level) have to be understood in order to improve triple-bottom-line indicators for the GBR region. Although higher level decision makers employ assumptions on environmental dynamics and land managers adaptation, lower-level decision makers such as land managers make their assumptions based on environmental dynamics and higher tiers of governance. Improving the understanding of land managers for how triple-bottom-line indicators might change at their level of resolution is likely to improve the adaptation to environmental changes and policy changes.

How would research be organised if the core question is to improve water quality and not to improve the understanding catchment authorities have of causalities in the GBR region? A single decision-making level would not be sufficient, especially if the targeted tier of governance is not the most relevant one. Instead, an effective foundation for integrated research is the identification of all the important decision-making layers. From here, methodologies have to be chosen in order to improve the understanding of decision makers on various tiers of governance, such as, in the case of the GBR region, land managers, catchment authorities and state-level decision makers.

This section summarises how methodological decisions shaped a research project that targeted the improvement of water quality in the GBR region. The underlying assumption was that quantitative modelling improves systems understanding on each decision-making layer, and coordinating information flows helps find a pathway to improved triple-bottom-line outcomes. This approach includes the development of a computable general equilibrium (CGE) model for the catchment scale and an agent-based model simulating land-use change on a paddock scale.

The CGE model PIA (policy impact assessment) incorporates physical realities such as hydrological dynamics and ecological dynamics into an economic framework. In general, CGE models are highly aggregated and simulate sectoral production processes and aggregated market dynamics. In order to capture non-market aspects of water quality (and quantity), PIA integrates the system variables that are based on ecosystem services, but not represented on markets. Firstly, a multi-criteria analysis based on a survey of about 1000 persons in the GBR region revealed the importance of quality of drinking water and fish-related aspects of biodiversity (Hajkowicz 2006; Smajgl and Hajkowicz 2005). Secondly, a dynamic, catchment-scale CGE model was developed for the GBR region and fish biodiversity was integrated with 'non-market production functions' calibrated with Eco-Path (Smajgl and Gehrke 2007). This allows for the quantification of not only the economic aspects of the triple bottom line, but also relevant ecological and social aspects. Hydrological system variables act as linking system components (Smajgl 2005).

This innovative tool quantifies triple-bottom-line outcomes of policy options related to the Reef Plan. For instance, impacts of a trading scheme for nutrients can be quantified in terms of sectoral production, regional GDP, fish populations and water quality indicators. Although the information generated by the PIA model incorporates catchment decision makers of totals and averages, the spatial distribution can be critical for economic, ecological and social aspects. Additionally, inherent to the highly aggregated model design are assumptions on behavioural responses of land managers to incentive changes. In order to make these behavioural aspects of individual decision making of land managers explicit, an agent-based model is developed.

The agent-based model SEPIA (Single Entity Policy Impact Assessment) simulates daily decisions by land managers – mostly farmers and graziers – and links it to social dynamics and environmental processes. Social dynamics include the diffusion of beliefs changing individual attitudes and knowledge bases. Environmental processes include growth functions for various flora and fauna, hydrological processes and physical processes such as sediment movement (Smajgl *et al.* 2007). Simulation results specify how adaptation processes change management practices in response to policy-based changes to individually perceived incentives. Following from farm-level indicators such as fences, stocking rates and fertiliser application rates, the spatial contribution of water-quality indicators is quantified. Visualising system connectivity and how system variables respond to changes in management practices on their farm is important for the decision support of land managers. Because SEPIA allows testing policies in a regional simulation, as well as from a farm perspective, it serves farm-level decision makers as well as catchment authorities. Additionally, information on the effectiveness of the spatial focus and design of incentive schemes such as bush tenders (Stoneham *et al.* 2003) can be tested and contribute to the Reef Plan goal on a regional level.

CASE STUDY 2: FOREST MANAGEMENT IN EAST KALIMANTAN

Background

This section describes a multi-scale assessment approach similar to the decision-support work in the GBR. The context is described by high deforestation rates in several provinces of Kalimantan (FWI/GWI 2002) while, in a period of decentralisation, power was handed over from federal- to district-level governance (Resosudarmo 2004). The initiating research question was what impact would further changes on the level of macro policy have on natural resources such as forests and poverty? For instance, how do decreasing fuel subsidies affect logging activities? How do poverty levels change in Indonesia?

In summary, Indonesian stakeholders articulated the clear goal to reduce poverty and avoid unsustainable usage rates of natural resources. Therefore, indicators such as unemployment rate, Gini coefficient and the per capita GDP are crucial socioeconomic indicators, while the deforestation rate is an important environmental indicator.

The multi-scale assessment approach

Disciplines such as economics and ecology have to form a shared system understanding in order to shape a decision-support tool for such a context. In addition to this type of integration, the problem perspective adds another dimension of complexity: although macro-policy decisions have a major impact on the system, they do not affect deforestation rates directly. Instead, incentives are changed for forest users and, depending on their behavioural response, deforestation is increased or reduced. Maintaining forests and reducing poverty concurrently through economic development is a major challenge. Essential decision makers at the macro-policy level are the Ministry of Forestry, Ministry of Energy and Ministry of Regional Planning; at the district level mainly Bupati, as the head of district; and at the land-manager level households. Both of these lower tiers of governance will respond to macro-policy changes as incentives change.

Creating decision-support tools for the lower levels of decision making is more promising from a problem perspective because assumptions of behavioural responses inherent to highly aggregated macro-policy analysis tools are themselves explicitly analysed. Additionally, system understanding can alter decision making at the district and household levels, quantifying flow-on effects of their potential response strategies.

Although fuel subsidies are determined at the macro-policy level, behavioural responses occur at the micro level. Fuel prices have an impact on transportation costs and indirectly affect forests as well as poverty levels. Quantifying triple-bottom-line outcomes for decision-making processes at the macro-policy levels would require quantifying highly aggregated indicators. National policy simply does not operate on household level data. Instead, the regional and sectoral trade-offs macro-policy interventions might create are highly significant in order to keep regional stabilities and employment figures on track.

Discussion with federal departments led to a decision to develop a multi-regional and multi-sectoral CGE model. Because the poverty-related and environmental impacts across Indonesia are very important, the CGE model differentiates between about 50 different income groups.

Although this approach serves the national information requirements, it lumps household types within a bigger region such as Kalimantan into one group. The inherent assumption is that all forest users respond in the same way to incentives changed by macro-policy decisions. While it is crucial to understand adaptation dynamics in order to simulate triple-bottom-line outcomes that cover flow-on effects (or unintended side-effects), forest users have to be distinguished according to their likely response. The response itself depends on what forest use means for a specific household, the reasons for the current uses, and what responses might be related to a specific macro-policy change.

In order to simulate such behavioural responses, an agent-based model is in development for East Kalimantan as a hot spot area for forest management. This agent-based model simulates land-use decision making on a household level. Well-being elements based on forests and their use and non-use values are included, which enable the cost–benefits that several policy options have in terms of economic development, financial gains and non-financial losses to be quantified. Because this is simulated over time, short-term and long-term impacts can be differentiated.

CONCLUSIONS AND RECOMMENDATIONS

This chapter argued for a meta-level understanding of integration that develops research projects according to the problems that they are representing. Such a perspective aims for improved understanding on multiple decision-making scales in order to solve environmental problems. One level of decision making in isolation is not likely to achieve targeted real-world outcomes because responses from other decision making levels are excluded.

This chapter argued that each level of decision making perceives the real world (problem) from a different perspective and that each perspective faces different levels of complexity. Some decision makers perceive (nearly) linear system behaviour, while others face (highly) non-linear or even chaotic system behaviour. Thus, if assessing the real-world impact requires designing research projects that target decision makers on multiple levels, and if decisions on each level are based on perception of real-world dynamics at varying levels of complexity, then research project have to incorporate a blend of methodologies. Research methods are predominantly developed from a disciplinary perspective and serve a very narrow domain of research questions, and therefore a certain level of complexity.

Two examples showed how CGE models are used to simulate outcomes of macro-scale interventions in order to inform high-level policy makers, while agent-based models are developed to simulate the behavioural responses of land managers on the micro-scale to such policy interventions. Covering multiple scales enables researchers to make explicit the assumptions of responses on other decision-making levels. Feeding this information back to the core decision makers who are relevant to the problem domain makes solving real-world problems more likely than concentrating on just one decision-making level.

In conclusion, effective integration should not just (a) imply multidisciplinary (or trans-disciplinary) research and (b) build explicit linkages between policy makers and researchers from research design to implementation. It should also target decision makers at multiple scales and employ a blend of methods that provide the diverse information required by these decision makers who operate at various levels of complexity. Such an integration approach includes the active development of linkage between multiple levels of decision making, which decreases the gap between policy making and research.

ACKNOWLEDGMENTS

The author wishes to thank Sally Way and Peter Wiegand for their editorial help.

REFERENCES

FWI/GWI (2002) *The State of the Forest: Indonesia*. (Ed. E Matthews). Forest Watch Indonesia, Global Forest Watch. Bogor, Indonesia and Washington DC.

Hajkowicz S (2006) Multi-attributed environmental index construction. *Ecological Economics* **57**, 122–136.

Jakeman AJ and Letcher RA (2003) Integrated assessment and modelling: features, principles and examples for catchment management. *Environmental Modelling & Software* **18**, 491–501.

Parker P, Letcher R, Jakeman A, Beck MB, Harris G, Argent RM, Hare M, Pahl-Wostl C, Voinov A and Janssen M (2002) Progress in integrated assessment and modelling. *Environmental Modelling & Software* **17**, 209–217.

Productivity Commission (2003) 'Industries, land use and water quality in the Great Barrier Reef catchment'. Research Report. Productivity Commission, Canberra.

Queensland Government (2003) 'Reef water quality protection plan. 25.' Department of the Premier and Cabinet, Brisbane.

Resosudarmo IAP (2004) Closer to people and trees: will decentralisation work for the people and the forests of Indonesia? *The European Journal of Development Research* **16**, 110–132.

Smajgl A (2006) Quantitative evaluation of water use benefits – an integrated modelling approach for the Great Barrier Reef region. *Journal of Natural Resource Modelling* **19**(4), 511–538.

Smajgl A and Gehrke P (2007) Integrated multi-scale modelling in the Great Barrier Reef catchments. In: *Reducing the Vulnerability of Societies Against Water Related Risks at the Basin Scale.* (Eds A Schumann, M Pahlov, JJ Bogardi and P van der Zaag) pp. 107–115. IAHS Press, Oxfordshire, UK.

Smajgl A and Hajkowicz S (2005) Integrated modelling of water policy scenarios in the Great Barrier Reef region. *Australian Journal of Economic Papers* **24**, 215–229 .

Smajgl A, Heckbert S and Bohnet I (2007) 'Simulating the grazing system in the Bowen Broken catchment: an agent-based modelling approach'. Water for a Healthy Country working paper. CSIRO, Townsville.

Stoneham G, Chaudhri V, Ha A and Strappazzon L (2003) Auction for conservation contracts: an empirical examination of Victoria's Bush Tender trial. *Australian Journal for Agricultural and Resource Economics* **47**, 477–500.

UNCTAD (2001) 'Greenhouse gas market perspective: trade and investment implications of the climate change regime'. United Nations, New York and Geneva.

Chapter 12

Conclusions

Wendy Proctor, Lorrae van Kerkhoff and Steve Hatfield Dodds

In this book, we have argued that the achievement of truly sustainable outcomes in natural resource and environmental management can only be obtained by an integrated mission-directed approach to research. An overview of research methods and practical case studies has been presented here to show how this type of research can be carried out to get these desired outcomes. This vast array of case studies from around the world has, however, enlightened us about some of the difficulties that may be involved in effectively carrying out such research and about some of the challenges that we face in achieving these outcomes. In conclusion, we summarise some of the challenges that we face in reaching these goals and provide some implications for future research efforts in this field. Firstly, we provide a set of challenges for researchers that wish to become involved in this field and some key questions that should be answered when trying to set up this type of research. Secondly, a list of potential benefits that could be obtained from effective integrated mission-directed research is provided along with a list of questions related to these benefits that should be assessed by researchers of the projects that they have undertaken to see if such benefits have been truly obtained.

CHALLENGES

An overview of some of the science and society related literature suggests a number of broad challenges that may be faced by those undertaking integrated mission-directed research.

A first set of challenges relates to how we ensure the integrity and quality of our science in this often complex and difficult area:

(1) How do we develop deep empathy for, and understanding of, the issues and problems of others without losing our distinctive (science) skills and contribution?

(2) How do we meet external needs for clarity and confidence in our research outputs, including ensuring appropriate theoretical rigour, relevance, data quality, aggregation or integration across issues, and effective communication?

(3) How do we achieve 'deep integration' of methods and frameworks through mutual interdisciplinary critique?

A second set of challenges relate to crafting constructive responses to more general tensions at the science–society interface:

(4) How do we respond to issues raised by the moral implications of knowledge?

(5) How do we respond to status quo bias in human behaviour, and the responsibilities implied by the influence of 'scientific knowledge' in framing social choices?

(6) How do we respond to issues of impulse control in public debate, such as through harnessing different forms of knowledge creation and articulation ('documenting' or 'validating' community opinion, or producing science consensus documents).

These questions deal with the big issues that surround integrated mission-directed research. Yet they are also manifested in research practice – in the 'everyday' decisions researchers need to make – in a variety of ways. With these broader challenges in mind, we held a workshop with most of the authors that contributed to this book as well as other integration scientists in which the participants identified a set of key themes or challenges that drew upon their experience as integrated mission-directed researchers. These themes, and the associated questions they imply, are shown in Table 12.1. They serve as practical lenses through which we could seek out lessons and compare experiences across different projects and could be used by future research practitioners in this field to develop the research case studies and processes more effectively.

Benefits and implications for research practice

A second outcome of the research and workshop was the process of articulating what we felt were the *benefits* of undertaking this more complex and

Table 12.1. Themes and questions for integrated, mission-directed research.

Key themes – challenges	Illustrative questions
Problem definition and identifying win–win projects	What strategies have proven effective in developing projects that provide 'valued' benefits to key stakeholders, as well as the outcomes required by researchers and research agencies (such as publications and reports)? How can projects be structured and implemented to meet multiple agendas? How can researchers deal with multiple stakeholders, and contested objectives and world views?
Technical integration issues	What challenges did the case studies present in integrating across disciplines, data and scale issues, ensuring appropriate confidence and quality assurance? What worked? What did not?
Role definition	How did project teams respond to pressures to fulfil 'knowledge broker' or 'community development' roles? Were these in tension with knowledge generation and research goals? To what extent did projects address knowledge transfer or adoption? How were these issues decided? What are the underlying goals of those involved in the research? What indicates success? (For example, goals might include the creation of new knowledge and insights, recognition through publications, recognition by clients or stakeholders, or change in practice by key stakeholders. Which of these would be considered most important?)
Creating a favourable organisational environment	Did the organisational environment and culture support integration within the project? If so how? What are the incentives and disincentives for researchers to undertake integrated research? Is there anything distinctive about the organisational arrangements or the research team that helps (or hinders) integrated mission-directed research?

difficult research process, and some questions to confront whether we actually realised those benefits in our research projects (Table 12.2). Documenting successes (or failures) is only useful as long as we have a clear understanding of the criteria against which we are judging – or being judged. A list of potential benefits of integrated mission-directed research has been provided here to assist future researchers to frame their research in such a way so as to obtain these benefits. In assessing the outcomes of such future research, the authors can draw on this list of benefits and related questions to determine if the research has met the objective of being truly integrative and mission directed and how such research could be improved in the future.

Table 12.2. Benefits of integrated mission-directed research.

Key themes – potential benefits	Illustrative questions
Catalysing new knowledge and insights	Did the case study project result in new knowledge or new types of knowledge that would have been unlikely to be produced by discipline-based (or non-integrated) approaches? Did engagement with stakeholders or an external orientation in defining the research questions have an impact on the nature of the research outcomes?
Developing more useful knowledge	Were the research outputs different or more useful?
Achieving greater impact	Did the process or results lead to different outcomes? How did the case study differ from other disciplinary based or curiosity driven research? Did this affect the nature or level of impacts? Were the impacts better (rather than just 'different')? How or why?
Increasing adaptive capacity across society	Did the research process or outputs affect the capacity of key stakeholders or groups outside the research community? Are there risks or disadvantages?
Responding constructively to values, ethics and power in the practice and impact of research	Did researchers, or others involved in the process, identify ethical issues associated with the role or impact of researcher or the research project? What were these? How were these issues regarded within the team or the wider constituency of the case study? How were these issues addressed or managed?

INDEX